TURKEY

*Bronze stag statuette,
Ankara Museum*

Gilbert Horobin is a playwright and poet who lived for a number of years in Turkey before making his home in Athens, Greece. Horobin has travelled extensively throughout the Middle East, Egypt and the Sudan, North Africa, East and Southern Africa, the Indian Ocean islands, India and Nepal, and the Far East. He has produced handbooks on Africa, the Middle East and the Far East. Horobin's published work includes *African Notes and Other Poems*. He is presently at work on a novel set in the 1940s and a long narrative poem that interlaces three experiences of Crete.

Grateful acknowledgement is made to the following authors and publishers for permissions granted:

Pantheon Books for *Anatolian Tales* by Yashar Kemal

Collins Harvill Publishers for
The Birds Have Also Gone © Yashar Kemal, 1978

John Murray (Publishers) Ltd for
The Lycian Shore by Freya Stark

Eland Books for
Portrait of a Turkish Family, © Ates D'Arcy Orga 1988

Distribution in the UK, Ireland, Europe and certain Commonwealth countries by Hodder & Stoughton, Mill Road, Dunton Green, Sevenoaks, Kent TN13 2YA

Editor: Jeris Stevenson
Picture Editor: Caroline Robertson
Map Design: Bai Yiliang
Photography: Adam Woolfitt
Design: John Ng
Cover Concept: Raquel Jaramillo

ISBN: 962-217-140-0

British Library Cataloguing in Publication Data has been applied for.

Printed in Hong Kong

Cover: Tyche, Goddess of Fate

TURKEY

Gilbert Horobin

Photography by Adam Woolfitt

ODYSSEY GUIDES
Hong Kong

Contents

6

Maps

Excerpts

Introduction

For the traveller in Turkey, there could be a sense of romance at this close brush with oriental mystery, even if tempered by an awareness of historical facts and events. Whether sauntering through the streets of İstanbul, one of the oldest cities of our era, or any other of Turkey's major centres, the visitor finds the past everywhere to be savoured. Homer is believed to have lived near İzmir, Midas was king at Gordium (near Ankara) and Croesus ruled at Sardis (inland from İzmir). Modern Bodrum was Halicarnassus for Herodotus, the first great European historian. The cynic philosopher Diogenes kept to his tub at Sinop, St Paul was born in Tarsus and St Nicholas, or Santa Klaus, was a bishop at Demre. The

appellation 'Christian' may have been used for the first time at Antioch, today's Antakya.

Asia Minor's history is apocalyptic with invasions, migrations, devastations and the displacement of one culture by another. When Alp Arslan led his Seljuks into Western Anatolia after his defeat of the Byzantine Emperor Romanus IV at Manzikert in 1071, he rode under the banner of Islam, but not every subsequent Seljuk sultan was absolutely opposed to Christianity, and Mongol khans even toyed with the idea of conversion. Early Ottoman sultans did not refuse to accept Christian Slavs and Byzantine princes as allies or as vassals, nor were Byzantine emperors averse to employing Turkish contingents against Christian monarchs.

Venice, Genoa, Pisa and Ragusa, the Italian maritime republics, all enjoyed trading agreements with the sultans, and 17th-century France was the first Western kingdom to sign reciprocal military agreements with the Ottoman Sublime Porte.

Archaeological discoveries of the 1960s established human habitation back beyond the Palaeolithic, while in southwestern Turkey evidence of very early artistic and technological accomplishment came to light at Çatal Hüyük,

Hacîlar and Yumuktepe (see Ankara Archaeological Museum, page 226). For Turkey is also a history of peoples: Hittites, Urartians, Phrygians, Mysians, Carians, Ionians, Aeolians, Assyrians, Galatians, Cimmerians, Paphlagonians, Pamphylians, Armenians, Greeks, Persians, Romans, Slavs, Arabs, Kurds, Jews, Lazes, Georgians, Circassians, Seljuks, Mongols, Osmanlis. Today over 45 million Turkish-speaking peoples, among whom there are minorities who retain their ethnic identities within the state, occupy a land with an area of 780,000 square kilometres (301,000 square miles).

From the western frontiers with Greece and Bulgaria to the eastern ones with the USSR and Iran, Turkey's length is 1,760 kilometres (1,100 miles). Its average depth between the Black Sea to its north and the Mediterranean Sea and the Syrian and Iraqi frontiers to its south is 400 kilometres (250 miles). The Bosphorus is a narrow waterway between the Black Sea and the Sea of Marmara, and this latter sea is connected to the Aegean and Mediterranean seas by another narrow waterway, the Dardanelles. Until 1973 these water-ways physically separated Asia from Europe, but in that year the opening of the first Bosphorus suspension bridge ended that historic dichotomy. East of the Bosphorus, Turkey's land area is known as Anatolia.

Because of its maritime connection with three seas, Turkey can offer count-less beaches for private or public pleasure, along with beachside hotels, motels, camping sites and yacht marinas, as well as the gamut of aquatic pas-times. The interior of the country east of the Bosphorus, however, is almost wholly mountainous. In the northeastern section, a high central plateau along the Black Sea coast has peaks rising to an average of 3,300 metres (10,800 feet), including Noah's Mount Ararat, 5,165 metres (16,950 feet) in height. In the extreme southeastern region, the wild Hakkari mountains spread into Iran and Iraq. The Taurus Mountains run impressively along Anatolia's southern edge, while, on Turkey's border with Syria, the Amanus Mountains form a con-genial backdrop at the eastern end of the Mediterranean. Facilities for moun-taineering, skiing and hunting are therefore legion.

Throughout western Anatolia, a European cultural way of life, blended with inherited Turkish mores, predominates. In the eastern area of Anatolia, with the exception of the major cities, a pastoral and semi-nomadic culture is prevalent. Although the Turkish Republic has no established religion, Turks are in the main Moslem, and the principal Islamic feasts, festivals and fasts are observed. Ethnic minorities maintain their places of worship, but under a law of the Republic no priest or cleric of any denomination may appear in public in clerical garb.

Because of its long history as the cradle of European cultures, Turkey offers unlimited opportunities for archaeological, scholarly or simply enjoyable ex-ploration.

Facts for the Traveller

Getting There

By Air
İstanbul's international Atatürk Airport, at Yeşilköy, west of the city, has separate terminals for international and domestic flights. Large and modern, it has banking and other facilities, and its international terminal has a duty-free section for incoming and outgoing passengers, though purchases have to be made in foreign currency. This duty-free service is available in the major airports of Turkey — Ankara, İzmir, Dalaman, Antalya — and has been extended to the cities where tax-free shops have been established. Turkish Airlines (Türk Havayollari or THY) is the national carrier.

From the United Kingdom, British Airways and Turkish Airlines have direct daily flights to İstanbul from Heathrow; flying time is approximately 3 hours 45 minutes. Charter flights operate regularly in high season from Gatwick and UK regional airports to İzmir, Dalaman and Antalya airports for holiday packages on the Aegean and western Mediterranean coasts. A charter operator such as Valuair, 24 Crawford Place, London W1H 1TE (tel. 01-4024262), can be a source of information and tickets.

From Athens, Olympic Airways and THY each have a daily flight to İstanbul, and there are less frequent flights to İzmir.

From America there are no direct flights to Turkey, but PanAm, Lufthansa, Alitalia, Air France, KLM, Swissair, Sabina and SAS all have European stopover connecting flights to İstanbul or Ankara. Lot, Jat, Balkan and THY have services to İstanbul from most major European cities.

There is a 30-minute passenger service from Atatürk airport to the THY terminal at Şişhane in the new city (Beyoğlu). All taxis have meters and you pay only what is on the meter, except after midnight when there is a 50 percent surcharge. The approximate taxi fare from the airport to Şişhane is 15,000TL.

The airport bus fare is 1,000TL. Taxi fare from the THY Terminal to Taksim Square at the centre of Beyoğlu is about 1,500TL.

By Car
From London the distance to İstanbul is approximately 3,000 kilometres (1,870 miles). There are any number of alternative routes through western Europe, but, for example, from Graz in Austria, take the road over a moderate pass through to Maribor in Yugoslavia, then to Zagreb and Belgrade, from where the journey to İstanbul continues through Niş to Sofia in Bulgaria, to Plovdiv and Edirne in Turkey.

Map of Turkey

0 20 40 60 80 100 km
0 20 40 60 miles

Black

BULGARIA

Edirne

Bosphorus

Zonguldak

Kastamonu

Şile

Akçakoca

Çankiri

Tekirdağ

İstanbul

Marmara Sea

İzmit

Adapazari

Sakarya

Kirikkale

Gallipoli
Peninsula

Bandirma

İznik

Bursa

ANKARA

Dardanelles

Çanakkale

Balikesir

Eskişehir

İyvalık

Bergama

Kütahya

Afyonkarahisar

Lake Tuz

GREECE

Manisa

A N A

Çeşme

İzmir

SMYRNA

*Beyşehir
Gölü*

Konya

Selçuk

Aydin

MTS

Kuşadasi

Priene

Denizli

Burdur

TAURUS

Lake Bafa

Milas

Perge

Bodrum

Marmaris

Termessos

Aspendos

*Aegean
Sea*

Antalya

Side

Alanya

Fethiye

Demre

Anamur

Kaş

Mediterranean Sea

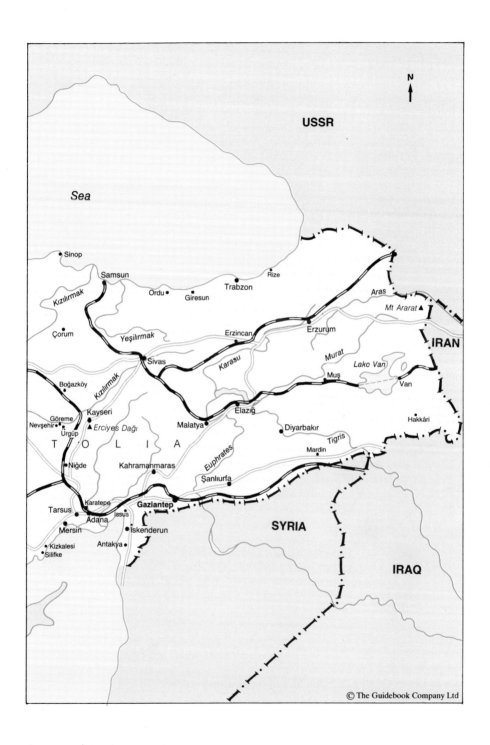

N

USSR

Sea

Sinop

Samsun

Kızılırmak

Çorum

Yeşilırmak

Ordu

Giresun

Trabzon

Rize

Erzincan

Erzurum

Aras

Mt Ararat ▲

IRAN

Sivas

Karasu

Murat

Lake Van

Muş

Van

Boğazköy

Kızılırmak

Göreme

Nevşehir

Ürgüp

Kayseri

▲ Erciyes Dağı

Malatya

Elazığ

Diyarbakır

Hakkâri

Mardin

Tigris

T O L I A

Niğde

Kahramanmaras

Euphrates

Şanlıurfa

Tarsus

Karatepe

Issus

Gaziantep

SYRIA

Adana

Mersin

İskenderun

Kizkalesi

Antakya

Silifke

IRAQ

© The Guidebook Company Ltd

Formerly the Byzantine city of Adrianopolis, Edirne was also an Ottoman capital before the fall of Constantinople and has several fine mosques, including the architect Sinan's Selimiye. At an annual festival held in the vicinity of Edirne, a national oil-wrestling championship is held (see page 46). The distance from Edirne to İstanbul is 250 kilometres (155 miles). Taken at average speed, and allowing for overnight and other stops, a journey from London to Istanbul by this route should take about five days.

British citizens do not need a visa for Yugoslavia, though Americans need a transit one. Citizens of both countries need transit visas for Bulgaria that are valid for only 48 hours. These should be obtained beforehand but can be got at the frontier with local currency by changing money at none too favourable a rate. The distance from Sofia to Edirne is 300 kilometres (188 miles).

An alternative but longer route from Belgrade can be taken by continuing south from Niş to Skopje, then on to Thessaloníki (Salonika) in Greece. From here the road east through northern Greece via Kavala to Alexandroupolis is taken, and so on to the Turkish frontier at İpsala. The distance to İstanbul from İpsala is approximately the same as from Edirne. Turkey's main border crossings have duty-free shops for ingoing and outgoing travellers.

Car insurance is required, and if your insurance or Green Card is not endorsed for Turkey, temporary third-party cover can be bought at the frontier. A personal driving license is acceptable in so far as your own car is concerned, but possession of an international driving license could make for ease of communication in an out-of-the-way place, and particularly if you are considering hiring a car.

Passenger — car train
There is a weekly service from Flushing in the Netherlands or from Brussels in Belgium as far as Ljubljana in Yugoslavia (direct road from here through Zagreb to Belgrade). For information contact DER Travel Service, 18 Conduit Street, London W1R 9TD (tel. London 4080111).

Passenger — car ferry
Türk Denizyolları (Turkish Maritime Lines) has a car-ferry service, summer months only, from Ancona in Italy to İzmir. The length of the voyage takes 48 hours. For information contact TML directly at the World Trade Centre, St Katherine's Way, London E1 9UN, or their agents Walford Lines, London (tel. London 4805621). Libra Maritime Lines, too, has a service from Brindisi to İzmir, crossing to Patras and calling at Piraeus, with sailings on Mondays, Wednesdays and Fridays — David Walker Travel, Littlegate Street, Oxford OX1 1QT (tel. 0865 728136). British Ferries also sails each Friday from May to September from Venice via Piraeus to İstanbul and Kuşadası. Their address is 20 Upper Ground, London SE1 9PF (tel. London 9285550).

Greek and Turkish maritime companies have services from Piraeus to İstanbul, and Italian boats touch on Turkish ports, as well as those of other countries. Potential passengers who find themselves in the Piraeus can inquire at the offices of shipping lines on Akti Miaouli, the main avenue on the waterfront at Piraeus, as there are frequent sailings by one or other line.

The Aegean Islands of Mytilini, Chios, Samos, Kos and Rhodes all have passenger or passenger-car ferry sailings to towns on the Turkish coast, as indicated in those sections of the text concerned with the Aegean and Mediterranean.

By Coach
Bosfor Turizm and Travel Inc, a Turkish company, has a daily coach service from Athens to İstanbul, while two other Turkish companies, Varan and Derya, run a daily service from Thessaloníki (Salonika) in northern Greece.

From Western Europe this company has a weekly service (twice-weekly in high season) from Amsterdam, The Hague, Hamburg, Cologne, Bonn, Berlin, Frankfurt, Munich, Vienna, Geneva, Paris, Lyon, Milan and Venice; while Varan Turizm has services from Venice, Salzburg, Strasbourg and Zurich.

From London, International Express has a summer service to İstanbul (Coach Travel Centre, 13 Regent Street, SW1Y 4LR); but as several coach companies co-operate under this service, bus changes are likely to occur at one or other scheduled stop. Eurolines has a daily service from Victoria Coach Station to Munich, from where it operates in tandem with Bosfor Turizm. Bosfor Turizm's office in Munich is Seidelstrasse 2, Munich 8 (tel. 592496; tlx. 529388 ABOS); in Vienna at Argentinerstrasse 67 1040 (tel. 650644, tlx. 136878). In İstanbul it is at Mete Caddesi 14, Taksim Square (tel. 143 25 25; tlx. 24324 IBOS TR).

By Train
Express trains to İstanbul tend to lose their epithet (and sometimes their sleeping compartments) on their journey through Yugoslavia and beyond. Check carefully when booking.

From London the İstanbul or Orient Express runs daily via Paris to Dijon, Lausanne, Milan and Venice, from where it continues to Zagreb, Belgrade and Niş in Yugoslavia, Sofia and Plovdiv in Bulgaria, and so to Edirne in Turkey. The total time for the journey is about 72 hours, with sleeping cars as far as Venice.

From Munich the İstanbul Express runs daily through Salzburg Ljublijana, Zagreb, Niş, Sofia and Plovdiv to Edirne and İstanbul. The Balkan Express to Istanbul starts daily from Vienna, through Maribor to Zagreb and on through Yugoslavia and Bulgaria to Edirne. The journey by either train takes about 40 hours, and transit visas for Yugoslavia and Bulgaria are needed.

In general, rail travel beyond Vienna or Venice is recommended only for the truly Spartan traveller. Comfortably, a train can be taken to Munich, or Salzburg, or Vienna, from which chosen place a transfer could then be made to one or other of the coach services or, at Venice or Ancona, a transfer to one of the ferry services to İzmir or Kuşadasî. From Venice there is a rail service to İstanbul with second-class couchette supplement available. The *Thomas Cook Continental Timetable* is an invaluable publication when planning extensive rail travel, as is *Spot on Turkish Travel*, a comprehensive manual published by Biltin Toker of Panorama Productions, 11 Lamartin Caddesi, Taksim, İstanbul.

Train and Ferry Connections
As well as from Venice and Ancona, there is a ferry crossing to Patras in Greece from Brindisi in southern Italy. Once in Greece, Greek National Railways has a daily rail service from Athens through Thessaloníki (Salonika) to İstanbul, the track passing through that section of Bulgaria where the three frontiers of Greece, Bulgaria and Turkey conjoin. This journey could in fact begin at Patras by taking the train from there to Athens. Again, once in Greece, by taking one of the daily sailings from Piraeus to one of the Greek Aegean Islands mentioned in the section on passenger-car ferries, you could then cross by ferry to the Turkish coast. There are also local flights by Olympic Airways, the Greek national carrier, to each of these islands.

The İstanbul railway terminus for trains coming from the west is at Sirkeci, near the waterfront at Eminönü on the western side of the Golden Horn. For continuing a rail journey through Anatolia, east of the Bosphorus, the railway terminus is at Haydarpaşa, which is reached by ferry boat from the quays of Eminönü, or those of Galata on the opposite side of the Golden Horn. However, plans for a railway tunnel under the Bosphorus are in an advanced stage of preparation and in a year or two an unbroken railway journey will become possible.

Visas

A valid passport or equivalent international document is required, however, British visitors can acquire a simplified form of passport. Valid for one year and non-renewable, it can be obtained from the Post Office or Employment Office in Britain.

Citizens of western European countries, the United States, Australia, Hong Kong, Japan, Morocco, New Zealand, Saudi Arabia, Tunisia and the United Arab Emirates are among those who need no visa and may stay up to three months. If you wish to stay longer, apply for an extension. Romanians and Yugoslavians must apply for an extension after two months; citizens of Malaysia must apply after two weeks. Other nationals who are granted a three-month residence without a visa are those of Bahrain, Barbados, Fiji, Gambia, Jamaica, Kenya, Kuwait, Malta, Mauritius, Oman, Qatar, Seychelles, Singapore, South Korea and Trinidad and Tobago.

To apply for permission to extend your stay, visit the offices of the Aliens Bureau, Yabancilar Şube Müdürlüğü, situated in the main police stations of towns. The Aliens Bureau in İstanbul is at Cağaloğlu, Sultanahmet, north of Divan Yolu (tel. 528 51 73). Or apply through the *vali* (governor) of a province in a city or his representative, the *kaymakam*, in larger towns.

Customs Regulations

A visitor may take the following items into Turkey duty free: 400 cigarettes, 50 cigars or one kilogram of tobacco; one kilogram of tea or coffee; five litres of spirits, of which three may be whisky; one kilogram of chocolates and five phials of perfume. Personal effects can include sports and camping equipment, guns and ammunition for hunting, still and cine cameras, ten rolls each of still and 8-mm film, spares for a car, a portable typewriter, a record player and up to ten records, a portable radio and a musical instrument. Items of value, however, such as cameras, a radio or typewriter, should be entered in the passport to facilitate export on leaving the country.

There is no limit to the amount of any foreign currency that can be imported and exported. Receipts for the exchange of foreign currency should be kept to enable re-conversion on leaving the country and as proof of currency conversion for the purchase of souvenirs such as jewellery or carpets valued at the equivalent of US$3,000 or more.

Climate and Clothing

A Mediterranean climate dominates on Turkey's Aegean and southern coasts. In general, hot, rainless summers offset spring and autumn showers, followed by mild winters with the rare excitement of a snowfall. Along the coast of the Black Sea the summer weather is akin to that of eastern Europe — plus a degree or two. The sea is less tranquil at times than off the other two coasts, and rain showers or a sudden storm can occur.

With sea or waterways seldom out of sight on three of its sides, İstanbul can still be hot and dusty on summer days, and somewhat close with humidity on others, but some rain should be anticipated. In winter, rain, sleet and snow are not exceptional in the city.

Inland on the central plateau of western Anatolia, summers are hot and dry, winters cold and crisp. Ankara experiences heavy frosts and snowfalls, lightened frequently by meridian blue skies and untroubled sunshine. The inland summer of eastern Anatolia resembles that of the western plateau, but in winter it is a colder place altogether, with some mitigation along the southern region that borders Syria and Iraq and between the two great rivers of the Euphrates and the Tigris.

Winter sports can be enjoyed in several locations without the anxiety of a sudden or premature thaw. Innumerable mountain ranges are seldom without snow on their upper slopes and peaks, in particular, on Mount Olympus in Mysia in the Bursa region and on Mount Ararat, the mother and father of mountains in far eastern Turkey.

For clothing along the Mediterranean and Aegean coasts, beachwear is quite clearly the order of the day, with something a bit less non-existent than a g-string perhaps on the Black Sea, and wind cheaters should be at hand for those who aspire to international yachtsmanship. Night-wear can be light and casual, with a pullover or cardigan available against a cooler breeze or an appreciable drop in temperature between sunset and moonrise.

Casual travellers going by bus and minibus throughout this extensive country should pack items such as shirts and underwear that can be dipped in a hotel's or pension's bathroom and dried overnight on the balcony. Slightly heavier woollies than those for the coast will be appreciated when eating at open-air restaurants in mountainous regions or beside lakes.

Women are advised to dress conservatively once among the less-Westernized inhabitants of the inland regions of eastern Turkey, and when visiting a mosque anywhere skirts and covered heads are expected. Sometimes the sacristan is able to provide a length of cloth for wrap-round use. Everyone goes shoeless, but at many of the larger mosques overshoes are available at the entrance.

Sandals help keep the feet cool and protect from blisters on burning sands. But for those who intend to visit at least some of Asia Minor's countless ancient and historic sights, a stout pair of walking shoes and frequent changes of socks are recommended.

Turkey is a thirst-making place throughout summer, but bottled water, mineral and otherwise, abounds, and in general tap water is safe. On long distance buses bottled water is available free of charge to the passenger, and all you have to do is to ask the *su lutfen* (conductor).

Health

Visitors are not asked to present a vaccination certificate.

Although frequently on ration to households in Istanbul, tap water is considered safe for drinking.

In any personal medical crisis, go into an *eczane* (chemist's) and ask for a *doktor* (doctor). Repeat the request until the chemist understands that you are in need of one. For first aid treatment there is a First Aid Hospital (Taksim Ilkyardim Hastanesi) on Siraselviler Caddesi, Taksim, down on the right-hand side of the street (tel. 143 10 40). Another recommended emergency hospital is the state-run Tip Fakultesi Hastanesi, Kocamustafapaşa Caddeşi, Cerrahpasa (tel. 585 21 00), or the private American Hospital, Guzelbahçe Sokak, Nişantaş (tel. 140 84 84). In place of the Red Cross, Turkey's medical symbol is a *kĭzĭlay* (red crescent moon) on a white ground.

In dire emergency, telephone 77 for an ambulance or mobile medical assistance.

Money

The unit of currency is the Turkish Lira (TL), divided into kuruş (krş), 100 krş to 1TL. The rate of exchange (August 1990) is 2,262TL to US$1 or 4,940TL to £1. Banknotes are issued in 500TL, 1,000TL, 5,000TL, 10,000TL, 20,000TL and 50,000TL. Care should be taken not to confuse the 1,000 and 10,000 notes. Kuruş coins are no longer of value. There are four aluminium lira coins for 1TL, 5TL, 10TL and 25TL, three nickel coins for 50TL, 100TL and 500TL and two small bronze coins, over which care should be exercised, for 100TL and 500TL.

There are over 60 major banks in Turkey. The largest ones have branches throughout most major cities and in the towns or centres where visitors in general find themselves. Some of the better publicized with exchange facilities are Akbank, Koc-Amerikan Bankasî (American Express), Citibank, Egebank,

Garanti Bankasi̇, Osmanli Bankasi̇, Ziraat Bankasi̇ and Yapi ve Kredi Bankasi̇. Banking hours are from 8.30 am to 12 pm and from 1.30 to 5 pm, Monday to Friday. Banks close on Saturdays, Sundays and public holidays. Most approved hotels are permitted to exchange currency, and this facility is also applicable to post offices (PTT). Visitors are likely to be solicited by non-licensed dealers who offer more favourable rates than the official rate of exchange, but extreme caution in such an encounter is advisable.

Eurocheques are accepted on the evidence of a Eurocard; traveller's cheques require that a passport or other universally accepted identification card or document be presented. American Express, Diners Club, Barclaycard, Carte Blanche, Eurocard and Visa are accepted credit cards, though there might be difficulty making use of these outside the cities and major towns.

Transportation

By Air
Flights from İstanbul leave from the domestic terminal at Atatürk Airport. There are daily flights to Ankara (45 minutes), Adana (80 minutes), Antalya (45 minutes), Dalaman (75 minutes), Diyarbakir (95 minutes), Elaziğ, stopover Ankara (3 hours 35 minutes), Erzurum, stopover Ankara (2 hours 35 minutes), İzmir (40 minutes), Kayseri (75 minutes), Malatya, stopover Ankara (3 hours 45 minutes), Samsun, stopover Ankara (2 hours 45 minutes), Trabzon, stopover Ankara (3 hours 10 minutes) and Van, stopover Ankara (3 hours 25 minutes). The above flights are by the national carrier THY, and the more popular schedules are augmented during the summer season.

On THY domestic flights married couples are entitled to a 10 percent discount on one ticket; sports groups (minimum of ten persons), 30 percent; journalists, 50 percent; infants (children under two years of age), 90 percent; and children from two to 12 years, 50 percent.

On international flights married couples and infants enjoy the same discount as on domestic flights, while students are entitled to a 60 percent discount.

Students who hold a card issued by TMGT (The Turkish National Youth Organization), with offices at İstiklâl Caddesi 471/2, Tünel, İstanbul, or TOGTO (Turkish Tourism Organization for Students and Youth), Samanyolu Sokak 62/8, Şişli, İstanbul, can claim discounts of 20 percent on Turkish Railways, 10 percent on domestic air flights, 60 percent on international flights out of Turkey and 15-50 percent on Türk Denizyollari̇ (Turkish Maritime Lines).

In addition to THY, Sonmez Holidays Hava Yollari̇ (tel. 573 29 20), a private company, flies to Bursa each morning and afternoon, with return flights, Monday to Friday and on Saturday morning. Marmara Hava Yollari̇ ve

Turizm A.S., another private company, has a schedule of internal flights, as well as one for its charter operations to overseas destinations. Its office is at Meşrutiyet Caddesi 164/3, Şişhane (tel. 144 51 65) The private company Emair has an office at the domestic terminal of İstanbul's Atatürk Airport. Its head office is in Ankara, at Necatibey Caddesi, 88/6, Bakanlıklar, with an office at Ankara's Esenboğa Airport.

The company can arrange sightseeing or aerial photography flights at a cost of about US$175 per hour minimum. Note that film makers or simple photographers need a military permit to film or photograph from the air. For permit application and information, contact Türk Kusu, Ankara (tel. 311 17 39).

For helicopter tours, Sancakair, with offices at Londra Asfalti, Florya, İstanbul, and at the domestic terminal of Atatürk Airport, has helicopters for hire for two, four or six people.

Sancakair also flies city tours on Saturdays and Sundays from its own heliport at Abide-1 Hurriyet Caddesi, Sehit Ahmet Sokak 1, Mecidiyeköy, İstanbul (tel. 172 79 52).

Nesu Air, at Valikonaği Caddesi 30/B, Nişantaşi (at the north end of Cumhuriyet Caddesi), İstanbul, operating from Atatürk Airport, offers executive air charter and an air taxi service, along with sightseeing tours and short-distance helicopter transportation from the Hilton Hotel.

By Car

To hire a car in Turkey, you must present a valid national driving license and be 19 years of age or over.

Outside the main cities and holiday centres, unleaded petrol may not be so easily available as in western European countries. Motorists are advised to obtain information from the offices of the Türkiye Turing ve Otomobil Kurumu (Touring and Automobile Club of Turkey). Its head office, (tel. 131 46 31; tlx. 27800 RING TR) is in the Şişli district of İstanbul at Halâskârgazi Caddesi 364, a continuation of Cumhuriyet Caddesi in Taksim. This organization has also undertaken tourist development projects such as the rehabilitation of old buildings in the Sultanahmet area of İstanbul and the reconstruction of tourist accommodation, restaurants and the Artisan Centre there. It has branches at İpsala and Edirne (Kapikule), frontier posts with Greece; Derekoy, the frontier post with Bulgaria; İzmir, Atatürk Bulvari 370, Alsancak; Mersin, Mucahitler Caddesi 55, Karadağ Iş Hani; Trabzon, Çomlekci Yokusu; İskenderun, Maresal Fevzi Çakmak Caddesi 8/2; Çilvegozu, the Turkish – Syrian frontier post; Gaziantep, Ali Fuat Cebesöy Bulvari 5D; Habur on the Turkey – Iraq border; Gorbulak, the Turk – Iranian frontier post near Doğubayazit; and Ankara, Adakale Sokak 4/1, Yenişehir.

By Yacht
Those wishing to charter a yacht should contact Albatross Yachting and
Marine Services at 3 Yerebatan Caddesi, Salkimsogut Sokaki 20/6, Cağaloğlu,
İstanbul (tel. 522 28 08; tlx. 22615 MOTE TR); it has branches at Bodrum and
Marmaris. Two other possibilities in İstanbul include Atlantis Yachting and
Tourism Company, OTIM, Ihlamur, Beşiktaş, or Fora, Comhuriyet Caddesi 2
43/4, Harbiye. Or in Bodrum, Ege Yacht Service Company, Neyzen Tevfik
Caddesi, 202, may be able to help you.

Communications

The main post office in İstanbul, Büyük Postane, is in Şehinşah Caddesi 22,
Sirkeci, in the old city, behind the buildings opposite the main railway station
there. Another main post office is at Kadîköy, Damga Sokak 1, on the Asiatic
side of the Bosphorus. Both are open 24 hours a day. All post offices are distinguished by a yellow sign with PPT in black lettering.

Branch post offices are less numerous than in western European countries.
Beyoğlu, the new city, has offices at İstiklâl Caddesi 190, Galatasaray; at the
start of Cumhuriyet Caddesi from Taksim Square; and in Osmanbey on
Halâskârgazi Caddesi, the extension of Cumhuriyet Caddesi; all are open from
8 am to 8 pm. After 8 pm there is an office at Yeniçarşisi Caddesi 3,
Galatasaray, or at Büyükderes Caddesi 8, Şişli. Minor branches close at 6 pm.
Some post office services such as stamps and posting can be handled, of
course, by reception staff at major hotels or, as at the Hilton, by a sub-post office on the premises. Telex messages can be sent by residents from major
hotels, and there are facilities at some, if not all, major post offices. The post
offices at Sirkeci, Beyoğlu and Kadîköy have a public facsimile service.

A *jeton* (token) is needed for use in public call boxes. They can be bought
at post offices, from concessionaires at public call boxes or at ferry stations as
jetons are also used on the ferries. When making an international call from a
public call box, make sure the instrument has the second slot for this purpose
and have an ample supply of *jetons*. They come in small-sized *küçük* (40TL)
for local calls, *orta* (200TL) for trunk calls and *büyük* for international calls.
Should you need to make a local call and there is no unoccupied call box in
sight, ask at an *eczane* (chemist's) — there are plenty, and it is a common practice.

The dialling code for an intended trunk call to another part of Turkey is 03,
and for international calls dial 528 23 03. Operators on international lines
speak at least one language other than Turkish, mainly English. When placing
international calls, the country code is 99 44 for the United Kingdom and 99 1
for the United States and Canada. The *Spot on Turkish Travel* directory has a
complete list of international dialling codes. Calls can be booked for a normal

connection, but for a rush call, place your request with the word *acele* (pronounced ajela) or, if extremely urgent, *yildirim* (lightning). The cost of *acele* is three times that of a normal call; *yildirim* is five times that of *acele*. Reduced rates are applicable for international calls made on Sundays or between 8 pm and 8 am daily.

Most familiar foreign language newspapers from European countries and America are on sale a day after publication. The Sunday papers are available about the middle of the week. The *Daily News*, in English, is published in Ankara but circulates in İstanbul and elsewhere. It has extensive international and local news coverage. *Apoyevmatini* is a Greek language newspaper, as is *ISO*.

Haşet at 469 İstiklâl Caddesi, Tünel, is the largest of the multinational booksellers and also stocks international newspapers and magazines. Among its branches in İstanbul, Haşet has outlets at both the Hilton and Sheraton hotels, while in Ankara there is a branch at Ziya Gökalp 14, off Kizilay. Back in İstanbul on Halâskârgazi Caddesi — a continuation of Cumhuriyet Caddesi — at Harbiye, Hitit has a selection of paperbacks and perhaps even an out-of-print edition of a book you have been seeking for a long time. Sander, also on Halâskârgazi Caddesi, 275, is a larger, enterprising bookseller with a good range of English books, including Penguin and Pelican, and some French and German offerings. The International Bookstore is on Valikonaği Caddesi 85, at Nişantaşi (at the north end of Cumhuriyet Caddesi). Net has a shop opposite the Yerebatan Cistern at Sultanahmet; Redhouse has one on Riza Paşa Yokuşu, 50, at Sultanhamam — telephone 527 81 00 for its location as the shop is not in one of the more familiar districts of the city. Taş Yayincilik is on Meşrutiyet Caddesi, Asi Han 13, not far from the British and American consulates. Bilimsel Eserler is at Siraselviler Caddesi, Ayla İş Hani 66, off Taksim. For secondhand books, the Sahaflar Çarşisi at Beyazit Square, down below the Grand Bazaar, is one of the oldest and most fascinating of bibliophile establishments. Türk-Alman (Deutsche Buchhandlung) at İstiklâl Caddesi 481, near Tünel, has been established there since the 1950s.

Time and Measurements

Turkey is two hours ahead of Greenwich Mean Time and observes the extra hour of daylight saving between 30 March and 25 October. Government office hours are Monday to Friday, 9 am – 12 pm and 1.30 – 5.30 pm. Shopping hours are 9 am – 1 pm and 2 – 7 pm daily except Sunday and national holidays. Some shops close all day or for half of the day on Saturday throughout the summer months — 1 June to 31 August. Many shops in the Covered Bazaar area stay open all the time. Modification of these shopping hours is under consideration, and changes are expected, which could mean a sudden alteration or perhaps no change at all.

Electricity is generally 220 volts AC, although in some older parts of İstanbul it is 110 volts. This is unlikely to cause a problem for the visitor, but prudence suggests a check before plugging in.

Weights and measures are metric.

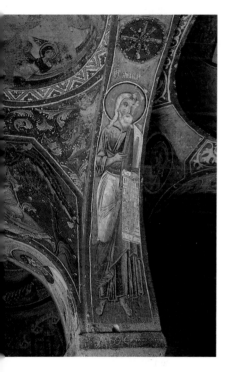

Public Conveniences

These are few and far between in Turkey, and where they exist often leave much to be desired in the way of hygiene. Cubicle or closet installations tend to be of the seatless kind — in themselves superior in terms of posture and hygiene rather than inferior, eschewing personal comfort.

In general, other than in hotels in the approved categories, the cleanest conveniences are in mosques, which are open to all.

Tourist Information

The head office of the Turkish Ministry of Culture and Information is in Ankara, but it has centres throughout the country, in almost every place in which a visitor might feel he or she is in need of help or advice. Brochures, and sometimes regional maps, can be got at these centres.

There are offices of the Ministry of Culture and Information in London at 170 – 3 Piccadilly, in New York at 821 UN Plaza, NY 10017, and in Washington at 2010 Massachusetts Avenue, Washington DC 20008. Other offices around the world include the Paris office at 102 Avenue des Champs Elysees; Frankfurt am Main at Baseler Strasse 37, D-6000; Munich at Kalsplatz 3/1, Munchen 2; Rome at the Piazza della Republica 56, 00185; Tokyo at 33 – 6 2-Chome, Jungumae, Shibuya-ku, 150; Amsterdam at Herengracht 51, 1017 BS; Madrid at Plaza de Espana, Piso; Stockholm at Kungsgatan 3 S-111 43; Zurich at Talstrasse 74, 8001; Kuwait, PO Box 15518, Deaya; Jeddah at Medina Road Kilo, A1 Musaidiya Street.

Language

Turkish, considered to be among the Uralo-Altaic group of languages, has some affinities with Hungarian and Finnish. As the languages of this group of the Indo-Aryan tongue do not differ appreciably, the language can be understood and spoken throughout Turkic populations from the borders of China to southeastern Europe. Until 1928 Turkish was written in Arabic script, but Kemal Atatürk changed this by introducing the Latin script and reforming the language, clarifying it and eliminating its accumulation of alien words and expressions.

Atatürk himself travelled the country, introducing the new script and teaching it to villagers. Along with reforming the language, he reformed the clothing by introducing European styles and abolishing the fez, which has been replaced by the cloth cap as a national headgear.

Turkish has only one anomalous verb and one irregular noun. It is an agglutinizing language with an unchanging root to which suffixes are added for tense, number and case. In general, in spoken Turkish the accent comes on the first syllable of a word, with a tendency to raise the pitch of the voice on the last syllable.

The Turkish alphabet has 29 letters, eight vowels and 21 consonants. Some of these letters do not occur in English, namely, ç, ğ, ş, ı, ö, ü. For near rather than exact pronunciation: 'c' occurs but is pronounced like English 'j' followed by a vowel, as in the word 'jug'; 'j' occurs but is pronounced with a soft sound as in French 'gendarme' or 'jour'; 'g' occurs but is hard as in 'ghost'; while 'ğ' is not pronounced but lengthens the preceding vowel.

Turkish 'ç' is as in 'change'; 'e' is as in 'bed', not as in 'her'; 'h' is always pronounced and never elided, except with the name 'Mehmet', in which the first syllable is lengthened; 'o' is as French 'eau', while 'ö' is the umlauted German 'lowen' or French 'deux'; 'ş' is as in 'should'; 'ü' as the umlauted German in 'tur' or as the French 'u' in 'tu'; and, finally, the undotted 'ı' is exclusively Turkish and has a shortened, slightly guttural sound as the 'u' in 'mum'.

Some everyday language:

sabah	morning	*anlamak*	to understand
bugün	today	*almak*	to buy
dün	yesterday	*bakmak*	to look
gün	day	*görmek*	to see
günaydin	good morning	*gördum*	I saw
yarin	tomorrow	*calişmak*	to work
akşam	evening	*gelmek*	to come
iyi akşamlar	good evening	*gitmek*	to go
hafta	week	*etmek*	to do

ay	month	*birakmak*	to leave
para	money	*bülmak*	to find
kaç para?	how much?	*satmak*	to sell
bir	a, an	*kahve*	coffee
bir	one	*çay*	tea
kiki	two	*kahvalti*	breakfast
üç	three	*otobüs*	bus
dört	four	*otogar*	bus station
beş	five	*istaşyon*	railway station
altı	six	*tren*	train
yedi	seven	*iş*	work
sekiz	eight	*kitap*	book
dokuz	nine	*pek*	very
on	ten	*çok peki*	very much
yirmi	twenty	*güzel*	good
otuz	thirty	*fena*	bad
kırk	forty	*vapuri*	steamer
elli	fifty	*evet*	yes
altmış	sixty	*bilet*	ticket
yetmis	seventy	*erken*	early
seksen	eighty	*gece*	night
doksan	ninety	*iy-geceler*	goodnight
yüz	one hundred	*Pazar*	Sunday
bin	one thousand	*Pazartesi*	Monday
by	this	*Sali*	Tuesday
şu	that	*Çarşamba*	Wednesday
hayır	no	*Perşembe*	Thursday
yok	none	*Cuma*	Friday
sicak	hot	*Cumartesi*	Saturday
soguł.	cold	*su*	water
mektup	letter	*süt*	milk
pul	postage stamp	*ekmek*	bread
lokanta	restaurant	*yumurta*	egg
hesap	bill	*biraz*	a little
sifir	zero	*tereyag*	butter
arkadas	friend	*büyük*	big
deniz	sea	*küçük*	small
Akdeniz	Mediterranean	*sonra*	later
kara	black	*ussak*	far
beyaz	white	*yakin*	near
oda	room	*yeni*	new
yatak	bed	*anahtar*	key

kapalı	closed	*çatal*	fork
açık	open	*bıcak*	knife
hasta	ill	*kaşık*	spoon
hastanesi	hospital	*bardak*	glass
lütfen	please	*şişe*	bottle
güle güle	goodbye	*tabak*	late
saat	time	*yemek*	food
kaç saat?	what time	*iskele*	quay

Food

Turkish cuisine has been classified with those of France and China among the innovative delights of the culinary world. Opinions on eating, however, and the comparative excellence of dishes can be very personal to a diner, whose health, weight and susceptibility to ulcers might well influence his or her assessment of quality. Others, enflamed by environmental or ecological convictions, might consider a bowl of porridge a banquet compared to a veal cutlet cooked rare on a French grill, bird's-nest soup or braised dog — whatever the Chinese call this domestic animal — or the raw liver served in an Arab restaurant (which is not a Turkish way of presentation since a Turkish chef will spice his liver and fry it with onions, or he will dice it and serve it well-seasoned as a salad with olive oil).

Since Turkish cooking originated in the Central Asian plains and the mountainous Altai, in a pastoral and nomadic setting, lamb is preferred to beef as a staple of meat dishes. Lamb is spitted, stewed, grilled in kebabs or minced *köfte* (meatballs or rissoles); mutton is roasted or casserolled. Beef is served as steak, less often roasted, or as *döner* kebab, spiced and compacted into a huge inverted cone and turned on a verticle rotating grill, from which fine slices are carved. There are regional variations in the way in which *döner* and other kebabs are prepared and served. Stuffed vegetables, including tomatoes, peppers, vine leaves, aubergine, marrow, pumpkin and squash (courgettes); stuffed mussels and shelled mussels dipped in batter, deep-fried and served with a garlic sauce; chicken boned and spiced (Chicken Kiev) and chicken cooked in a Circassian way with walnut sauce; a variety of *pilâv* dishes — all very simple to explain, and nothing out of the ordinary, many might say. But it is far from simple to describe the taste that expert hands and the professional mind of a dedicated chef can concoct. Those who have travelled in Greece might brush off any special claim made on behalf of such dishes, assessing them as mediocre on palate and low in satisfaction, which could be true of Greece but is an error where its neighbour's kitchen is concerned. The difference is not so much one of temperament as of obeisance to culinary art and care in preparation and presentation, as well as a willingness to please the diner.

As an alternative to meat kebabs, try pieces of swordfish grilled on a skewer interspersed with peppers and onions. There are fish of all varieties, particularly from the Black Sea, perhaps seeking their escape to an illusory freedom by way of the Bosphorus. Fish, large or small, for grilling, frying or baking on a brick or tile, can be chosen alive from the restaurant's tank in an inland city such as Ankara, where sea bass are flown in and trout are caught from nearby mountain streams.

The danger is for the weight-watcher, the traveller on a diet who cannot avoid the overpowering temptation of honeyed sweetmeats: the baklava, a tiny roll of leaf pastry enriched with crushed nuts and soaked in honey, *bülbül yuvasi* (nightingale's nest, a variety of baklava), *tel kadayif* (shredded wheat subjected to a similar process of preparation), *kabak tatlisi* (baked pumpkin served with pounded walnuts) and walnuts in strained yoghurt and served with honey; these are a few of the available honeydew amongst the wealth of paradise. Not to ignore Turkish Delight: most visitors probably will have tasted this sweet, or 'pudding' as it is sometimes translated, prior to their arrival but now will discover in what variety it can be enjoyed.

It has to be confessed, though, that with the development of international tourism the variety of dishes in tourist centres is becoming minimal.

Guide to a Turkish Menu

Soups (*Çorba*)
Düğün çorbasi	Lamb soup with egg and lemon sauce
İşkembe çorbasi	Tripe soup with egg and lemon sauce
Mercimek çorbasi	Lentil soup
Şehriye çorbasi	Chicken soup with noodles
Yayla çorbasi	Rice soup

Eggs (*Yumurta*)
Çilbir	Poached
Menemen	Scrambled
Pastirmali yumurta	Fried with bacon (*pastirma*)
Sahanda yumurta	Fried

Meat (*Et*)
Düğün eti	Chopped leg of lamb or mutton roasted in spicy tomato sauce
Haşlama	Chopped leg of lamb or mutton cooked with celery and carrots
Küzü dolmassi	Roast leg of lamb with rice, raisins and pine nuts
Küzü guveçi	Casseroled lamb with potatoes and tomatoes

Küzü incik patlîcanli	Lamb stew with aubergine
Küzü karamasi	Grilled lamb with salad
Papaz yahnisi	Diced beef with onions, spices and cinnamon

Kebab
Bahçivan kebabi	Diced lamb or beef with carrots, potatoes, peas
Çomlek kebabi	Lamb with green beans, eggplant, potatoes, carrots, ochra and green beans
Çop kebabi	Diced (small) beef on stick grilled on charcoal
Döner kebab	Sliced mutton off vertical spit
Işlim kebabi	Lamb in pastry with tomatoes, peppers, etc
Ka'git kebabi	Lamb cooked in foil with carrots, potatoes, peas
Orman kebabi	Roast lamb with tomatoes, carrots and peas
Şiş kebabi	Lamb on a skewer grilled on charcoal
Taş kebabi	Sliced beef in sauce

Köfte
Adana kebabi	Heavily spiced and peppered mincemeat
Cizbiz	Grilled meatballs
Içli Köfte	Mince with crushed walnuts, spices and parsley
Terbiyeli köfte	Meatballs with egg and lemon sauce
Kadin büdü köfte	Meatballs with rice dipped in egg yolk and fried

Fried and Grilled
Arnavut ciğeri	Diced fried liver
Beyin tava	Sauted lamb's brains
Böbrek izgara	Grilled kidneys
Ciger izgara	Grilled liver
Ciger tava	Fried liver
Dil	Tongue
Koç yumurtasi	Lamb's sweetbreads grilled with herbs

Poultry
Bğendili tavük	Chicken with aubergine and cheese
Çerkez tavügü	Circassian chicken
Hindi dolmasi	Turkey with spiced rice
Bildircin pilâvli	Quail with rice

Cooked Vegetables
Biber dolmasi	Stuffed green peppers
Domates dolmasi	Stuffed tomatoes
Kabak dolmasi	Stuffed marrow

Patlican dolması	Stuffed eggplant (aubergine)
Yaprak dolması	Stuffed vine leaves
Bamya etli	Ochra with slices of mutton or beef
Enginar dolması	Stuffed artichokes
Etli fasulye	Green beans with mutton or beef
Havuç kızartması	Fried carrots - *yovgurtlu* (with yoghurt)
Ispanak kavurması	Saute spinach and mincemeat - *yogurtlu*
Kabak kızartması	Fried squash
Kapüska	Cabbage with mincemeat
Karnabahar kızartması	Fried cauliflour dipped in egg yolk and flour
Kis türlüsü	Potatoes, celery, carrots, leeks with pieces of lamb
Patlican beğendi	Aubergine with cream and cheese
Patlican tava	Fried aubergine
Pirasa	Leeks with lamb
Yaz türlüsü	Green beans, aubergine, tomatoes, green peppers, potatoes, squash, with lamb

Fish (*Balık*)

Barbunya kagitta	Red mullet baked in foil
Hamsa tava	Fried anchovies
Kiliç şiş	Swordfish portions on a skewer
Levrek kagitta	Sea bass grilled in foil
Mersin şiş	Sturgeon grilled on a skewer
Papaz yahnisi	Bonito fish cooked in olive oil
Uskümrü dolması	Fried mackerel
Sardalya asma yaprainda	Sardines in vine leaves
Midye plakisi	Mussels in olive oil
Midye tava	Deep-fried mussels in batter

Salads in oil and hors d'oeuvres (*meze*)

Ayse fasulye	Green beans
Bakla zeytiynagli	Broad beans
Barbünya plakisi	Red beans
Imam bayildi	Aubergine stuffed with sliced onions and garlic
Kereviz zeytinyagli	Celery
Lahana dolması	Cabbage leaves stuffed with spiced rice
Midye dolması	Mussels stuffed with spiced rice
Beyin salatası	Sheep's brains in olive oil and lemon juice
Cacik	Chopped cucumber and garlic in strained yoghurt
Ciroz salatası	Dried mackerel and dressing
Patlican salatası	Mashed aubergine salad
Tarama salatası	Fish roe salad
Tarator salatası	Sesame seed ground with walnuts and garlic

Rice dishes and savoury pastries

Bühara pilâvî	Rice with carrots, almonds and mutton
Ciğerli pilâv	Rice with liver
Bulgar pilâvi	Cracked wheat with onions and tomatoes
Firinda makarna	Baked macaroni
İç pilâv	Rice with chopped liver, raisins and pine nuts
Manti	Turkish-style ravioli
Bohça boreği	Meat and cottage-cheese pie
İspanakli börek	Spinach pie
Muşka boregi	Small triangular shaped meat and cheese pies
Peynirli börek	Cheese pie
Sigara boreği	Meat and cheese in roll of flaked pastry
Talaş boregï	Diced beef in flaked-pastry pie

Puddings

Fîrîn sütlaç	Baked rice pudding
Keşkül-U fukara	Cream pudding with pounded almonds
Sütlaç	Creamed rice
Tavuk göğsü	Pounded chicken's breast in cream

Selection of fish

Hamsi	Anchovy
Levrek	Bass
Palamut	Bonito
Pisi	Brill
Yengeç	Crab
Yilan baliği	Eel
Çipura	Bream
İstakoz	Lobster
Üskümrü	Mackerel
Kefal	Mullet
Tekur	Red mullet
Midye	Mussel
Ahtapot	Octopus
Mexit	Cod
Kerevit	Prawn
Karides	Shrimps
Kalamar	Squid
Dil	Sole
Kalkan	Turbot
Mezit/bakalyaro	Whiting
Kîlîbalîgi	Swordfish
Mersin balîg	Sturgeon

Drink

Turkey has a large wine-producing industry, based on domestic strains of vine and on recognized imported ones from France. Currently on offer are over 52 varieties of red wine, 50 varieties of white, 16 rosé and eight sparkling wines. Of the red, the wines of Atatürk Orman Çiftliği can be recommended: Ankara, Ankara Altini, Boğa Kani, and Kilis; of Doluca Bağcilik ve Sarapilik: Villa Doluca, Doluca Antik, Doluca; of Tekel: Büzbağ, Büzbağ (Madalyali), Güzel Marmara, Hösbağ, Trakya; of Kavaklidere şaraplari: Yakat, Kavaklidere Eski, Dikmen. In light wines Ankara and Ankara Altini have white versions; Tekel has Barbaros and a white Güzel Marmara, Narbağ and Trakya; Doluca has white versions of Villa Doluca, Doluca Antik and Doluca; Kavaklidere has its Cankaya and Kavak. Among the rosé there are Aral (Aral şarap Ltd), Bortacina (Yiğitler şarap Islt), Dona Villa (Mütük şarap San Ltd) and Truva (Talay şaraplari); the other companies mentioned above all have their rosé wines. Among the sparkling wines, Altin Köpük is a Kavaklidere champagne. This is only a selected list, and other labels you might come across in major cities and towns, or outside of them, are not to be excluded from palatability.

Not all Turkish restaurants serve wine or alcoholic drinks, and those that do add an extra 15 percent on to the bill. Therefore, if you like to drink with your meal, make sure the service is offered before taking a table.

Bottled drinking water is a Turkish industry almost as major as wine production. Citizens who have acquired a palate for the water of a particular spring will travel distances to obtain a magnum of it, and itinerant vendors with their carts or motorized transport circulate with giant jars of water from one natural spring or another. Many Turks are as expert in their connoisseurship of water as a taster of vintage wines. Claims are made for the medicinal effectiveness of some bottled waters — for stomach or kidney disorders — such as Circir from Sariyer on the Bosphorus, which is also a location of other springs. There is recommended water from Alemdağ, Beyköz and Büyükdere. Maden Suyu is a palatable bottled mineral water that is stocked by most restaurants, and there is a Maden Sodasi, too, which is good as a mixer. Of many labelled products Kızılay, from Afyon Karahisar, is highly recommended.

Raki is the national alcoholic beverage. It is distilled from raisins, and anise is added, making it a similar product to Greek ouzo, Arabic arak or French pastis. The principle brands are made by Tekel, Yeni Raki or Altinbas. Drunk as an apéritif, a *meze* (or hors d'oeuvres) is generally served with it. Tekel also manufactures *kanyak* (cognac), *votka* (vodka), *cin* (gin) and whisky, and there is a variety of liqueurs from Tekel and other manufacturers. The import of noted international brands of alcoholic liquor is now being considerably increased.

The Dogs of Constantinople

I am half willing to believe that the celebrated dogs of Constantinople have been misrepresented—slandered. I have always been led to suppose that they were so thick in the streets that they blocked the way; that they moved about in organized companies, platoons and regiments, and took what they wanted by determined and ferocious assault; and that at night they drowned all other sounds with their terrible howlings. The dogs I see here can not be those I have read of.

I find them every where, but not in strong force. The most I have found together has been about ten or twenty. And night or day a fair proportion of them were sound asleep. Those that were not asleep always looked as if they wanted to be. I never saw such utterly wretched, starving, sad-visaged, broken-hearted looking curs in my life. It seemed a grim satire to accuse such brutes as these of taking things by force of arms. They hardly seemed to have strength enough or ambition enough to walk across the street—I do not know that I have seen one walk that far yet. They are mangy and bruised and mutilated, and often you see one with the hair singed off him in such wide and well defined tracts that he looks like a map of the new Territories. They are the sorriest beasts that breathe—the most abject—the most pitiful. In their faces is a settled expression of melancholy, an air of hopeless despondency. The hairless patches on a scalded dog are preferred by the fleas of Constantinople to a wider range on a healthier dog; and the exposed places suit the fleas exactly. I saw a dog of this kind start to nibble at a flea— a fly attracted his attention, and he made a snatch at him; the flea called for him once more, and that forever unsettled him; he looked sadly at his flea-pasture, then sadly looked at his bald spot. Then he heaved a sigh and dropped his head resignedly upon his paws. He was not equal to the situation.

The dogs sleep in the streets, all over the city. From one end of the street to the other, I suppose they will average about eight or ten to a block. Sometimes, of course, there are fifteen or twenty to a block.

They do not belong to any body, and they seem to have no close personal friendships among each other. But they district the city themselves, and the dogs of each district, whether it be half a block in extent, or ten blocks, have to remain within its bounds. Woe to a dog if he crosses the line! His neighbors would snatch the balance of his hair off in a second. So it is said. But they don't look it.

They sleep in the streets these days. They are my compass— my guide. When I see the dogs sleep placidly on, while men, sheep, geese, and all moving things turn out and go around them, I know I am not in the great street where the hotel is, and must go further. In the Grand Rue the dogs have a sort of air of being on the lookout—an air born of being obliged to get out of the way of many carriages every day—and that expression one recognizes in a moment. It does not exist upon the face of any dog without the confines of that street. All others sleep placidly and keep no watch. They would not move, though the Sultan himself passed by.

In one narrow street (but none of them are wide) I saw three dogs lying coiled up, about a foot or two apart. End to end they lay, and so they just bridged the street neatly, from gutter to gutter. A drove of a hundred sheep came along. They stepped right over the dogs, the rear crowding the front, impatient to get on. The dogs looked lazily up, flinched a little when the impatient feet of the sheep touched their raw backs—sighed, and lay peacefully down again. No talk could be plainer than that. So some of the sheep jumped over them and others scrambled between, occasionally chipping a leg with their sharp hoofs, and when the whole flock had made the trip, the dogs sneezed a little, in the cloud of dust, but never budged their bodies an inch. I thought I was lazy, but I am a steam-engine compared to a Constantinople dog. But was not that a singular scene for a city of a million inhabitants?

Mark Twain, The Innocents Abroad

Sira is a delicious non-alcoholic grape drink, often available in non-alcoholic restaurants. Another drink for a cold day is *salep*, made from hot milk and orchis root, sprinkled with cinnamon. On a warm day *ayran*, a sour milk drink, can be a first-class thirst-quencher, often made in local neighbourhoods and sold out of large porcelain or metal tubs, in the way ice cream is sold elsewhere.

Best made locally, it is also available in bottles from grocery shops. Turkish coffee, too, is back, served black, *sade* without sugar, as *şekerli* with little sugar, *orta şekerli* medium sweet or *şekerli* sweet. Tea-drinking is a national habit. The tea is prepared in a samovar, or metal urn, and served in a small glass brought on a saucer. The tea is not milked, but sugar lumps are placed on the saucer alongside the spoon.

Tuborg Gold, Tuborg Pilsner and a rarer Draught Pilsner are beers produced in conjuction with Danish Tuborg; a dark beer, Ozel, is also on sale. There is Efes Pilsen, Pilsen on draught and a Lowenbrau. Tekel manufactures a light, dark and a *fici bira* (draft beer), too. Tekel is the state monopoly organization for cigarettes, spirituous liquors and other commodities, but present-day Turkey has begun to relax its state corporation economy and has extended production and marketing responsibilities to the country's private sector, with appreciable results.

Tobacco

Turkey has a large tobacco industry; its cultivation is centred principally on the Black Sea coast. Turks are heavy smokers too, and according to one Turkish commentator cigarette consumption is growing, not diminishing as in western European countries. In the present freer market economy of the country, with the state monopoly in tobacco and other commodities relaxed, the availability of imported brands of cigarettes, tobacco and cigars has increased, and multinational manufacturers are moving in for business. Of local cigarette brands, the extra strong Birinci is popular. Bitlis is a newer brand that is available mainly in the east of the country. Among those brands that claim lower tar and nicotine content in their cigarettes, and the filter-tipped varieties, king-sized Maltepe or the stronger-flavoured, well-established Samsun brand are recommended. Cigarettes for export, in particular a brand called Best, are also being produced. For prestige smoking, Tekel introduced the packing of cigarettes in individual wrappers, printed with a person's initials, company name or a submitted emblem or idiosyncratic motto.

For cigars, Ankara in boxes of 20 and İstanbul in packages of five are well regarded. For the cigarello and panatella type, Marmara in packets of five and ten and Pazar in packets of five are considered favourites.

Industry

Since the 1960s Turkey's economy has switched from being predominantly agricultural to a heavily industrialized one. Over 30 percent of the country's industrial activity occurs in İstanbul and vicinity, where 350,000 workers produce something like 60 percent of the country's industrial output. Among the largest enterprises are shipbuilding, pharmaceuticals, automobiles, machine assembly plants, building materials, household appliances, machine and automobile spares, food, textiles, leather, tobacco, glassware, cement, sugar, iron and carpets. Other than the appropriate government department, the Yapi-Endustri Merkezi (The Building and Industry Centre) has an information service for those who are interested in setting up cooperative industrial or contracting enterprises in the country. The office is on Cumhuriyet Caddesi 329, Harbiye. Tusiad, also on Cumhuriyet Caddesi, 233/4, Harbiye, is the Turkish Industrial and Businessmen's Association, and therefore a repository of the kind of information needed by an overseas businessman or industrialist who is contemplating activity in Turkey. Yased, an Association for Foreign Capital Coordination, offers information and assistance on capital investment in the country. Contact can be made at Ihlamur Sergi Sarayi, Beşiktaş.

Museums, Galleries, Sound and Light

Museums throughout Turkey are open from 9 am to 5 pm but do close on at least one day, usually a Monday. There are some variations of closing day, and a local check should be made. The entrance fee to most museums is variable, but usually fairly modest.

Where a museum has been established on an archaeological site, there is usually a charge for visiting the museum in addition to the site charge.

In İstanbul and Ankara there are a number of private galleries where special exhibitions of Turkish art and artists, rather than international ones, are held from time to time. Opening hours are usually from 10 am to 7 pm daily except on Sundays. A few selected galleries are Berk at Cumhuriyet Caddesi 69, Elmadağ; Atatürk Kültür Merkezi (Atatürk Cultural Centre), Taksim Square; Galeri Baraz, Kurtulus Caddesi, Kurtulus; Bestek Art Gallery, Abdi Ipekçi Caddesi 75, Maçka; İlhami Atalay Art Gallery, Alemdağ Caddesi 28/2, Sultanahmet; Kobi Art Gallery, Valikonaği Caddesi Pasaj 85, Nişantaşi; İmaj, Rumeli Caddesi, Villa Iş Hani 4-6, Nişantaşi; and Kolekşiyon, Sheration Hotel, Cumhuriyet Caddesi.

Moda Kültür Merkezi at Bahariye Caddesi 53, Kadiköy, is an art centre where international art films are screened, plays performed and art exhibited. Ortaköy Kültür Merkezi at Dereböyü Caddesi, Barbaros Passaj 110/1, Ortaköy, on the Bosphorus, and Bilsak, Siraselviler Caddesi, Soğanci Sokak 7,

Cihangir, are similar centres. Bilsak also runs a restaurant and bar.
Sound and light performances are held at the Sultan Ahmet Cami (The
Blue Mosque) from May until September and are given in English, German, French and Turkish. Evening performances start at about 8.30
each evening. In Ankara similar performances are given at the
Anit Kabir (Atatürk's Mausoleum) from 19 May to 30 September. For details of programmes, call at Türk Anit,
Ceyvre ve Turizm Değerlerini Koruma, Vakfi (Foundation for the Preservation of Monuments, Environment
and Tourist Attractions) Meşrutiyet Caddesi 57/3,
Tepebaşi. The performances are given free of charge.

National Holidays, Festivals and Folklore

The two principal religious feasts of the Turkish year are
the four-day Kurban Bayrami and the three-and-a-half-day
Şeker Bayrami. The first commemorates Abraham's willingness to obey God's command to sacrifice his son Isaac (for
whom the ram in the thicket was then substituted). The second, the Sugar Festival, follows the month-long fast of Ramadan, the anniversary of the Hegira
(Mohammed's flight from Mecca to Medina). The timing of these feasts varies
each year in accordance with the Moslem calendar, which is 11 days shorter
than the western one.

One-day holidays:

1 January	New Year's Day
23 April	National Sovereignty and Children's Day
19 May	Youth Day (anniversary of Atatürk's arrival at Samsun in 1919 and the beginning of the resistance that ultimately led to the foundation of the republic)
30 August	Victory Day
29 October	Republic Day

There are annual international and/or local festivals in over 30 cities and towns
throughout Turkey. Complete details can be obtained from the Ministry of
Tourism and Information at its information centres at airports, harbours and in
major cities, towns and tourist centres. The following is a selection of those
most publicized:

Antakya Flower Festival, 23 April
Tulip Festival, 23 April – 1 May
Ephesus Festival, first week in May
Konya Culture and Arts Festival, May 16 – 19
Marmara Folk Dancing Festival, 28 – 30 May
Bergama Festival, 30 May – 3 June
Kirkpinar Oil Wrestling (Edirne), second week in June
Rize Tea Festival, 11 – 12 June
Van Culture and Tourism Festival, 18 – 20 July
İstanbul International Arts Festival, July – September
İzmir International Trade Fair, 20 August – 20 September
Urgüp Wine Harvest, 14 – 16 September
Mevlana Anniversary Ceremonies, 14 – 17 December

Turkish music, making use of quarter tones, betrays no polyphony, or harmony in an accepted western sense, but is nevertheless pervasive with a modal line that has some resemblance to monastic plainsong. Some dances have no musical accompaniment; the dancers perform to the rhythmic hand-clapping of those watching. Often an instrument when used is simply a reed pipe or a form of bagpipe. The Zeybek is a dance of the Aegean region (a similar dance is performed in Greece and the Balkans). There are Bar dances from the eastern regions, a Halay dance from central Anatolia and a Horon dance from the

Black Sea. The Karşilamalar is from the Marmara region, and a sword and spoon dance, the Kiliç Kaşik, is from Bursa. There are also spoon dances, Kaş ‚ik, from the south. Men predominate in the dance, which can be acrobatic at times, but there are professional troupes now of men and women dancers who perform wearing traditional and regional costumes at dance festivals throughout the country.

Nasreddin Hoca is a figure out of the remote past of Turkish folklore and legend. He was a humble teacher but wily, practical and earthly wise in his dealings with fellow villagers. His concerns were the intricacies of marital and domestic life, town manners and mores, bazaar intrigues and gossip, and the cupidities of government officials. Stories of the Hoca's contemporary adventures are a matter of continuous invention in *çay ev* (tea house) and *külüp* (club), as with invented folk heroes of other countries. The shadow theatre of and Hacivat goes back into a remote central Asian beginning, migrating through Persia into Anatolia and further west into Greece. The repertoire is traditional, as evergreen for children and enthusiasts as Punch and Judy or the tales of the Arabian Nights. Scripts often have a bearing on contemporary foibles.

Crafts and Souvenirs

At Sultanahmet, an 18th-century *medrese* (theological school) has been restored as the Artisan Centre (İstanbul Sanatlari Çarşisi). It is a court surrounded by a portico, and the cells of the students have been restored as workshops. Artisans work on embroidery, lacework, calligraphy, bookbinding, doll-making, gilding and ebru (papier-marbre, the art of decorating paper for use on the inside covers and flyleaves of fine books). The artisans are happy to be observed at work, and orders are welcome.

Carpets: A prayer rug from Kula in northwestern Anatolia or from Gördes in the İzmir area can be a good buy, if found.

Modern carpets in traditional patterns come mainly from Kayseri. Valuable ancient carpets have either been sold or grace a museum or a private collection. Unless you happen to be an expert, you simply have to trust in the honesty of the merchant or employ a reputable agent to advise or buy for you. *Kilims* are rugs that may be referred to elsewhere as 'peasant rugs'. Colourful and in bold patterns, they are suitable for floors, bed covers or for wall decoration. Traditional *kilim* weaving is encouraged, among other crafts, by the Association for Promoting Turkish Handi-crafts (Türk El Sanatlari Derneği) at Yenis ‚ehir in Ankara; their showroom is located at 30/32 Selanik Caddesi.

Jewellery: Genuine antique heirlooms are as hard to find as valuable carpets. If a reputable dealer has an item that interests you, he will weigh the gold or silver item and charge according to the current market price of the precious metal. There are many acceptable reproductions and imitations. Mehmet Kabaş, of Urart, has the reputation of being the best jeweller of Istanbul. Some of his designs are based on originals belonging to ancient Anatolian civilizations. His workshop is on the Bosphorus at Bağlarmevkii, Yunus Sokak 2, Yeniköy, with a showroom at the Maçka Hotel, Maçka, near Nişantaş.

Copper: Traditional ware is handmade, but what is on view in souvenir shops is mostly machine made. If the products of a master craftsman, Alaeddin Yanik, can be found, the additional cost over a machine made product will be amply justified.

Ceramics: This traditional craft was brought by potters transplanted by Sultan Selim I from Tabriz. After İznik, Kutahya became the most important centre of pottery, along with İstanbul, but today the products of Kutahya, based on traditional patterns, are pre-eminent. The best designers are said to be teenage girls, who follow a two-year course of training after selection.

Brass: This is another, though deteriorating, Turkish craft. There are some traditional craftsmen still who are not mass-producing for the tourist trade. Look at the work at Bronze Is (Riza Paşa Yokuşu, Uzunçarşi, Beyazit).

Marble and Onyx: Onyx objects (colour-layered quartz) proliferate in stores and souvenir shops throughout the country. The acquisition of onyx and marble items is very much a matter of personal taste, perhaps, or that of friends for whom a purchase is being made.

Musical instruments: One of the most traditional and unusual of Turkish instruments is the *saz*, which might be described as an elongated mandarin but with a very long fingerboard and a much smaller — minute almost — sounding base. There are three sizes of this instrument; *cura*, the smallest, medium-sized *bağlama* and *divan sazi*, the largest.

Silk: Bursa is today's centre of the *ipek* (silk) industry, which flourished in Byzantine times but declined in latter Ottoman days. Bursa, too, produces excellent cotton-towelling items.

Leather goods: Turkey, justifiably, is noted for the high standard of its leather and suede. By all accounts, though this could deter a sensitive buyer, the use of the skins of young animals rather than the tougher hides of older ones explains the quality. The range throughout countless shops in the Grand Bazaar and elsewhere is enormous. Items of clothing are tailored in a matter of hours for a customer in a hurry.

Meerschaum: This absorbent clay is quarried near Eskişehir, southeast of Bursa. Smoker's pipes, some in fanciful shapes, cigarette holders and many other assorted decorative items, both large and small, are manufactured out of it.

Hunting and Sport

A favoured hunting ground for animals and birds is in Trakya, the section of
the country between İstanbul and the Greek and Bulgarian frontiers. The
season, with quail the favourite quarry, starts in mid-September and runs
through to March. The season for the wild boar, also a hunter's favourite
throughout Turkey, begins in late autumn. A hunting license can be arranged
through one of the 30 or more hunting clubs of the country. In İstanbul there is
a Hunters and Shooters Club (İstanbul Avcilar ve Aticilar Ihtisas Külübü) at
Sîraselviler Caddesi, 58/1, off Taksim Square. The brown bear can be hunted
in the Hakkâri Mountains of southeastern Turkey, in the Taurus Mountains and
in some Pontic Mountain areas. The hunting of jackal, hyena, lynx and wolf is
permitted at all times, while there is a total prohibition on the fox, gazelle,
chamois, otter, deer of all kinds and wild sheep. If birds interest you, note that
total prohibition is extended to the crane, bustard, flamingo, francolin,
pheasant and swan, while seasonal permits are given for partridge, quail, wild
duck and wild goose.

The favoured viewing area for bird-watching is on the hills of Çamlîca behind Üsküdar on the eastern shore of the Bosphorus. Tours to other favourable
sighting areas can be arranged through, or advised by, the Bird-watchers As-
sociations throughout Europe and America. In İstanbul a good season for
watching is between 15 September and 10 October when birds are migrating
south, and an estimate of something like 40,000 storks cross İstanbul each day.
Not far from Bandîrma in the Balîkesir province near the southern shore of the
Sea of Marmara, the Kuşcenneti (Bird Paradise) is an ornithological reserve
where some 200 species have been identified.

In İstanbul many Turks obtain a meal by fishing off Galata and Atatürk
bridges or at Rumeli Hisar and at Tarabya on the Bosphorus. There are no pis-
catorial clubs. Boats can be hired, or fishing trips can be arranged with in-
dividuals at harbours along the coasts of the various seas. Trout fishing can be
indulged to the heart's and mind's content in the mountain streams of Anatolia,
particularly in the Pontic Mountains of the northeastern area and in the hinterland of Trabzon and Rize. There is lake fishing in Lake Abant (southeast of
Adapazari mentioned in the Black Sea Coast section), İznik Gölü (the lake at
İznik), Bafa Gölü (Lake Bafa, south of İzmir) and elsewhere. However, the
water in some lakes, such as the large Lake Van in eastern Turkey, is too
sodium-slaked to harbour fish. No permit is needed for fishing. There is a
balîk müzesi (fish museum), which has a collection of more than 4,000 species
of fish, on Kennedy Caddesi 11, Kumkapî, the area southwest of Beyazît
Meydanî (Beyazît Square) in İstanbul. The sea products wholesale market —
balîkhane or *su urunleri hali* — is in this area, too.

Mountain ranges occupy the largest area of Anatolia and the opportunity for mountaineering that is challenging —hazardous, even, in the case of Ararat, Erciyes and other peaks — is unlimited. In Ankara at Ulus Işhani, Ulus Meydani, there is a Federation of Mountaineering and Skiing that can put visitors in touch with local alpine clubs in Ankara, Agri (Ararat), Erzurum, Adana, Elaziğ, Van, Kayseri, Mersin and Hakkâri.

Oil wrestling is a sport indigenous to Turkey, and an annual championship (over 600 years old) is held in June each year at Kirkpinar, near Edirne, in which more than 500 wrestlers participate. With their arms and bodies covered in oil and wearing only leather breeches, competitors wrestle for a fall. The İstanbul Gures Ihtisas Külübü at Çingirakli Bostan Sokak, 39/41, Aksaray, is a club for freestyle and Graeco-Roman wrestlers and can offer a special arrangement for non-members. Camel fighting, which sounds terrifying, is in fact a bloodless and harmless sport in which the camels push and shove rather than wrestle and tear each other. Matches are arranged during rutting periods, and an annual competition is held at Selçuk.

Association football (soccer) has become a spectator sport as popular as in every other country in the world. The performances of Turkish players, and club football, have improved appreciably in recent years: in 1989 one İstanbul club, Galatasaray, reached the semifinal of a European Champion's Cup competition, while the national team performed well in the preliminaries of the 1990 World Cup Competition. Players and managers from other countries are now contracted to indigenous clubs.

Golf can be played at İstanbul's nine-hole course and club, the İstanbul Golf Ihtisas Külübü, Büyükdere Caddesi, Ayazaga, a district to the north of Beyoğlu, inland through Şişli. Non-members are permitted for an arranged membership fee and a course fee.

Tennis players may like to visit Dalyan Spor Teşişleri (at Adlihan Sokak, Dalyan, Fenerbahçe, on the Golden Horn) which runs an instruction course from June to September. İstanbul Tennis Külübü has courts at Bayildim Yokusu, Taşlik, while Tennis Eksrim Dagçilik Külübü is at Askerocagi Caddesi, Taksim. To play on the above courts, which are for members only, a visitor would have to pay the annual fee or sign up for Dalyan Spor's instruction course. Tacspor, however, accepts non-members, and their courts are at Yenigelin Sokak, Suadiye (tel. 358 41 25).

The Eurasia Marathon is an annual event, started in 1983, which attracts runners to the tune of 10,000 and more. On the shorter ten-kilometre (six-mile) course, more than one waiter carrying a serving napkin and tray, and perhaps a fully rigged, newly wedded couple, will be seen among those participating for the sheer fun of it. They start from Beylerbeyi on the eastern shore of the Bosphorus, cross the first Bosphorus bridge and end at Sultanahmet course which also starts from the eastern shore and crosses the Bosphorus, but then it runs north to Büyükdere and, returning by another route, finally concludes near the Dolmabahçe Palace. Interested athletes are able to obtain full information from the Intercontinental Eurasia Marathon, Cumhuriyet Caddesi 187/4, Elmadağ.

Yacht chartering companies are covered in the Transportation section. If you wish to pursue scuba diving, coaching can be arranged through Satt-Sub Aquatic Tourism and Travel Corporation, Gazi Caddesi 39/1, Sinop.

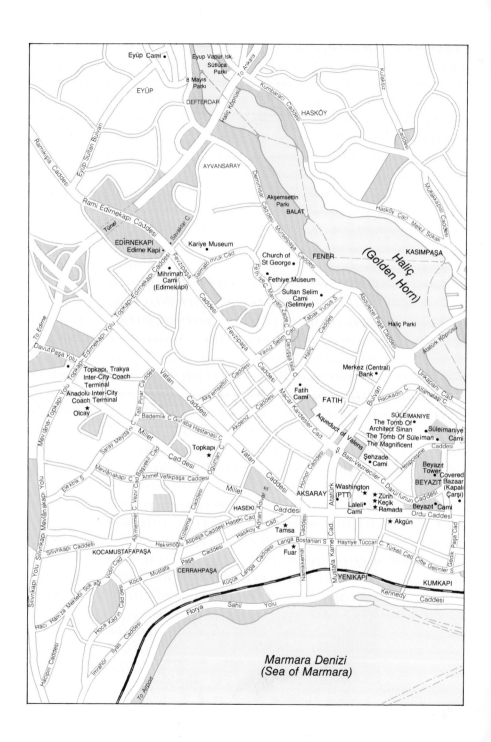

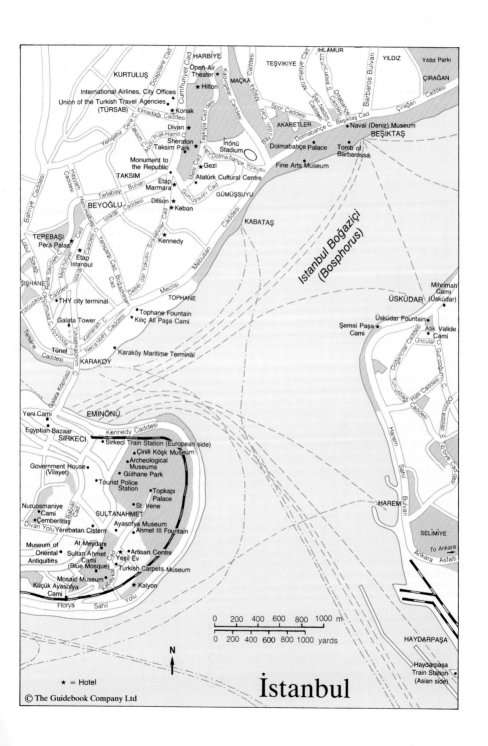

KURTULUŞ
HARBIYE
Open-Air Theater ★
Hilton ★
MAÇKA
TEŞVIKIYE
IHLAMUR
YILDIZ
Yıldız Parkı
ÇIRAĞAN
Çırağan Caddesi
International Airlines, City Offices
Union of the Turkish Travel Agencies (TÜRSAB)
Konak ★
Elmadağı Caddesi
Spor Caddesi
AKARETLER
Naval (Deniz) Museum •
BEŞIKTAŞ
Divan ★
Sheraton ★
Taksim Park
İnönü Stadium
Dolmabahçe Palace
Tomb of Barbarossa •
Dolmabahçe Yokuşu
Fine Arts Museum •
Monument to the Republic
Gezi ★
TAKSIM
Atatürk Cultural Centre •
Etap Marmara
GÜMÜŞSUYU
BEYOĞLU
Tarlabaşı Bulvarı
Dilson ★
Keban ★
KABATAŞ
Kennedy
TEPEBAŞI
Pera Palas ★
Etap İstanbul ★
İstiklal Caddesi
İstanbul Boğaziçi (Bosphorus)
ŞIŞHANE
Meclisi
Mihrimah Cami
THY city terminal •
TOPHANE
ÜSKÜDAR (Üsküdar)
Galata Tower •
Tophane Fountain •
Kılıç Ali Paşa Cami
Üsküdar Fountain •
Şemsi Paşa Cami •
Atik Valide Cami
Tünel
Karaköy Maritime Terminal •
Uncular C.
KARAKÖY
Halk Caddesi
Yeni Cami •
EMINÖNÜ
Egyptian Bazaar •
SIRKECI
Kennedy Caddesi
Sirkeci Train Station (European side) •
Çinili Köşk Museum •
Government House (Vilayet) •
Archeological Museums •
Gülhane Park •
HAREM
Tourist Police Station •
Topkapı Palace •
St Irene •
Nuruosmaniye • Cami
SULTANAHMET
Ayasofya Museum •
Çemberlitaş •
Divan Yolu
Yerebatan Cistern •
Ahmet III Fountain •
SELIMIYE
At Meydanı
Museum of Oriental Antiquities
Sultan Ahmet Cami (Blue Mosque) •
Artisan Centre ★
Yeşil Ev ★
Turkish Carpets Museum •
To Ankara
Mosaic Museum •
Ankara Asfaltı
Küçük Ayasofya Cami
Kalyon ★
Florya
Sahil
HAYDARPAŞA

| 0 | 200 | 400 | 600 | 800 | 1000 m |
| 0 | 200 | 400 | 600 | 800 | 1000 yards |

N ↑

★ = Hotel

© The Guidebook Company Ltd

İstanbul

Haydarpaşa Train Station (Asian side) •

İstanbul

Its beauty etched in dome and minaret at dusk, İstanbul announces its un-
abashed longevity. Divided by waterways, the city mounts and descends on
seven hills, pulsating as a living entity should. For the vitality of this city owes
as much to its citizens of today as it does to past Byzantine emperors and Ottoman sultans.

Getting Around

The airport bus runs along Florya Highway and eventually turns left into
Atatürk Bulvari to go through Aksaray to Unkapani, where it passes under the
Aqueduct of Valens. If you intend to stay in the old city near the district of Sul-
tanahmet, dismount from the airport bus at Aksaray. New road construction
now carries incoming traffic from Unkapani along the Golden Horn to Galata
Bridge where a revamped road system leads either to the THY air terminal station at Şişhane or by way of the reconstructed Tarlabaşi Caddesi to Taksim
Square. Another route from Galata Bridge takes traffic past the main quay at
Karaköy and along the Bosphorus waterfront through Kabataş to Beşiktaş. A
new Galata bridge is under construction alongside the old one, and on both
sides of the waterway a revised complex of roadways is changing the layout of
the area.

An alternative form of transport in İstanbul and elsewhere in Turkey is the
dolmuş, or shared taxi. The service runs between fixed destinations and has
passenger stops and a single charge as with buses. Though a *dolmuş* can be of
the taxi-type, the customary vehicle today is the more serviceable minibus.
Dolmuş services seem to operate no longer within the city but only on routes
taking you away from the centre. Trolley buses have also been withdrawn
from service.

To take the ferry to Üsküdar on İstanbul's Asian shore, go to Kabataş, a little to the south of the Dolmabahçe Palace. Although there are the Bosphorus
bridges, and your taxi or *dolmuş* is likely to take one or other rather than the
ferry, the opportunity the boat offers to observe the outline of the city with its
hills, domes and minarets is recommended.

It may not be long before a planned tunnel to create a direct railway link between west and east İstanbul will be in operation. In the meantime, there is a
regular ferry service leaving from Karaköy near the Galata Bridge. Its destination is Kadiköy where Haydarpaşa, the main railway terminal for Anatolia, is
located.

If your stay is to be short, or even if it is to be a longer one, the best plan
would be to find your way to the Sultanahmet district where the monuments

you will want to see can be found. The Topkapı Palace, St Sophia, The Blue
Mosque, the Archaeological Museum and the Grand Bazaar are within
reasonable walking distance. These are in the area of the original walled city
of Byzantium on the western side of the Golden Horn. If you are staying in
Beyoğlu, the new city, you can travel by taxi, bus or *dolmuş* down to the Gold-
en Horn and then cross the Galata Bridge to the old city.

Historical Background

When Mehmet II breached the walls of Constantinople in May 1453, the
Byzantine Empire had been reduced in size to little more than the area of the
city. For the last emperor, who died in the breach, the battle had been fought
courageously with few defenders, a lack of arms and money and almost no
Western support — a Genoese naval contingent arrived too late to participate.
On entering the city, Mehmet went at once to St Sophia and, prostrating himself at the altar, rededicated the building to Allah, after which he rode to what
was left of the Great Palace where he reflected philosophically on triumph,
time and mortality. His troops were then allowed to indulge in three days of
looting and licensed mayhem — the customary privilege of a conquering army
whatever its creed — after which the rehabilitation of the city as an Ottoman
possession began.

Mehmet repopulated the city with Turks, but he also encouraged people of
other nationalities, Greeks and Jews in particular, to set up businesses to help
restore the city's commercial prosperity that throughout the latter years of the
Byzantine Empire had seriously declined.

Gennadius, a Byzantine scholar, was installed as Patriarch of the Greek Orthodox Church. Mehmet allocated the Church of the Holy Apostles as the seat
of the patriarchate and, as with other ethnic communities, established the
Greeks as a *millet* (self-administrating unit) under the patriarch, which included judicial control, though not for criminals, who were subject to trial in
the Turkish courts. The authority of these *millets* would decrease with time.
The patriarchate was later moved to the Pammakaristos Church and Monastery
on the fifth hill overlooking the Golden Horn, while the Fatih Cami (Mosque
of the Conqueror) was built on the site of Holy Apostles, on the fourth hill of
the city, to the northwest of the Aqueduct of Valens. The church had been the
burial place of emperors, and later Mehmet himself would be buried on the
same hill. Murat III took over the Pammakaristos in order to build the Fethiye
Cami, and the patriarchate was then established at St George's Church in
Phanar (now Fener) on the Golden Horn, where it is today.

In the initial period of occupation, the Ottomans converted many existing
churches but later built mosques that within the complex often included a
medrese (theological school), a *hastanesi* (hospital) and an *imaret* (soup

kitchen). As well as Turkish architects, craftsmen of other nationalities were employed, and many high officers of state were selected from among foreigners who had converted to Islam.

With the first four sultans, up to the reign of Suleiman the Magnificent, the Ottoman Empire achieved its apogee of influence and expansion. Imperial control lasted until this century, but in the aftermath of the country's defeat in the First World War and the repulse of the Greek invasion of 1920–2, the empire ended with the declaration of a republic. Kemal Atatürk, its first president and great reformer, established the capital at Ankara. Besides Parliament and the embassies, the head offices of banks and large commercial and industrial enterprises are located there. İstanbul, though, retains much of its principal city aura, and its acquired authority as a former imperialistic masterpiece.

The Early History

About the middle of the seventh century BC the Megarans, neighbours of the Athenians, are believed to have built a first city on the site. Its name of Byzantium is said to derive from their leader Byzas, but authentic records of this early time are scant. In 506 BC it was occupied by the Medes but seems not to have been all that important to the Persian Xerxes who built a bridge of boats across the Hellespont at the lower end of the Dardanelles when launching the invasion of Greece. The Spartan general Pausanias captured it in 478 BC, and due to its strategic and political importance in the long power struggle between Sparta and Athens, the city changed hands on several occasions. Byzantium repulsed Philip of Macedon when he besieged it in 340 BC, and Alexander a year or two later chose to ignore it and made his crossing into Asia Minor by way of the Gallipoli Peninsula. As an independent city, its coinage bore the stamp of the crescent and star, a symbol that in a much later age was to spread panic among those in the path of Ottoman expansion.

In the second century BC the city elders signed a treaty of alliance with Rome and agreed to pay tribute, but Vespasian annexed it for the empire in AD 73. A civil war followed on the death of Commodus (AD 192), and the Byzantines made the mistake of supporting the rival of Septimius Severus who, after a three-year siege, revenged himself on the citizens by thoroughly sacking the city. Then, in recognition of its unique strategic value, he rebuilt it; his new city of Antoninia occupied the snout of high land above the Marmara Sea. Temples to Artemis, Aphrodite and Apollo are associated with Antoninia. Apollo's temple was located between those to Artemis (where St Sophia now stands) and Aphrodite (on the St Irene site). Of Antoninia, only some sections of the city's walls remain.

In AD 330 after Constantine had defeated Licinius, his last rival in the civil war that followed the death of Diocletian, he chose Antoninia as the site for his capital of New Rome, which on completion was designated Constantinople.

Constantine extended the boundaries of Antoninia, building his walls further to the west. With Constantine's declaration in favour of Christianity — his mother Helena was a convert who had been on pilgrimage to the Holy Places of Jerusalem and had returned with relics of Christ — the city became the Christian capital of the Eastern Roman Empire, though Constantine himself is thought not to have been baptised until his deathbed. For a brief spell under Julian (361–3), there was a reversion to paganism. But Julian died in battle in the Middle East, and the future of Christianity was assured when Theodosius I (378–95) declared the empire Christian and ordered the destruction of all remaining pagan shrines. Rome fell to the Goths in 476, and Constantinople became the sole political capital of a developing Christian world.

In Justinian's time (527–65) much of the city was destroyed in the Nika Riot, but Justinian, one of the greatest of East Roman rulers and, as Hadrian had been, a prolific builder, reconstructed the city on a magnificent scale. His brilliant generals Belisarius and Narses regained most of Italy, Spain and the North African provinces for the empire, though the cost of doing so was to damage irrevocably the economic resilience of the state. Some historians base the switch from Roman Empire to Byzantine during the reign of Justinian. He codified the laws that until that time had existed only in decrees. He recognized the predominance of Greeks among the empire's citizens by making Greek an official language of state along with Latin, and later Greek became the empire's sole official language.

Throughout the ensuing centuries Constantinople successfully repulsed many assaults, from Goths, Alans, Serbs, Bulgarians, Russians and seventh-century Arabs. Its defences held, reinforced by new walls built in the fifth century under Theodosias II. (Standing to the west of the walls that Constantine built, they are the ones that can be seen there today.) In the 12th century, though, the knights and soldiers of the Fourth Crusade attacked and took the city, establishing a Latin Empire and occupying it until 1261 when the Byzantines reoccupied it. They continued in possession, warding off a serious and sustained late 13th-century Ottoman assault by Beyazit I, until Mehmet's assault and victory of 1453.

Sights

Sultanahmet — The Old City

Topkapi Palace

First Court
Sultan Ahmet III loved fountains and tulips. He became sultan in 1703 and

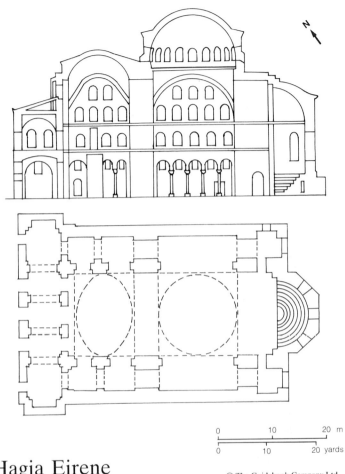

0   10   20   m

0   10   20   yards

Hagia Eirene

© The Guidebook Company Ltd

each April held a Tulip Festival. The Seraglio Gardens were decked with cages of canaries hanging in the trees and lighted candles on the backs of roving tortoises. One of his fountains, decorated with marble tulips, is outside the Royal Gate of the palace. It was erected in 1728, but two years afterwards Ahmet was deposed because of his extravagance.

The **Royal Gate,** or Bab-i-Humayun, is in the walls of Septimius Severus's rebuilding of Byzantium, which he called Antoninia after his wife. The gate opens on to the First Court and entrance grounds of the palace.

Over to the left after entering is the Church of St Irene, **Hagia Eirene** (in Greek), or Church of Divine Peace. It was never converted to a mosque and is classified as a museum with, ironically, a display outside of military armament of past ages. A first church, in all probability built over an earlier Temple to

Aphrodite, was burned down during the Nika Riot of the sixth century and afterwards rebuilt. Still remaining is the basilican ground plan of the church — rectangular with semi-circular apse on the eastern end — but structural modifications and rebuildings followed another fire and an eighth-century earthquake.

The Janissaries

Near St Irene stood the Mint, and in front of this building a great plane tree was known as the Tree of the Janissaries, the Ottoman Royal Corps of Guards. By tradition the Janissaries would assemble at this tree whenever they wanted to dispute their conditions of service or, more drastically, depose a sultan. Their method of protest was to bang their cooking pots or 'kettles' or, in a serious revolt, overturn them. Under Mahmut II (1808–39), the Janissaries had become such a menace to the court and to public order that the sultan secretly deployed artillery units about the palace. When the Janissaries overturned their kettles and called for the sultan's deposition, murdering the emissaries he had sent to parlay with them, the sultan mounted a white charger with the Banner of the Prophet unfurled and ordered the artillery to open fire at point-blank range. The Janissaries who survived this onslaught took refuge in their barracks which were then pounded mercilessly. The handful of Janissaries that escaped this massacre fled to the Basilican Cistern where each was individually hunted down and killed. The corps was never re-formed.

An **Executioner's Fountain** stands close to the Ortakapi, the Middle Gate and entry to the Second Court. The gate had a prison, and the executioner doubled as the palace head-gardener. After execution the head of a ranking person was displayed on the Ortakapi but a lesser privileged person had to be content with an ear or a nose set up outside the Royal Gate among the mass of the executed.

Second Court

The **Middle Gate**, Bab-i-Salam, or Selam Kapisi (Salvation Gate), is a double one designed to prevent unlawful entry. This is where the entrance fee is paid, with an extra charge for visiting the Harem. In the vicinity evidence of the Byzantine Magnaura Palace has been found by excavators.

On the right side of this Second Court are the **domestic quarters** where the main kitchen and its enormous fireplace and huge cooking pots and cauldrons, as well as iron and copper kitchen utensils, can be seen. In another section is a large display of porcelain and china, gifts to the court from kings, queens and potentates; in other sections are copperware, glassware and silver.

On the east side of the court is the **Divan**, or Kubbealti (Council Chamber), in which the grand vizier, the empire's executive officer, conducted affairs of state. Until the time of Süleiman the Magnificent, the sultan himself used to preside at meetings here, but Süleiman constructed a room with access to his own quarters in the Harem, allowing him to overlook proceedings incognito. Ahmet III discontinued this use of the Divan, and thereafter the grand vizier conducted meetings outside the palace in his own quarters, which became universally known as the Sublime Porte. There is a private entrance to the

Harem behind the Divan; the public entrance is at the back of the Armoury, the next building up on that side.

Third Court

The entrance to the Third Court is the **Gate of Felicity**, or Bab-us-Saade, and the building immediately inside the entrance is the sultan's **throne room**, or audience chamber. Ambassadors often had to wait on benches at the gate before being summoned to an audience. Here were the quarters of the White Eunuchs, who served the sultan and the palace and were therefore neutralised, not castrated as were the Black Eunuchs. They served in the Harem and had their quarters there.

Under a colonnade on the right-hand side, there was a palace school for boys in the **Court of the Enderun**. On graduation the pupils first served the sultan as pages. The rooms here now have a display of royal clothing and ceremonial costumes. Next to it, in the former **Treasury**, is the royal collection of jewellery, along with jewel-encrusted daggers, swords, thrones, cots and gewgaws into which jewels have been indiscriminately imbedded. The **Library** of Ahmet III, which is at the centre of the main court, has a collection of illuminated manuscripts.

The most sacred building in the Third Court is the **Pavilion of the Holy Mantle**, or Hirka-i-Saadet Dairesi, containing Mohammed's cloak, brought back along with his sword and standard by Selim I after his conquest of Egypt. These three sacred items conferred the title of Caliph on the holder, the highest religious office in Islam.

Lower down on the left of this court is the 15th-century **Agalar Cami**, and behind it is the discreet **Küshane Kapisi** entrance to the Harem. The **Harem** complex consisted of 250 rooms situated on varying levels, and in the time of Süleiman the Magnificent there were 1,000 selected inmates, as well as other girls in training. Sinan designed part of the **Seraglio** for Süleiman, and a concealed passageway led from that sultan's quarters to the room of his current favourite. The Valide Sultan, the mother of the sultan, was nominally in charge of the Harem and had her quarters there. Another section consisted of the **Kafes** which was in fact a royal prison for the heir to the throne. Those who lived there were cut off from all contact with society outside the palace: Osman III spent 50 years in the Kafes prior to his elevation as sultan.

Mehmet II, the conqueror of Constantinople, on his accession promulgated the Law of Fratricide — given credence by Koran interpreters — whereby a newly elected sultan, as a safeguard against palace rebellion and conspiracy, had his brothers and other near relatives executed by means of a silken cord. A later sultan suspended this law and restricted action to confinement in the Kafes of only the immediate heir to the throne. In the 19th century the mad Abdul Hamid II temporarily revived this law.

Fourth Court

Notable in the Fourth Court is the **Baghdad Kiosk**, or Bavgdat Köskü, which Murat IV built, modelled on a building he had seen in Baghdad at the time of his capture of that city in 1638. It has exquisite tiling and faience work, and the rooms, complete with divans, look out to a courtyard with a fountain and views of the Golden Horn. In the same court the **Revan Kiosk** is an earlier building, again modelled on a building that Murat had noted on campaign. This kiosk has for company the **Sünnet Odasi** of 1641, built by Sultan Ibrahim for the circumcision ceremonies of princes. The Mustafa Pasa Kiosk, Kara Mustafa Köskü, or Sofa Kiosk, was so named because of its low-set sofas in the window bays. Kara Mustafa was the grand vizier responsible for restorations at the palace. Pierre Loti, the French novelist of the late 19th and early 20th century, was given the sultan's permission to stay at this kiosk during his residence in İstanbul.

With its pools, gardens and marble terraces, the Fourth Court is an agreeable place to linger. It has a restaurant situated in a kiosk that was a favourite retreat of Abdül Mecit I and overlooks the Marmara Sea. A gateway out of this fourth court leads to **Seraglio Point** where wayward and offending ladies of the Harem, tied into weighted sacks, were dropped into the Bosphorus.

Abdül Mecit (1831–61) abandoned Topkapi in favour of Yildiz Kiosk near Besiktas on the Bosphorus, on the other side of the Golden Horn, and lived there until the building of the Dolmabahçe Palace was completed.

In their Revolution of 1908 the Young Turks, whose political aim was to bring Turkey out of the dead past and into the 20th century, broke up the Harem and invited relatives of inmates to reclaim their kin. Circassia in the Caucasus region had been a favoured recruiting ground for girls, and many villagers arrived from Circassian villages, as from elsewhere. Not every odalisque was claimed, nor did every inmate welcome release from the security the Harem had provided. Unclaimed residents were given house room in the Eski Saray, the Old Palace near the Fatih Cami, which had been the Harem prior to Süleiman's day.

Hagia Sophia

On leaving Topkapi, and passing Ahmet's fountain, **Ayasofya** (in Turkish), or **St Sophia**, the Church of the Holy Wisdom, is on the right. The church from this southeast side looks massive, partly because of the heavy buttresses that were erected during the Latin occupation at the beginning of the 13th century. The Belfry on the west façade is a Latin addition too. Flying buttresses had been constructed in the ninth century. After the Byzantines reoccupied the city in the 1260s, Andronicus II Palaeologus put up other buttresses, setting these against the main piers. On its conversion to a mosque, Mehmet II erected a wooden minaret on the southeast corner, replacing this later with a brick one.

Beyazit II added a stone minaret at the northeast corner, and Sinan was employed by Selim II to erect another on the southwest, and finally in the cause of harmony Murat II added the fourth. Murat also donated two large alabaster urns taken from Pergamum to serve as an ablutions fountain in the forecourt. To add to the mounting clutter, several large tombs were placed on the west side. In general, the exterior aspect of this great church might well discourage a visitor prior to entering it. In fairness, the massive nobility of the structure is best seen from the Marmara Sea on a ferry boat making its way to the Princes' Islands.

Constantine, or his son and successor Constantius, is thought to have erected a first church over what had been a Temple to Artemis on a site sacred to even earlier deities. This church, as with St Irene, was among the buildings burned down in the Nika Riot of 532. Afterwards, Justinian commissioned Anthemius of Tralles and Isadore of Miletus to build a new and larger church, which was completed in 537. The unique feature of the new building was the round dome set on a square by use of squinches, pendentives and soffits. Twenty years later, weakened by earthquakes in 553 and 557, the dome collapsed; a new, higher one was erected by a nephew of Isadore of Miletus. In 986 the western arch collapsed, and the dome was rebuilt by an Armenian architect.

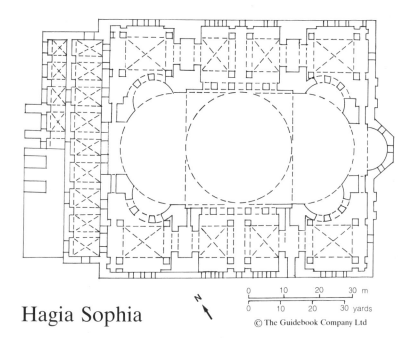

Hagia Sophia

N

0   10   20   30 m
0   10   20   30 yards

© The Guidebook Company Ltd

The eastern arch fell in 1347, and this time three Italian architects were employed to undertake repairs that took seven years. In the 19th century Sultan Abdül Mecit I commissioned Swiss engineers, the Fossati Brothers, to put an iron girdle about the dome.

In magnificence of concept, Justinian believed he had built better than Soloman with his Temple at Jerusalem. Its gold, silver, priceless brocades and precious ornamentation are no longer here: much of it disappeared with the Latins. Its mosaics and frescoes have been plastered over and whitewashed under Islam, and its windows have been boarded up or blocked. Kemal Atatürk ended Moslem worship there and declared it a museum, but the low-hanging chandeliers remain, as do the large medallions with their calligraphic inscriptions of Allah, Mohammed and the first four caliphs.

The tall wooden structure with a stairway leading up to the mimbar (a pulpit) is Moslem, and in the apse is the mihrab (the shallow niche that represents the cave in which Mohammed hid from his pursuers on the night of his escape from Mecca to Medina). Aligned on Mecca, the setting of a mihrab in a converted church can often look off-centre, because the altar end of a church is seldom built to face east with such precision. The great dome, which spans 32 metres (105 feet), is supported on four main piers with arches between them and half-domes on the west and east. The eight pillars of the nave are of green Molossian marble and probably came from Ephesus. The porphyry columns of the porticoes are likely to have been cut in Egyptian quarries at Thebes.

Work on the restoration of the mosaics was begun in the 1930s by Thomas Whittemore and his team from the Byzantine Institute of America and was continued by Paul Underwood after Whittemore's death in the 1950s. The lunette (wall in which windows are set) over the main entry from the narthex — the vestibule between the church entrance and the nave — has a detail of Christ between roundels of the Virgin Mary and the Archangel Gabriel, with a prostrate interceding emperor, Leo VI. In the dome of the apse is a portrait of the Virgin Mary. In the lunette over the southwestern entrance to the narthex, Constantine offers his city to Mary, while to Justinian, he offers his church. In a room over the southwest porch, there is a mosaic of Christ between Mary and John the Baptist (St John Prodromos), and there are other portraits of Apostles and of patriarchs. The dome of the apse has a portrait of the Virgin. In the south gallery, the Empress Zoe and the Emperor Constantine IX Monomachus are on either side of an enthroned Christ. Near it another panel has John II Comnenus and his wife Irene in company with Mary, and in another damaged mosaic Christ is again with Mary and St John Prodromos. All these works date between the mid-ninth and early 12th century.

Henry Dandolo, Doge of Venice, who was the evil counsellor at the time of the Latin assault on Constantinople and its subsequent occupation, has rated at least a modicum of sanctity in that an inscribed stone in the women's gallery commemorates him.

Two of the original bronze gates that stood at the southwest entrance have survived. Entrance is now by way of the exonarthex and narthex on the northwestern end. A café is available to the public within the enclosure, near the entrance.

Sultan Ahmet Cami — The Blue Mosque

Go southwest from Ayasofya, through the open area of the former Augusteum to the site of the Hippodrome to arrive at the Blue Mosque; the entrance into the walled forecourt is on the northwest side. If St Sophia is a paean to the revealed Wisdom of God, Sultan Ahmet is celestial illumination through blue and green Iznik tiles: Allah is conveyed in a less-delineated form for the faithful than the son of God in Christian mosaic, portrait and sculpture. Four massive pillars support the 43-metre- (141-foot-) high dome, 23.5 metres (77 feet) in diameter, with half-domes on each side. The somewhat austere effect is set off by filtered and reflected light on the beautiful tulip-patterned tiling. Birds nest in the dome and are in almost constant flight, as in an enormous birdcage.

The mosque, begun under Ahmet I in 1609 and completed in 1616, was built over part of the ruins of the Byzantine Great Palace, the Daphne. Its architect was Sedefker Mehmet Aga, a pupil of Sinan. From the fine spacious forecourt with its elegant fountain on six pillars with floral carvings, the exterior mass of the building lightens impressively as it rolls back and rises in ascending curves to the dome. There are six slender minarets. An apocryphal story says that Ahmet was considered presumptuous in erecting six minarets since the only other mosque with six was the Ka'aba at Mecca, and so as not to jeopardize his hope of eternal felicity the sultan donated a seventh to Mecca, which in fact already had seven minarets.

For a Moslem, ritual ablution accompanies the five canonical daily periods of prayer. In the larger mosques, the şsadirvan (ablutions fountain) is in the mosque's forecourt, though in some, such as the Ulu Cami at Bursa, the fountain is inside the mosque; in small mosques it is likely to be a tap above a basin in the wall near the entrance.

One must go shoeless into a mosque, and women are expected to be soberly dressed with covered heads. At large mosques galoshes-like overshoes or slippers can be obtained at the entrance; they are not for hire, but a small tip can be given to the custodian when returning them. Shoes can be left in his care or carried. In general, no objection is raised to the discreet use of a camera inside a mosque.

The Hippodrome

The main gateway from the forecourt of the Blue Mosque leads into the **At Meydani** which was the site of the Hippodrome. The Daphne section of the Great Palace here had an entrance into the Royal Box, the Kathisma.

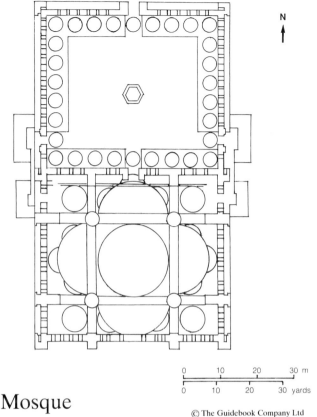

N

Blue Mosque

| 0 | 10 | 20 | 30 m |
| 0 | 10 | 20 | 30 yards |

In Constantinople, chariot racing was the principal spectacle, not gladiatorial contests as in the Colosseum in Rome. This was interspersed with light entertainment — dancers, acrobats and singers — or heavier spectacles in the form of a public execution or the humiliation of a captive of distinction or perhaps a fallen emperor, as with Andronicus I. The display could be gruesome, as when Basil I blinded 15,000 Bulgarian prisoners, or idiosyncratic, as with Constantine V's mustering of the city's monks and nuns and ordering them to copulate on pain of execution or blinding. The humiliation of a captive, however, not unusually might have ended with an act of clemency, such as granting permission to stay on in the city, with accommodation and a job. Draperies were hung in the Royal Box to indicate the form of entertainment for the following day. The Emperor, the human being with the closest edge on divinity, adjudicated from the Kathisma.

Competing charioteers wore the colours of one or other of the factions, a legacy from Rome, though they seem not to have been politically organized at first. Later the Greens were recruited from and supported by the lower social

groupings; the Blues came from the better off. There had been Whites and Reds as well, but the Whites joined the Blues, and the Reds merged with the Greens. Inter-faction fighting was frequent, more often than not with casualties, even fatalities. Some civil responsibilities were expected of the members, such as serving as supplementary police or as standard bearers in civic processions or triumphal marches.

The Nika Riot lasted eight days and culminated in the Hippodrome, with a great part of the city destroyed, damaged or burning. According to the historian Procopius, Justinian's nerve, about to crack, was held firm only by the greater determination of Theodora, his empress. About 30,000 Greens were massacred by the imperial troops, and Justinian rebuilt the city.

Of the monuments that were set up along the centre spine of the Hippodrome, only three have survived. The one that attracts most attention is the **Serpent Column**, transferred by Constantine from its original site at Delphi in Greece where it had been placed to commemorate the victory of the Greeks over the Persians at Plataea in 478 BC. Only part of one head of three entwined serpents exists now, and this is in the Archaeological Museum. According to Rene Guerdon, this monument once dispensed wine, milk and honey through its three mouths, but the Patriarch Theophilus in his day considered it a source of evil and went out one night to axe the heads of the 'dragon'. He succeeded in destroying two before the night watch stopped him.

The benignity of the serpents, though, was made manifest when one sultan, also considering the monument malign, had the remaining head removed, and the city afterwards became infested by snakes.

The **Theodosian Column** was brought from Karnak by Theodosias I (379–95). Carvings in relief with inscriptions in Latin and Greek at the base of the granite column record events in the emperor's career.

The **third obelisk** is one that was rededicated to Basil I (867–86) by Constantine Porphyrogenitus (913–59) in honour of the former emperor's deeds. The gilded plaques that once adorned this monument were removed for their value by Dandolo's soldiers, as was the sculptured group of four Bronze Horses now set up above the portal of St Mark's in Venice.

The fountain at the northeast end of the Hippodrome, the **Alman Çesmesi**, or Kaiser's Fountain, was a gift from Kaiser Wilhelm to Abdul Hamit II in 1898.

At the rear of the belediye (town hall) building at the southern end of the At Meydani, excavation and reconstruction have established part of the Hippodrome's curved retaining wall, which had been built up to counter the steep slope of the hill at that end.

Other Old City Sights
On the opposite side of the At Meydani from where the Blue Mosque stands, the **Museum of Oriental Antiquities** is housed in the former 16th-century Palace of Ibrahim Pasa, named for a grand vizier of Süleiman the Magnificent. Besides the exhibits, the building itself is of considerable interest.

The Artisan Centre (see Crafts, page 42) can be found on Kabaskal Caddesi by going out of the open place in front of St Sophia at its southwest corner. The courtyard of this restored *medrese* can be a cool, quiet place in

which to rest. There is a fountain. Its workshops are under the arcade that surrounds the central court. Next to the Artisan Centre on Kabaskal Caddesi is **Yesil Ev**, a restored timbered mansion which has been converted to a hotel and restaurant. The garden here has a marble pool, a conservatory and flowered arbours. Reconstruction of these two buildings was sponsored by the Turkish Touring and Automobile Club.

The **Basilican Cistern** is located on Sogukçesme Caddesi, which is off the roadway that runs downhill from the north side of St Sophia. It is on the line of the walls built by Septimius Severus. The cistern, which has been dry for a long time, has now been converted by the Touring and Automobile Association into an attractive restaurant, with its tables among the ancient columns. Beside it, and along Antoninia's ancient wall behind St Sophia, is a row of timbered houses which has become the TTOK Pension with tourist accommodation and restaurants.

On the opposite side of the open place in front of St Sophia, the site of these former **Baths of Zeuxippus** has been refashioned and landscaped as a park. When the silk worm was first brought to the city from China by two Byzantine monks, the baths were converted to an imperial silk factory. Beside the park on the southwest corner of the open place, a former **Turkish bath** has been reconstructed and opened as a museum. The many rooms have been fitted out in keeping with their purpose, and throughout the building there is a display of fine Turkish rugs and *kilims* (pileless, double-sided carpets). In one section, carpets or rugs may be bought or ordered. Its rear exit leads into Kabaskal Sokak. Entrance to this building is without charge.

Beyond the northeast end of the At Meydani and the Kaiser's Fountain is the entrance to the remarkable **Cistern of Philoxenos** or **Yerebatan Saray**, constructed in the time of Justinian. Water was brought to it via the aqueduct built by the co-emperor Valens (364–78); it spans the valley between the city's third and fourth hills. The cistern has 336 columns supporting arched vaults in brick and covers an area of 9,800 square metres (11,720 square yards). Effective flood-lighting and a wooden walkway that surrounds the whole area have been installed. Most of the columns have their capitals still and probably were brought here from pagan sites. At least two of the columns are set on carved Medusa heads that most likely came from Ephesus or Didyma. A café is in operation on a platform below the entrance stairway where the walkway starts. Above the cistern is a brick water tower, one of several in the city. Entrance fee to the cistern is 2,000TL.

In Byzantine times the main street of the city was the Mese, which ran westward from the Augusteum and through the city walls at Hadrian's Gate to link up with the Egnatian Way, the great road east from Rome. The **Milion** was the post from which all road distances were measured. Alongside the entrance to the Yerebatan Cistern at the start of Divan Yolu, an excavation located the site of this milestone, and a broken section has been uncovered.

Almost a complete ruin at the time of the building of the Blue Mosque, the former **Great Palace** on the summit was a vast complex of buildings and pavilions, with gardens, stairways and stoas on the hillside down to the Marmara. What has survived is a number of fine, mainly floor, mosaics of the sixth century, some of which are *in situ*; others have been moved and reset in what is now the **Mosaic Museum**. The museum is on Torun Sokak, downhill from the northwest corner of the open place in front of St Sophia but also reached from the southeast end of the Hippodrome. Entrance is in the arcade of the Arasta Bazaar, a reconstructed unit of tourist boutiques and carpet sellers.

The First Court of Topkapi Palace is part of **Gülhane Parki**, which is encompassed within the walls of Septimius Severus's city, and on the north side runs downhill to the Bosphorus shore. From Ayasofya follow the line of the walls northeastwards down towards the Bosphorus to reach the entrance into the park. Exhibits include many from early and prehistoric periods as well as Hellenistic, Roman and Byzantine. A notable exhibit is the item know as the **Alexander Sarcophagus**, excavated at Sidon in the Lebanon and believed by some to be that of the Macedonian conqueror. It has fine relief carvings, including that of a dramatic hunt. A companion sarcophagus is that of the **Weeping or Mourning Woman**, which also has beautiful carvings and is assigned like the other to the fourth century BC. An exhibit from Cyprus is of a savage caveman-like Heracles with club.

In the close neighbourhood of the museum is the **Çinili Kiosk** of 1472, one of the very earliest Ottoman buildings in the city, where Mehmet II is said to have resided while the new Topkapi Palace was under construction. Its style is pleasingly Persian with those large open-fronted tiled and vaulted chambers known as *eyvans*. Now a **tile museum**, among its exhibits is a Seljuk mihrab from Karaman, in dark-blue faience with traditional stalactite pattern.

Lower down in the park, towards the shore, the **column**, known as that of the **Goths**, is of obscure origin. It has been attributed to Claudius II (268–70) but also to Constantine, though it may have been set up by Septimius Severus: an inscription of a much later date assigns it as a victory monument to the defeat of a Gothic incursion.

In the park is a small zoo containing a section of birds of prey that is not without its mesmeric fascination. Many visitors might feel outraged by the caged dogs on display.

A shopper's paradise, the Kapali Carsi (covered market) or Grand Bazaar

Vicinity of Sultanahmet

Çemberlitass
Set off westward along Divan Yolu from the Milion. After several hundred metres, a little off to the right is the Çemberlitass, or Burnt Column of Constantine, so called because of its having been damaged by fire.

In Constantine's day there was an oval forum situated here at what may have been the west gate of Antoninia. On its erection, the column of nine high drums was surmounted by a statue of Constantine as Apollo, and the orb he carried was said to contain a fragment of the True Cross. At the foot of the column was a sanctuary in which were relics claimed to be from the crosses of the two thieves who had hung with Christ on Calvary, the baskets from the loaves and fishes miracle, a jar belonging to Mary Magdalene and presumably used by her in the washing of the feet, the palladium of ancient Rome and a wooden statue of Athena from Troy.

In 1150 a gale blew three drums and Constantine's statue off the column. Bronze wreaths had covered the joins between the drums, but these were likely to have been taken as loot by the Latins, or perhaps lost in a fire. After the column had again been damaged, Sultan Mustafa II (1695–1703) made good the loss of the wreaths with iron bands.

The Grand Bazaar and Vicinity
Between Constantine's Column and the Kapali Çarsi, the Covered or Grand Bazaar, there are two mosques of interest, the **Atik Ali Pasa Cami**, which is one of the oldest in the city, and the **Nuruosmaniye**. The Atik Ali was built in 1497 by a grand vizier of Beyazit II. It is on the same side of the road as the Çemberlitass. A little further on again, and off to the right, is the Nuruosmaniye (Light of Osman), a mosque begun in 1746 under Mahmut I (1730–54) but completed by Osman III (1754–7). The interior is impressively uncluttered, and a multitude of windows let in light. By going through the courtyard of this mosque one of the ten or more entrances to the Grand Bazaar can be reached, though the main entrance to the **Iç Bedesten** (Old Bazaar) is further along on Divan Yolu.

The bazaar is a complex of market areas. The Iç Bedesten was in origin Byzantine; Mehmet II began extensions in 1461, and the complex grew. Although fire has on more than one occasion destroyed sections, and there has been damage by earthquakes, repairs and reconstructions were undertaken on an almost permanent basis. Within the complex are several main avenues and something like 100 cross streets or arcades.

A *bedesten* is a separate vaulted court, each a centre for a particular trade. The jeweller's is among those most advertised, but the merchants of fine rugs are numerous, as are those dealing in leather and suede. The *bedesten* for brocades is also an auction hall, where the items on display in the morning are for sale in the afternoon. One needs a visit or two to become acquainted with those *bedestens* of your particular interests. You may harbour a belief that bartering and oriental bazaars go hand in hand, but fixed prices are more the order of the day now, although vendors can be found who enjoy a haggle for its own sake. If you happen to be in a hurry over the purchase of a leather garment and cannot find one off the peg, there are tailors who can measure and make one in a matter of hours, including a fitting. The bargain hunter should perhaps temper enthusiasm with the realization that a rare bargain is an exception rather than the rule, particularly in jewellery.

There are over 3,000 shops, including restaurants and cafés, in the covered market. Streets on the northeast side of the bazaar lead down, shops all the way, to the Mirsir Çarsisi, the **Egyptian** or **Spice Bazaar**, which is situated just off the waterfront at Eminönü on the Golden Horn, close to the western egress from Galata Bridge.

Within the complex of the Grand Bazaar are several *hans*, or inns, in particular the **Valide Han**, built in 1651, and the **Zincirli** at the northwest corner. Throughout Turkey such *hans* provided accommodation for merchants, their animals and their merchandise, as well as for travellers. A *han* is a large rectangular structure that has an open central courtyard off which are the stables for the animals and storage space for merchandise; a balcony overlooking the court provides access to the rooms for merchants and travellers. Many an abandoned *han* can be seen during the course of travels, and you may find one — where refinements are few but the ambiance agreeable — still in use.

Süleimaniye Cami

This mosque is situated on a hill — counted as İstanbul's third hill — to the northwest of the Grand Bazaar. It was built by Sinan between 1550 and 1557 for Süleiman the Magnificent. In his ambition to create an individual Ottoman style, this great architect had already built two mosques, the Sehzade and the Mihrimah, but for this new mosque he seemed to revert to that unassailable achievement, Hagia Sophia, for his model. There are resemblances in the concepts of both buildings, though the Süleimaniye dome is smaller and set higher. Because they have been partially concealed within the walls, the buttresses supporting the dome are less conspicuous than those of the church, and the mass of the piers has been lightened by stalactite-patterned niches. Light comes from windows around the dome, and colour passes through 138 stained-glass windows designed by an artist known as Ibrahim the Drunkard, whose method was to pour lime into clay moulds into which his glass was then set. Calligraphic inscriptions within the mosque are by Hassan Çelebi. The mimbar is in carved marble with wood and inlaid mother-of-pearl, and the mihrab is in marble.

Süleimaniye Mosque

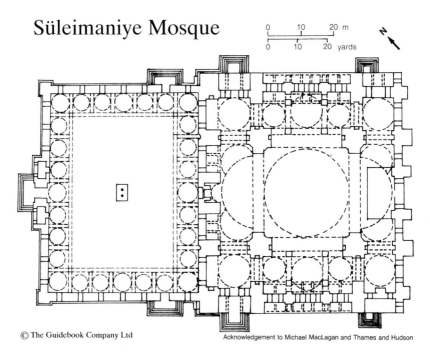

Acknowledgement to Michael MacLagan and Thames and Hudson

The courtyard of the mosque is as pleasing as the interior, with marble paving, columned porticoes all round and cupolas. There are four minarets, two on the east with three balconies each and two shorter ones on the west, each with two balconies. The number of minarets and the combined number of balconies are said to have significance in that Süleiman was the fourth sultan to reign in İstanbul but was the tenth in line from Osman.

Within the large complex of buildings surrounding the mosque, there are *medreses*, including two that have been turned into a library, a former *imaret* or soup kitchen for the poor, a former hospital and a hostel. In the grounds is the octagonal red and white marble tomb of Süleiman. Faience tiling on the interior of the dome is dark red in colour and set with crystal roses with emerald centres. Nearby is the tomb of his favourite wife, Haseki Hürrem or Roxellana, who may have been of Russian parentage and was revered as a woman of strong character. Sinan's tomb is also in this complex.

Church of St Saviour in Chora: Kariye Cami

Because it has outstanding mosaics and frescoes, a visit to this church, now a museum, is an imperative. It is situated off to the right of Fevzi Pasa Caddesi as you approach the Edirne Gate in the Theodosian Walls of the city. An earlier church existed on the site which at that time was outside the walls of Constantine's city. The church was rebuilt in the eighth century after the conclusion of the Iconoclast controversy, and again in the 12th century by Mary Ducaena, mother-in-law of Alexius Comnenus. Theodore Metochites (1303–26), the Grand Logothete of Andronicus II (1282–1328), rebuilt it again, adding not only the narthex, esonarthex and south chapel but also commissioning every inch of wall and ceiling space to be covered with mosaic and fresco decoration. It was a late-flowering of Byzantine art wherein Christian belief is illustrated through the depiction of Gospel stories and miracles, with apostles, saints and the holy family portrayed. All this remarkable work was hidden under plaster and whitewash until the building was declared a museum. Then Paul Underwood and his assistants from the Institute of Byzantine Studies in Boston, already mentioned in connection with the recovery of the mosaics of Hagia Sophia, began the restoration work that achieved such magnificent results.

Admiring the mosaics at the Kariye Museum calls for a great deal of looking up, and a visitor might well consider it an advantage to take along a small cushion for sitting, or even lying on the floor, and opera glasses for examining details of the work.

Beyazit II Cami

Divan Yolu (the former Mese) becomes Ordu Caddesi, and by continuing on beyond the Covered Bazaar, you reach Beyazit Meydani, which in Byzantine days was the Forum of Theodosius, or the Forum Tauri. Blocks of fallen Byzantine buildings line the main roadway on the left here, and over on the right is the university campus. Just inside the campus is the **Beyazit** Tower, built for fire-watching by Mahmut II (1808–39) to replace an original wooden tower.

Beyazit II's mosque is on the right of the square and has a large paved forecourt, serving as an assembly area for the city's pigeons. There is a story that a poor widow presented Sultan Beyazit (1481–1512) with a brace of pigeons, and ever since the birds have been under the protection of the mosque, commonly referred to as the Pigeon Mosque. Robert Liddell has maintained that if you feed the pigeons here you will get news of absent friends.

The mosque is one of the earliest Ottoman constructions, modelled after Hagia Sophia but with Seljuk undertones. Beyazit's tomb is in the garden, as is that of his daughter and the tomb of Mustafa Resat Pasa, a 19th-century statesman. On the east side of the mosque, in an enclosed court, is the Sahaflar Çarsisi second-hand book market. An 18th-century Turkish bath here is no longer in use as such, but at one of the entrances to the Grand Bazaar nearby are two reconstructed *hans*, the Hasan Pasa and the Simkes.

Church of Saints Sergius and Bacchus: Küçük Ayasofya

By going downhill from the southern end of the At Meydani, past Torun Sokak and the Arasta Bazaar, you can find Küçük Ayasofya down near the Marmara sea walls on Küçük Ayasofya Sokak. You may have to locate the warden to open up, but almost inevitably a small boy of the area will appear and run to fetch the warden or at least bring back the key.

The architects of the church, now in use as a mosque, were those chosen for the larger Hagia Sophia. Saints Sergius and Bacchus, known as the Little St Sophia, was dedicated at an earlier date in 527 than the greater church and may well have been its model. Sergius and Bacchus were soldier converts to Christianity and martyred under Diocletian and Maximium (284–305). Justinian believed these two saints had interceded successfully on his behalf when he was under sentence of death after being implicated in a plot against the Emperor Anastasius.

The church — an octagonal shape within an irregular quadrilateral — has a dome set without the use of pendentives. Columns stand back from the centre to contribute to semi-circular recesses; 18 columns in the gallery are connected by arches. A frieze running below the gallery has an inscription to Theodora, praising her charitable activities, and includes a reference to St Sergius. Monograms of Justinian and Theodora are set on some columns.

Below, the railway runs along the line of the sea walls. Against the walls was the **Bucoleon Palace** built by Theodosias II (408–50). Only three windows with their carved balcony supports exist still. On the man-made harbour was the sculpture of a bull in conflict with a lion. When Rhodes fell to the Turks, the lion, it is said, turned its head defensively to the east. Justinian restored this palace. One of its pavilions was known as the Porphyra, and a royal child born there was designated Porphyrogenitus, or born in purple, as was Constantine VII. Nicephorus Phocas (963–9) restored the palace, only to be assassinated here. Manuel I Comnenus (1143–80) brought back a porphyry slab on which he believed Christ's body had lain after being taken down from the cross, and carried it on his own back up the long stairway from the quayside.

The Landwalls

Remarkably, long stretches of the **Theodosian walls** of the city exist in surprisingly intact condition, and in a sense still control the city's entrances and exits as they did in the days of Byzantium. A recent mayor of İstanbul has tried to tidy up the past by reconstructing sections of the wall and the city entrances, as well as the roadway intersections, particularly between Hadrian's Gate and the Yedikule Tower on the southern Marmara section. Alas, this has not been done with strict fidelity to the antique model, even though the convenience of today's citizens has been enhanced.

Its first walls were built by Septimius Severus (193–211), enclosing his city of Antoninia, the area occupied now by Topkapi Palace, At Meydani, Baths of Zeuxippus and Gülhane Park. Restored sections of this old wall survive. When Constantine decided to build New Rome, he paced out the boundary of the city himself, marking the line of his new walls with the tip of his spear, while claiming that an invisible guide had walked ahead. His walls seem not to have survived. The **Aqueduct of Valens** (364–78), which stands in such prominent majesty still at Unkapani, a city entrance, may have replaced an aqueduct of Constantine's time. It was built perpendicular to the line of his walls which ran along present Atatürk Bulvari from the Yenikapi (New Gate) on the Marmara through the Aksaray road junction to the Atatürk Bridge.

In 413 Anthemius, the regent for Theodosius II (408–50), built new walls, the present ones, to the west of Constantine's, stretching from the Marmara to the Golden Horn. Anastasius (491–518) built additional walls even further to the west, running for 105 kilometres (65 miles) from the Marmara to the Black Sea; although there are no walls there now, this line is a recognized feature of Turkish defence strategy.

Topkapi, or **Cannon Gate**, the St Romanus Gate for the Byzantines, was the focal target of Mehmet II's assault on the city. Ordu Caddesi, which becomes Millet Caddesi after Aksaray junction, runs to it. Here, because the gateway was in the valley of the Lycus River, the attackers on the hills had an advantage of height over the defenders on the walls. A huge cannon designed and built by Urban, a Hungarian engineer, pounded the walls here. It took two months to haul this piece the 250 kilometres (155 miles) from Edirne. Loading the cannon took two hours, which gave welcome respite to the defenders and the opportunity to repair damage, and it had to be doused with gallons of oil after firing. After only a limited use, the cannon blew up, killing Urban himself and many members of the gun crew. Mehmet, however, had other smaller cannons at work on the walls. The last Byzantine emperor, Constantine XI

The Birds Of Florya Plain

*T*he boys were always up very early in the morning, but even before they had woken, at the first glimmer of dawn, Tugrul would be there already. How many times had I seen him rushing along the fringe of the wood towards the poplar tree, as though fearful of missing something, and then, if the boys were still asleep, he would draw a deep breath and slump down in his accustomed place in front of the barbed wire, resting his chin on his knees.

On Florya Plain, the bird hunt was in full swing now. So it is each year when October comes, when the north wind is blasting, ice-cold, keen as a razor's edge, or when the sea is churned into a furious foaming mass by the lodos that blows from the south. Then, clouds of tiny birds are tossed hither and thither, tracing zigzags in the air, flurrying down over the thistles, only to rise again in the same instant, veering swiftly over the sea, on to Çekmece Lake and back to the wood, grazing the crests of the trees, a scatter of many-coloured specks in the sky, vanishing from sight and appearing again. But on warm sunny days, they swarm down over the thistles in thousands, twittering madly, and devour with frightening rapacity the seeds of the dried shrubs that, in the summer, had flowered bright yellow, dyeing the whole plain saffron.

Ever since ancient Byzantium, through Ottoman times to this day, these tiny birds, coming no one nows whence and going no one knows where, have sojourned here, on Florya Plain, from October to the end of December. And ever since, the people of Istanbul town have set all kinds of snares to capture them. They capture them, and then sell them, in front of churches if they are Christians, synagogues if they are Jewish, or mosques if they are Moslems. "Fly little bird, free as the air, and meet me at the gates of Paradise." And so, all over Istanbul town, the sky will be swarming with little birds delivered from captivity by those who wish to ensure a place in Paradise cheaply. Children especially, and also the very old...

Many years ago, it must have been when I first came to Istanbul, I had seen in Taksim Square a very old gentleman, wearing a fur-collared coat, and a little boy of six or seven. From a barefooted youngster they were buying tiny wild-eyed yellow birds and casting them up into the air. They would take it in turns, first the old gentleman, then the little boy, and at every throw the three of them would cry out in pure joy. And there was that cat huddling in the bushes under the plane trees... Every now and again, one of the small birds, unable to take wing, would fall to the ground and flutter off into the bushes. No sooner there than that monster of a cat would pounce on it, tear it apart with claws and teeth, and devour it greedily. Then, licking its chops, the cat would lie in wait, quite still, its eyes on the air, for its next prey.

Nowadays, it is only in the courtyard of Eyup Mosque that children manage to sell a bird or two to be set free. So they prefer to take them to the bird market in Eminönü where the dealers select a few of the finest out of hundreds, in order to sell them at a high price to bird fanciers. And the children go back home, weary, disappointed, toting their cages still filled to the brim, wondering what to do with all these birds.

If the chroniclers of Istanbul city neglect the history of these birds and of the fowlers on Florya Plain, then their work, according to me, will not be worth much. Indeed, it will all have been in vain. The joy of millions of little birds set free in front of churches, synagogues and mosques for hundreds of years, and the joy of so many people too... Is that an adventure of small importance? One day, I know it, some person, imaginative, wise, pure of heart, will come forward and write the fine history, full of hope and gladness, of the birds of Florya Plain, and then Istanbul city will be a more beautiful, a more enchanting place. Is the magic of Istanbul only in its sea and sky, its rivers and monuments? And what of the Florya birds then?

Yashar Kemal, The Birds Have Also Gone

Dragases, died at this gate on the final day of the siege.

The next major gate to the north of Topkapi is the towered **Edirne Kapi**, the exit through the walls on Fevzipaa Caddesi. It is the principal gate in today's reconstructed road system. However, this was the Byzantine Charisios Gate, named after the leader of the Blues when an emergency wall construction programme was undertaken by the city prefect, Constantine Cyrus. The walls are at their highest elevation here, before descending to the Golden Horn. North of the gate is **Tekfur Saray**, the Byzantine palace of Constantine VII Porphyrogenitus, of which some good stonework and brickwork is left. Another gate in the walls here, the **Kerkoporta**, reportedly was left open by mistake after a Byzantine sortie, enabling a small body of Turks to gain entrance. By all accounts the incident need not have been disastrous, except that defenders elsewhere, seeing the standard raised by the Turkish infiltrators, panicked, believing the walls had been irrevocably breached, and their resistance crumbled. The walls from here to the Golden Horn now include that of the outer wall of **Blachernae Palace**, favoured by the Comneni emperors, and its gate the **Karsios** or **Oblique Gate**, outside which Alexius III Angelos allowed the army of the Fourth Crusade to camp, and from where they attacked the city.

At the Marmara end of the Theodosian walls was the **Golden Gate**. The present road from İstanbul's airport, Florya Highway, running along the Marmara, enters the city near this former gate. Triple-arched, the gate was used by royalty for whom the central, taller arch was reserved. The suburb of Hebdomon and the military Campus Martius lay outside the walls. Hebdomon had a port and a palace where an emperor returning from an overseas campaign stayed prior to his triumphal entrance into the capital. If he was a newly elevated emperor, acclaimed by the troops on the Campus Martius, his exaltation would be confirmed at the monastery church of **St John in Studion** inside the walls. The ruins of the church, protected by fencing, can still inspire appreciation. Between the Golden Gate and the shore was the Postern of Christ, said to have borne his monogram. What has survived of the Golden Gate is now incorporated in a fort known as **Yedikule** or the **Castle of the Seven Towers**, an Ottoman construction. The Byzantines had a prison at the Golden Gate, where an ambassador or a plenipotentiary might sometimes be imprisoned, as was Luidprand, the Bishop of Cremona, and the Ottomans used Yedikule for similar purposes.

The main city wall was four metres (13 feet) wide and 13 metres (43 feet) high. It had 96 towers — square, pentagonal or octagonal — 20 metres (66 feet) high. Ahead of this wall were protection ramparts with their towers, a moat and a sentry platform.

The Golden Horn

For an excursion up the Golden Horn, a ferry service starts from Eminönü in the old city. It calls at stations on either side of the waterway, which is now spanned by three bridges. Atatürk Bridge crosses from Unkapani on Constantine's line of walls to Azapkapi on the Galata side. Above Atatürk Bridge some ferry stations have historic connotations, such as Fener (on the left bank) which was the Phanar district where many Greeks settled after the conquest of the city and in time became known as Phanariotes. The **Church of St George** here became the seat of the Greek Orthodox Patriarch; it was rebuilt in 1720. Kasimpasa (on the right bank) is likely to have been the place where Mehmet II relaunched his boats — after hauling them overland from the Bosphorus. The Byzantines had closed the Golden Horn with a chain stretched from Seraglio Point to Galata, and Mehmet, his navy having failed to force an entry by frontal attack, hit upon this arduous surprise tactic and thereby completed the city's encirclement.

Hasköy, higher up on the right bank, was the quarter of the Sephardic Jews, who were given sanctuary here after their expulsion from Spain.

On the western or left bank, Ayvansaray was the quay for the Blachernae Palace and where the land walls met the sea walls, which ran all the way down the Golden Horn to Seraglio Point. The last surviving sections are disappearing now under development and cosmetic projects. In a street near the quay is the **Aghiasma of Mary**, the most holy Byzantine shrine in the city. Mary's robe was kept here as a talisman to be brought out for display whenever the city was threatened by assault. During the course of the annual celebration on 15 August, Mary's Day, the emperor would plunge three times into the sacred pool. The Koca Mustafa Cami here was formerly the Church of St Peter and St Mark, wherein the holy robe had been kept prior to its transfer to the Aghiasma.

Eyüp

The third bridge, the newest in construction, crosses the Golden Horn just above Ayvansaray; it links up with the Bosphorus bridges that carry traffic from Europe directly into Asia. Justinian had a bridge constructed about here which was called the Callinicus, and Mehmet II spanned it with a bridge of barrels. Passing under today's Halic Bridge, you reach the last quay on the left bank, Eyüp. This is a place of graves, from the tombs of sultans and princes to the tombstones of the humble and the meek. The **Eyüp Cami** here is dedicated to the Companion and Standard Bearer of Mohammed, who was killed during the Arab siege of Constantinople in 672 but whose burial place was discovered only after Mehmet II's capture of the city. The mosque was built in 1458, and as the saint was again laid to rest, Mehmet himself was present and ceremoniously accepted the Scimitar of Osman. It became the practice then for each newly acclaimed sultan to go to Eyüp to pray at the mosque and to receive the scimitar in confirmation of his role as spiritual and military champion of Islam.

The mosque was damaged during an earthquake of the early 1800s and was reconstructed. Light is admitted onto marble and carved ivory through lattice-patterned windows. The inner of two courtyards holds the saint's tomb, little more than a niche in a tiled wall, behind a grille through which a pilgrim may offer his prayers or beg a spiritual favour. In the vicinity of the mosque is a Sinan tomb built for Sokollu Mehmet Pasa, a grand vizier. Mehmet V (1909–18), the last sultan to die within Turkey's borders, also has his tomb at Eyüp.

Climb up the hill at Eyüp on a pathway through a forest of tombstones to a café on the crest. This is a café that Pierre Loti visited often, and it is named after him. In his day it would have offered a clear view of the Golden Horn as it opens up to the Bosphorus, or inland to hills, to the Forest of Belgrade and the Sweet Waters of Europe with their Ottoman aqueducts.

Beyoğlu — The New City

Taksim Square
Taksim is the centre of the new city. Buses run to it from the THY air terminal, but the distance to Taksim from there is little, taxi fares are low, and a taxi driver must now adhere strictly to his meter.

The **Monument to the Republic** in Taksim Square was erected in 1928 under the guidance of an Italian architect. Between it and the lower end of the square is a railed garden with the **Atatürk Cultural Centre and Opera House**. Standing with your back to the Opera House, the Etap Marmara Hotel is on the left-hand side. On the right-hand side is the stairway entrance to Taksim Park, and the several bus stops for the various districts.

From the top end of Taksim Square, by the monument, Cumhuriyet Caddesi (Republic Street), one of the two principal thoroughfares of Beyoğlu, leads off to the right. A broad twin-avenued thoroughfare with a central spine of trees, it is railed at the Taksim end to restrain haphazard pedestrians. Along this avenue, following the line of shops on the right-hand side, is the Sheraton Hotel, and then further along, beyond the Divan Hotel, is the Hilton. On Cumhuriyet, too, between the Hilton and the square, on both sides are the offices of the major airline companies, some of the larger restaurants and *pavyons* (nightclubs) and many boutique-type shops selling tourist souvenirs.

İstiklâl Caddesi (Independence Street), a one-way street leading into the square, is the other principal thoroughfare as you walk out of the square in a southwesterly direction. Less wide than Cumhuriyet, it is the main shopping street at the centre of Beyoğlu, with fashion shops, banks, cinemas, snack bars,

restaurants, patisseries, tailors, leatherware boutiques, bookshops, chemists' (*eczane*) and, lower down, the Pigalle-type nightclubs. Many old buildings on this street are under restoration. There is a plan to turn İstiklâl into a pedestrian precinct with an old-fashioned tramway operating for its entire length.

While the French Consulate is at the Taksim end of İstiklâl Caddesi, the Consulates of the Soviet Union, The Netherlands and Sweden are further down the street. For Britains and Americans, their respective consulates can be found by turning right about half-way down İstiklâl Caddesi just after passing the Post Office on the right, and then turning left immediately into Mesrutiyet Caddesi. The British Consulate is a large rail-enclosed building on the corner, and the American Consulate can be found on the right by following along this street for several hundred metres. Mesrutiyet Caddesi leads to Tepebasi, the district in which the hotel Pera Palace is located, and then on to the THY air terminal at Şişhane.

In the very lowest reaches of İstiklâl is the entrance to Tünel. Built in 1877, it is the city's single underground railway line which is really more of a funicular and runs down to Karaköy on the Golden Horn waterfront near Galata Bridge.

Tarlabasi Caddesi, running out of Taksim on the western side, is an old street that has been transformed into a highway and is now a principal thoroughfare in the re-vamped road system between Taksim and Galata. Yet another street leading out of Taksim, in a southeasterly direction, is Siraselviler Caddesi. At its near end are several medium-range hotels. Off the lower, eastern end of Taksim, on the right of the Opera House as you face it, Gumussuyu Caddesi runs downhill to reach the Bosphorus waterfront near the ferry station at Kabatas and the **Dolmabahçe Palace**. Atatürk, who chose to stay in this palace whenever he visited İstanbul, died there in 1938; all the clocks in the palace were stopped at the exact time of his death.

At its northern extremity, Cumhuriyet Caddesi becomes two prongs of a fork: the lower prong leads through Nisantasi, and the upper one passes through Osmanbey to Şişli (an inland route to the upper reaches of the Bosphorus and the Black Sea). Recently, Osmanbey and Nisantasi have developed as rival centres to İstiklâl for fashion shopping.

Galata District and Tower

Galata, or Pera, was the area of the merchants, the Genoese in particular. Under the Byzantines, the Venetians enjoyed greater and often exclusive trading privileges, with warehousing facilities on the western shore of the Golden Horn. In their mercantile rivalry, the two Italian republics were quite frequently at war with each other in these waters. Still the commercial, banking and shipping centre of the city, Galata stretches along the quays at Karaköy from Atatürk Bridge to the docks on the east side of Galata Bridge and up the narrow and hilly streets that rise above the waterway here. The most conspicuous building in the area is the **Galata Tower**, built with a fire-watching post up top by the Genoese in 1348 when timbered structures were the architectural order of the day. It may originally have been made of wood but was rebuilt in 1423. Reconstructed again in the 19th century, the tower had its more recent face-lifting a year or two ago when its top section was converted to a restaurant and nightclub. Sixty-eight metres (223 feet) high, the tower may be climbed by way of the spiralling stone stairway, or go up by lift. The views from the top will repay the small fee, even if you decide against eating there.

The Bosphorus and the European Shore

Taking Dolmabahçe Palace as the starting point, a tree-lined avenue, Dolmabahçe Caddesi, runs for about a kilometre (.6 mile) north to Beşiktaş. Two Ottoman palaces on this section of road, **Yildiz Kiosk** and the **Çiragan Palace,** have been revitalized recently. Yildiz, with its pavilions and lake, has become a public park, and Çiragan is an exclusive luxury hotel and restaurant on the waterfront. At Beşiktaş the **Tomb of Barbarossa**, designed by Sinan, is situated in a small garden near the ferry station. The notorious, red-bearded pirate became famous and successful as an admiral under Süleiman the Magnificent. Also nearby, sailing ships of many ages are the fascinating exhibits in a **Naval Museum**.

At Ortaköy, a little north of Besiktas, the road passes under the western stanchions of the first Bosphorus suspension bridge to reach Arnavütköy, the first of the waterway's residential villages, where there are some fine timbered houses on the waterfront as you enter the village street. There are restaurants here with terraces on the waterside.

Bebek is the next village, developing now into a substantial suburb, but it has some good restaurants and several large *gazinos*. In Turkey a *gazino* or casino is a blend of restaurant and music hall — with singers, raconteurs and dancers — and in general caters for family eating and entertainment, unlike a *pavyon* (nightclub) where the show might be considered *risqué* in the French sense. On the hills above Bebek is the campus of the Bosphorus University which in origin was an American foundation, Robert College. The grounds are lovely and offer fine views of the waterway.

The castle at **Rumeli Hisar**, put up in three months by Mehmet II and 3,000 workmen, was a principal item in his plan for capturing the city. The walls and towers are sound still, and the castle is used frequently as a theatre, particularly during the annual İstanbul Arts Festival. The second Bosphorus bridge spans the waterway from a little above Rumeli Hisar, however, the supporting access road system has not yet been constructed.

Emirgan has a modern harbour with a dry dock. It was Sosthenion for the Byzantines. The Argonauts built a temple here to a winged mentor who had come to their assistance in a crisis; Constantine built a church, dedicated to the Archangel Michael. Daniel, a notable stylite saint, occupied a column here.

Yeniköy was Neapolis, and a year or two ago a former Byzantine palace on the waterside was turned into a gambling casino, the only licensed one in İstanbul, until a manager, it was said, absconded with the profits. The casino moved to the Hilton Hotel, and the palace became a private bathing club and restaurant. The waterside Carlton Hotel is nearby. Today licensed casinos and machine-gambling saloons are numerous throughout the city.

Tarabya has an attractive bay and yacht marina, as well as a multitude of quayside restaurants, all serving indescribably good seafood. It was Therapeia in classical and legendary times when the blind king Phineas was tormented here by the Harpies. On the northern arm of the bay is the large Grand Tarabya Hotel, with its own private bathing beach.

Büyükdere, a village of very fine timbered buildings, has its waterside restaurants, too. **Sariyer**, a little to the north of it, has developed far beyond the rusticity of its simple village origins. With large waterside restaurants and *gazinos*, it has a sizeable fish market as well.

The roadway narrows beyond Sariyer and then arrives at Rumeli Kavagi, the furthest point to which you can go without obtaining permission from the military. Before reaching Rumeli Kavagi (Roman Poplar), **Tellibaba** has the shrine of a Moslem saint, whom infertile wives petition for the blessing of fecundity. **Rumeli Kavagi** has the ruins of a Byzantine fortress, and a public bathing beach at **Altnkum**. From the heights here, the Clashing Rocks of Homer, the gateway to and from the Black Sea, can be observed but not photographed.

Rumeli Kavagi is some 16 kilometres (ten miles) from Taksim Square, and a *dolmus* (minibus) from the Taksim area can be taken to the village of your choice up the Bosphorus, which is always a pleasure to be travelling along or eating beside. Buses also run to Sariyer. Restaurants are plentiful, and the cuisine is of a high standard. It might be well to remember, though, that less canopied restaurants are not necessarily less worthy than their gaudier neighbours and certainly are less expensive.

Ferry boats plying the Bosphorus zigzag from station to station, from shore to shore, providing a pleasant excursion of several hours. The station is at Eminönü beside Galata Bridge on the western side of the Golden Horn. A good way of enjoying the Bosphorus is to take the ferry to Rumeli Kavagi and then return by *dolmus* or bus, choosing one or other of the villages for a stop at a waterside restaurant.

Because the strength of the undertow can be dangerous, the Bosphorus is not an exceptional place for swimming. It is advisable to use the private or es-

tablished facilities along the shore. **Kilyos** on the Black Sea, however, has a long sandy beach, full bathing facilities, camping, hotels and other accommodation. It can be reached on the inland route from Taksim by taxi, bus or minibus or from Büyükdere on the Bosphorus.

Other bathing beaches near İstanbul are on the Marmara Sea at Florya, Ataköy and a little further west at Yesilköy, a pleasant residential suburb close to the international airport.

Üsküdar — İstanbul's Asian Shore

Kiz Kulesi or Maiden's Tower

This tower, set on a rock about mid-stream in the Bosphorus, has been erroneously associated with the legend of Leander and Hero. The true location of this event was at the Helespont, at the southern end of the Dardanelles, away to the southwest. At the time of the Athenian Empire in the fifth century BC a toll post on this rock exacted dues on all shipping passing through the Bosphorus. Later in history the rock acquired a lighthouse, and more recently it became a signals station.

Üsküdar

This was Scutari at the time of the Crimean War (1853–6) in which Britain, France and Sardinia were the allies of Turkey against the Russians. At a much earlier date it was Chrysopolis, the Golden City, which was plundered by the Goths in the third century. Prince Igor's Russians held it for a time in the tenth century until driven out by the Byzantine Emperor Romanus Lecapenus. There were Seljuk Turks serving as mercenaries in the forces of Nicephorus Botantiates during his attempt to seize imperial power in the city in 1078. This offered at least some Turks the chance to observe the great potential prize across the water.

On the quayside is the **Mihrimah Cami** built by Sinan in 1547, and, in front of it, a **fountain** erected by the tulip-loving Sultan Ahmet III. The mosque on the right of the quay is Sinan's Semsi Pasa Cami of 1580, and off to the right is the **Atik Valide Cami** of 1583.

The road leading away south from the quayside through the town was the former main road out to the E5 highway to Ankara. This route is bypassed now by the direct link to the E5 across the first Bosphorus bridge, and also by a feed road directly from the Üsküdar quayside. Out on the old road is the hospital where Florence Nightingale worked as a nurse during the Crimean War; it is attached to the Selimiye Barracks with, nearby, the cemeteries of the Allied dead of that war.

Travel south of the barracks to reach Kadiköy, once the ancient city of Chalcedon founded by the Megarans before Byaz settled on the site of Byzantium.

Though the earlier Megarans were sneered at for having been blind in their choice of a site inferior to that of Constantinople, they may not after all have been so stupid since the climate of Kadiköy is more equable than that of the former capital. Septimius Severus, punishing the citizens of Chalcedon for their opposition to him, demolished the city's walls and used the stone for his own building project of Antoninia. Held here in 451, the Fourth Oecumenical Council of the Church declared that the Monophysite doctrine was heresy.

The Eastern Shore
There are fewer urban villages along the eastern shore of the Bosphorus than along the western, and the roadway sometimes leaves the waterfront or is diverted by the road reconstruction system. Yet there are pleasures to be derived from an excursion along it, not least the number of old timbered houses, many of which have been or are being reconstructed.

Beylerbeyi, where the first Bosphorus bridge reaches land on the Asian shore, has a **castle** built by Sultan Abdül Aziz (1861–76). The mad Abdül Hamit II, who while occupying Yildiz Kiosk carried a pistol everywhere and threatened those he believed were plotting against him, was exiled here in 1909, bringing only his cat, the single being he appears ever to have loved. An interesting baroque-style mosque here dates from 1778.

Eight kilometres (five miles) north of Beylerbeyi, at Kandirli are two streams, the Küçüksu and the Göksu, known as the Sweet Waters of Asia. There is an organized bathing establishment on the Bosphorus here. In the vicinity, too, is an elegant waterside *yali* (18th-century timbered villa). An ornate gateway leads into the 18th-century **Göksu Palace** grounds, in which there is a handsome fountain. In the 1850s the meadows through which the Küçüksu ran was a picnic area for the fashionable of İstanbul and a trysting place. The lady accompanied by a eunuch or chaperone would stroll on one side of the stream, while on the other the gentleman would pass. By an exchange of wordless expressions and gestures, such as tossing a flower across the water, their affections and desires were demonstrated.

A little way north of Küçüksu, is **Anadolu Hisar** a fort built by Beyazit I. Unlike its partnering fort on the European shore, namely, the Rumeli Hisar of Mehmet II, Anadolu Hisar is pretty much of a ruin, if a picturesque one. The road system of the second Bosphorus bridge is going to have its effect on the landscape here. Kanlica to the north is noted for its yoghurt, and there is a mosque built by Sinan for a grand vizier of Süleiman the Magnificent. Another lovely timbered *yali* just to the south of Kanlica is a 17th-century construction.

The palace at Çubuklu was built for the Khedive of Egypt in 1900. Beykoz, three kilometres (two miles) to the north, must be considered the most urbane of the eastern shore villages, with an 18th-century fountain in the main square and at least one restaurant over the water. It was here that the Argonaut Pollux

An Autocrat
at the Hamam

ow and then, usually about once in a week, my grandmother had a
sociable turn of mind and when these moods came upon her she
invariably went to the Hamam. Hamams, or the Turkish Baths, were
hot-beds of gossip and scandal-mongering, snobbery in its most
inverted form and the excuse for every woman in the district to
have a day out. Nobody ever dreamed of taking a bath in anything
under seven or eight hours. The young girls went to show off their
pink-and-white bodies to the older women. Usually the mothers of
eligible sons were in their minds for this purpose for these would, it
was to be hoped, take the first opportunity of detailing to their sons
the finer points of So-and-sq's naked body. Marriages based on
such hearsay quite frequently took place, but whether or not they
were successful few of us had any means of knowing.

In the hot rooms of the Hamams little jealousies and rivalries
were fanned into strong fires and very often fights took place
between the mothers of attractive daughters vieing for the favours
of the same young man.

As against the mothers of daughters the mothers of sons took
pride of place. There was a sort of sharp dividing line drawn
between them and it was quite easy for a stranger to tell which of
the plump, matronly ladies had the best wares for sale. For whereas
the mothers of daughters were inclined to laugh a lot, to draw
attention to their family groups, the mothers of sons lay aloof on
their divans—too conscious of their own superiority to contribute
to the general noise and scandalising. They would lazily nibble
fruit, eye the simpering, posturing young girls critically and
sometimes accept the offer of having their backs washed by some
ravishing young creature but with such condescension that
immediately the wildest speculations were engendered in the other
female breasts as to why such an obvious favour had been shown at
all. The back-washing concluded, the ravishing young creature
would be dismissed and one by one the mothers of the ignored
daughters would sidle up to the devilish old autocrat who had just
had her back washed and whisper the most damning things about
the character of the recent, elated, now vanished back-washer.

Irfan Orga, Portrait of a Turkish Family

wrestled with and killed Amycus, the king who had boxed and killed any and every stranger who landed on his shore until that time. Out of Amycus's grave grew a bay tree with leaves said to induce madness if chewed.

Further north at Hünkar Iskelesi, the palace is in use as a hospital. Beyond the Tokat valley and inland a little, on top of Yusa Tepesi, or Hill of Josua, there is a grave which is 12 metres (40 feet) long and known as the Bed of Heracles. The next and last ferry stop is Anadolu Kavagi, whose fortifications, as with those of Rumeli Kavagi on the western shore, were built by the French.

Polonezköy

A day trip from İstanbul could be made to Polonezköy, or it could be included as part of a two-day trip to Üsküdar and the villages on the eastern shore. Lying inland from Beykoz, Polonezköy can be reached by road from Çubuklu or Beykoz, and an overnight stay could be planned. Polonezköy is not so much a village as an area settled by Polish refugees who were given land to farm here by the reigning sultan because of their service to the country during the Crimean War. The inhabitants have created a little Poland, in lifestyle and in the landscape with its individual farmhouses. Polish home-cooking can be enjoyed in any one, and rooms are available for brief or longer stays. Inevitably, the rapid development of tourism in parts of Turkey has had an effect here.

Sile

The western Bosphorus has its bathing centre at Kilyos on the Black Sea coast, and the eastern Bosphorus has Sile, also on the Black Sea, which is not quite so accessible from İstanbul but likely to be less onerously crowded as a holiday resort. Its beach is a good one, with accompanying bathing facilities, accommodation and a ruined **Genoese castle**. It can be reached from Beykoz, 73 kilometres (45 miles) away, or on road 020 that branches off the E5 after it has crossed the Bosphorus bridge and is about to join the coastal road south of Üsküdar. The distance by the latter route is 54 kilometres (34 miles). Sile could be the final destination of an excursion that takes in the eastern shore of the Bosphorus and a visit to Polonezköy.

Other Mosques and Churches

The **Fatih Cami** (Mosque of the Conqueror), begun in 1462, was the first to be built in the city after the conquest. It is on the fourth hill, to the northwest of the Aqueduct of Valens. This was the site of the Church of the Holy Apostles founded by Constantine I but completed by Constantius, his son and successor. Constantine was buried here, but was afterwards disinterred and reburied at Hereke. Justinian enlarged the church, and it became the burial place of a succession of emperors, whose tombs were looted during the Latin occupation of

1204–61. Mehmet II installed Gennadius as Greek Patriarch here, but in 1461 the Patriarchate was transferred elsewhere when the building of the mosque was begun. The architect of the mosque is said to have been Atik Sinan (no relative of the great Sinan), however, the structure is also attributed to a Greek architect named Christodoulou, which may have been Atik Sinan's name prior to his conversion to Islam. The mosque was badly ruined in an earthquake of the 1800s and was replaced by the present one. According to a 16th-century traveller's notes, the mosque had a central dome and a half-dome above the mihrab and above each lateral. This suggests that the design of the original building was founded on the designs of earlier Ottoman mosques of Bursa and Edirne. The structure of the Church of the Holy Apostles can be seen in Venice at St Mark's, which is said to have been modelled on the Byzantine church.

The **Yeni Cami** (New Mosque) is the impressive-looking mosque with twin minarets that you see as you cross Galata Bridge towards Eminönü and the old city. It was begun in 1592 for the mother of Mehmet III, Safiye, but building was stopped in 1602 on the death of the sultan, though renewed again in Mehmet VI's reign and completed for his mother, the Valide Sultan, in 1663. A feature of the exterior is a second mihrab in the east wall outside the mosque for use of latecomers or in the event of a full mosque. The fountain is a fine feature of the forecourt.

Mosques by the Architect Sinan

The Sehzade Cami is one of Sinan's first constructions, built by Süleiman the Magnificent for his son Prince Sehzade, who died young in 1543. It is close to Valens' Aqueduct. Supporting the central dome are four half-domes, instead of two half-domes as at St Sophia and the Süleimaniye. There is fine tile decoration on the prince's tomb.

Construction of the **Mihrimah Cami** may have followed that of Sinan's work on the Sehzade. Mihrimah was the sister of the young prince and was married to the Grand Vizier Rüstem Pasa. The mosque (1566) is on the sixth hill up near the Edirne Kapi (Edirne Gate). Sinan dispensed with half-domes here, replacing them with walls and corner turrets to support the squinches.

The **Rüstem Pasa Cami** — a major work of Sinan — stands to the right of the Yeni Mosque, near the waterside, and is dated 1561. The building is constructed on a terrace, with two enclosed stairways leading up to the forecourt. There is fine Iznik tiling on the exterior and interior of the mosque. The dome is supported on four pillars, with half-domes replacing the pendentives. The sadirvan (ablutions fountain) stands in its own enclosure.

You can find your way to this Sinan mosque, **Sokollu Mehmet Pasa Cami**, by going downhill from the Hippodrome (At Meydani), past the street with the Mosaic Museum and towards the Kucuk Ayasofya Cami but moving gradually to the right. Construction was begun in 1571. The architectural innovation here is the hexagonal support for the dome, having four laterals buttressed by half-domes. The building, too, is built on a slope. A porticoed court has a fine door-way into the mosque. Once again, İznik tiles have been used to attractive effect. Sokollu Mehmet, an admiral of Selim II's, was a convert to Islam (and the son of a priest). He married Esmekham, the sultan's daughter, who is said to have been a dwarf.

Sinan began the **Piyale Pasa Cami** in 1573 at Kasimpasa on the north-eastern shore of the Golden Horn. Piyale Pasa, as Grand Admiral of Selim II's fleet, was defeated by a combined Christian navy under the Venetian Andrea Doria. The design of the mosque is simple compared to the architect's more ambitious projects, and he broke with tradition by placing the single minaret in the centre of the façade, not to the right of the entrance as was customary.

The **Kiliç Ali Pasa Cami** is the mosque of yet another admiral, this time under Murat III. Sinan's commission for the structure came late in his career in 1580. It is at Tophane, near the Bosphorus in the Galata area. St Sophia may have been Sinan's influence here, with the installation of galleries along both aisles; the way the mihrab is built might even indicate that the architect had had the idea of an apse in mind when designing it.

The Iskelc Cami or **Büyük Cami** (Grand Mosque) is on the quayside at Üsküdar on the asiatic shore of the Bosphorus, beside the ferry station. Built on a platform, it dates from 1547 when Sinan was middle-aged. It is dedicated to the Princess Mihrimah.

The **Sinan Pasa Cami** was built for another unrelated Sinan, a sailor and the brother of the Grand Vizier Rüstem Pasa. This Sinan mosque is at Beşiktaş on the western side of the Bosphorus, on the way to where the first suspension bridge crosses the waterway. There is good brickwork and stonework on the exterior of this mosque.

The **Sultan Selim Cami** (the Selimiye) was built for Selim I by his son Süleiman the Magnificent, on his succession. This early Sinan mosque is on the fifth hill of the city at Yavuz Selim, northwest of the Fatih Cami. The central area has a dome with two adjoining cupolas and a portico. Again, there is excellent tilework and inlay decoration. From the courtyard there is a fine view of the Golden Horn.

Go south of Millet Caddesi, beyond the Aksaray road junction and to the west. In 1539 Süleiman commissioned Sinan to build the **Haseki Cami** for Roxellana, his favourite wife.

Early Mosques by Other Architects

In Aksaray near the road junction west of Beyazit Square, the **Mürat Pasa Cami** is an early mosque of 1466. Built on a T-shaped ground plan and erected by Mürat Pasa, a grand vizier of Mehmet II, the mosque's central area has two domes above it and a vestibule with cupolas leading into it.

In Cerrah Pasa on the Marmara seaboard, the **Cerrah Pasa Cami** is about halfway to the walls at the Golden Gate. The mosque was built in 1594 for a grand vizier of Mehmet III. The Forum of Arcadius was here, and there is the base of the column the emperor erected in 404.

18th- and 19th-century Mosques

Near the Dolmabahçe Palace and the ferry station at Kabatas is the **Dolmabahçe Cami**. It was built in 1853 by Sultan Abdul Medjid. It has the slenderest minarets in the city.

In Kocamustafa, west of Cerrah Pasa, is the **Hekimoglu Ali Pasa Cami**. The mosque was built for Mahmout I in 1735 by the architect Araboglu Meliton Kalfa.

Lâleli is the district to the east of the Aksaray junction. The **Lâleli Cami** is on the north side of Ordu Caddesi which extends from Divan Yolu. Dating from 1763, it is not especially distinguished except for its minarets and the large courtyard — a pleasing feature of most mosques.

Mosques That Were Formerly Churches

On the fifth hill at Yavuz Selim, the **Ahmet Pasa Mescidi** or **St John Prodromos in Trullo** is located near the Selimiye. The Church of St John Prodromos (John the Baptist) was a 12th-century construction. It has a smooth semi-circular apse in contrast to the more usual angled ones.

The **Fethiye Cami**, or **Church of the Pammakaristos**, is on the fifth hill, too, a little to the northwest of the Ahmet Pasa mosque and overlooks the Phanariote (Fener) area of the Golden Horn. The church was restored in the 14th century as the Church of Theotokos or the All Blessed, the Pammakaristos. It was within a monastery complex which became the seat of the Orthodox Greek Patriarch after it was moved from the Church of the Holy Apostles. It was converted into a mosque in 1586 under Murat III. The dome was built following its conversion. Some very beautiful mosaics were uncovered by the restoration team from the Institute of Byzantine Studies in Boston.

Close to the Golden Gate, **Imrahor Cami**, or **St John in Studion**, was a notable theological centre. Newly elected emperors were confirmed in their elevation here, and more than one emperor, either deposed or on relinquishing office, retired to it to end his days in prayer and contemplation. The St John of the title again is John the Baptist, and the monastery's most precious relic was the Baptist's severed head to which each emperor paid homage on the anniversary of the saint's execution by Herod.

The monastery was founded in 463 by the Patriarch Studios and became known as that of the Akoimetai, or sleepless ones, the liturgy being celebrated endlessly by relays of monks. Its famous abbot of the late seventh century was Theodore, who brought fame to it by his reforms and by the attainment of a high level of its theology, music and calligraphy. Theodore was a vigorous opponent of Iconoclasm and was exiled to Büyük Ada in the Princes' Islands, where he died in 826.

St John's was built in true basilican form with its long rectangular columned hall with aisles, the semi-circular apse and the entrance to it by porch and narthex. On its conversion to a mosque soon after the conquest, an ablutions fountain was installed in the court. The building was damaged by fire in 1782, by an earthquake in 1894 and by fire again in 1920 after which it was closed to the public. Observed within its present enclosure behind a railing, it is an evocative ruin of slender columns with lightweight capitals: note the verd-antique columns of the north aisle and the narthex colonnade with its architrave and Corinthian capitals. There is part of a mosaic pavement, too, that was contributed by Michael VIII Palaeologos on his return to the city as emperor after the expulsion of the Latins.

Located in the Kocamustafa district northwest of Cerrah Pasa is **Koca Mustafa Pasa Cami**, or **St Andrew in Krisei** — if indeed this is St Andrew's. The church was built under Basil I (867–86) over an earlier church. It was rebuilt or modified in 1284, and further structural changes were made when it became a mosque. Koca Mustafa was a grand vizier to Beyazit II (1481–1512).

Standing to the west of the Fethiye Mosque, the **Bogdan Saray** may have been the **Church of St Nicholas**. If so, it could have been founded by an Anglo-Saxon of the Varangian Guard, the elite Corps of the Byzantine Court, similar to that of the British Brigade of Guards or the American Marine Corps. The members of the Varangian Guard were recruited from northern Europe, with Swedes prominent among those from Scandinavia, but later on Anglo-Saxon recruits became numerous in its ranks. The Corps also was a forerunner of the Ottoman Janissaries.

The **Gül Cami**, or **Church of St Theodosia**, is at Balat, lying above Fener on the Golden Horn. It is ninth century in origin, with 14th-century brickwork, while the dome and minarets were added after the conversion. It is a mixture of styles — an early example of post-modernism! Ultimately, there is uncertainty about its true identification. Mehmet broke through into the city on St Theodosia's day, and according to legend this church is said to have been packed with people and decorated with roses, hence the name Gül (Rose) Cami.

Situated in the area of the Fatih Cami, the **Eski Imaret Cami**, or **Church of Christ Pantepoptes, the All-seeing**, was built by the mother of Alexius I Comnenus (1081–118). Its interior has not lost too much of its original identity, even though it has been put to use as a school. There is still some attractive exterior brickwork on the south side.

Arap Cami, or **Dominican Church of St Paul and St Dominic**, is in the Galata district. There could have been a mosque here when the Arabs occupied this quarter during their 717 siege of Constantinople. Later it may have been rebuilt, or the earlier building was converted for use by the Dominican Friars. In 1455 it seems to have reverted to a mosque for the use of Arab refugees from Spain. The building was badly damaged in a fire of 1808.

The **Zeyrek Kilise Cami**, or **Church of Christ Pantocrator, the All-ruling**, is northwest of the Fatih Cami and stands near the Aqueduct of Valens above Atatürk Bulvari. This monastery church — the monastery founded by the Comnenian Empress Irene or by her husband John II (1118–43) — is in fact a composite of two churches and a chapel. On the northeast side is the original church; the other on the southwest is a larger, later 12th-century building. In between is a funerary chapel which may have been built by Manuel I (1143–80) to house the tomb of his father, John II, and where other Comneni are buried. The marble slab on which Manuel believed Christ's body had lain, and which he had carried up on his back from the Bucoleon harbour to the palace, was eventually placed in this chapel. During the Latin usurpation, the Icon of St Demetrius, patron saint of Thessalonica, was held at the Pantocrator for safe-keeping, as was the image of the Panaghia Hodighetria from Blachernae, believed to have been a creation of St Luke. When Michael VIII returned to Constantinople in 1261, the Panaghia was carried at the head of the triumphal entry procession through the Golden Gate. Gennadius (George Scholaris) was confined in the Pantocrator by the last emperor, Constantine XI, because of his opposition to the emperor's policy of unification with the Roman Church. But on his release after the fall of the city, he was appointed Orthodox Patriarch by Mehmet II.

The **Bodrum Cami** is in the Zeytinburnu district of the city, southwest of Beyazit Meydani. It is considered to have been part of a monastery complex, the Myrelaion, established by Romanus Lecapenus (919–44), although there are doubts about this. Or it could have been built as a monastery or convent of the sixth century and rebuilt by Romanus. Two churches stood one above the other; the lower one was a basilica of the seventh century, while the upper, of a later date was built on a cross-in-square pattern. Conversion to a mosque occurred in the 16th century.

The **Sancaktir Mescit** (the Standard Bearer) is situated in Samatya, the district bordering the Marmara to the south of the Fatih district. The site is thought to have been that of the Gastria, a monastery built under the Emperor Theophilus (829–42). St Helena, mother of Constantine I, is said to have brought back plant cuttings from the Holy Land and planted them here, hence the title Gastria — a *gastra* is a plant pot in Greek. Mehmet II's standard bearer, Hayrettin, was buried here.

On the third hill of the city, to the northwest of the Aqueduct of Valens, the **Vefa Kilise Cami**, or **St Theodore in Tiro**, was restored in the 14th century, although its façade retains earlier work of the sixth century. Three domes cover the narthex, and there are remnants of mosaics, too. There is, however, doubt concerning the true identification of this structure.

The **Kalenderhane, Kalender Cami**, or **Church of Christ Akataleptos**, is southwest of the aqueduct. Christ the Incomprehensible is the designation of this monastery church. Built in the ninth century, it has undergone a number of rebuildings and reconstructions.

Fenâri Isa Cami, or **St Mary Panachrantos, the All-immaculate**, is on Vatan Caddesi where it approaches the military postern gate in the walls near Topkapi Gate. It is a two-church structure again, with a common narthex. Constantine Lips, a court official of Constantine VII Porphyrogenitus, dedicated the first church; he died in 917. The second church was built by Theodora, widow of Michael VIII. Both structures were badly damaged by a fire in the 1920s. Close by is the **Column of Marcian** (450–7), the Kiztasi or Maiden's Column, so named because of a carving of Aphrodite on the column. Five metres (16 feet) high with a Corinthian capital, it also has carved eagles on its pediment.

Churches

Other than the Church of St Irene in the First Court of Topkapi Palace, the most important church that has never been converted to a mosque is **St Mary of the Mongols** at Fener. Mary was the daughter of Andronicus I (1282–328). In order to secure an alliance treaty with the Mongol Great Khan against the Turks, the emperor offered Mary to the Khan as his bride. The account tells that by the time Mary reached the Mongol court the Great Khan had died, but his successor, Abaka, accepted Mary and married her. As her husband was shortly afterwards poisoned by his brother, Mary returned to Constantinople. There is, however, some doubt about her parentage; some claim that she was the bastard daughter of Michael VIII. The church was dedicated in 1265, within Michael's reign, yet Mary's journey seems unlikely to have taken place prior to the late 1270s, and by the time Andronicus had come to the throne both the Great Khan and Abaka were dead, which may also indicate that an existing church was rededicated to Mary.

Another church at Fener is St George's, already mentioned as the seat of the Greek Orthodox Patriarchate.

Marmara Sea and North Aegean Region

The Bosphorus separates the Black Sea from the Sea of Marmara which on its eastern extremity becomes the Gulf of İzmit. Nine islands, the Princes' Islands, or Kzil Adalar (Red Islands), lie in the Marmara Sea south of the eastern shore of the Bosphorus. The Turkish name derives from the red earth that is common to them all.

İzmit, a modern industrial port at the head of the gulf, is the first major city to be reached after leaving İstanbul on a journey into Anatolia.

İznik is a walled city with over 100 towers and three of its four gates still standing. Many Byzantine buildings are under the lake now, but the interesting parts of the present town are still contained within its walls.

Though evidence of Ottoman beginnings is scant, Söğüt does seem to be the centre from which the Osmanli tribe's later expansion into an empire began. Bursa became the first captial city of the Ottomans. It lies below Uludag (Mount Olympus in Mysian times) on a shelf above a fertile, watered plain stretching away to the north and east. A little to the west, there is the spa of Çekirge with its health-giving springs and baths.

On the north Aegean coast lies the peninsula where the Gallipoli campaign of World War I was fought. It is possible to join a group in Çanakkale to visit the site where the Allied forces came ashore. The trenches still remain.

Not far south is Truva, ancient Troy. You would find it hard to run round the walls of Troy today as Hector did in Homer's *Iliad*, not because of the distance, which seems absurdly short, but because of the uneven fall of the land on one side. There is an absence of towers and seemingly impregnable walls, but very little will interfere with personal feelings about Priam's city, or imaginings concerning the events that took place here as Homer recorded them.

The town of Bergama is modern and, like all Turkish towns on the Aegean, Marmara and Mediterranean coasts, has expanded enormously in the last year or two. The ancient acropolis of Pergamum is to the northeast of the town's centre; the Asclepium (Santuary of the Healing-god) is off to the west.

Getting There

There is a regular daily ferry service to the largest island, Büyük Ada, leaving from Eminönü on the shore of the Golden Horn at the western end of the Galata Bridge. After stopping at the island, the ferry continues across the Gulf of Izmit to Yalova on its southern coast, but check this because in the future the Eminönü station may restrict its services to the islands only.

Another ferry service leaves from Kabataş, on the Bosphorus near the Dolmabahçe Palace, for the islands of Heybeli and Büyük Ada and continues to Yalova with a travel time of about two hours. The cost is 3,500TL. The ferry station at Kabataş may become the sole one for Yalova, with sailings at 9.30 am and 2.15, 6 and 8 pm each day. However, 17 kilometres (ten miles) south of İstanbul, there is another ferry at Kartal. This is a car, truck and passenger ferry to Yalova, from where İznik, Bursa and Troy can be reached by road, thereby avoiding a journey round the eastern end of the gulf.

On the road from İstanbul to Ankara, İzmit is 93 kilometres (58 miles) from Üsküdar on the E5. The drive is not unpleasant once out of the city but becomes traffic-logged after Gebze.

İznik is 68 kilometres (42 miles) south and east of Yalova, at the eastern end of the Lake of İznik, or İznik Gölü. On a road which passes through Yenişehir and Bilecik, 90 kilometres (56 miles) to the southeast of İznik, is Söğüt.

There is a good bus service from Yalova to Bursa, a distance of 74 kilometres (46 miles) through attractive hill and mountain country. If travelling by car, you may want to take a detour to see Mudanya on the way. This is the Marmara Sea coastal resort for Bursa, 26 kilometres (16 miles) north of the city.

Çanakkale is not far from Troy and can be reached from Bursa by way of the Marmara coastal route on road 200 through Bandirma to Lapseki, then southwest down the Dardanelles to Çanakkale (on the E24), a total of 300 kilometres (186 miles). Or you may choose an inland route on road 545: 162 kilometres (101 miles) through Balikesir to Edremit, along the shore of the Gulf of Edremit to Ayvacik, 83 kilometres (52 miles), and then north to Ezine and Çanakkale (E24), 136 kilometres (85 miles).

An alternative route by road from İstanbul is to go west to Tekirdağ on the E25, cross the wide neck of the Gelibolu Burnu (Gallipoli Peninsula) to Kesan, then go south, down the peninsula to Eceabat (E24), 333 kilometres (207 miles), and cross by ferry to Çanakkale.

From Çanakkale the E24 runs south to İntepe, ten kilometres (six miles) away. After another eight kilometres (five miles), you turn seaward for five kilometres (three miles) to reach Troy. The site Alexander believed to be Troy, though, was in fact at Alexandria Troas, on the coast to the south. Taking road E24 to Ezine, a distance of 22 kilometres (14 miles), you cross the Scamander River and turn coastwards for Geyikli, a further 15 kilometres (ten miles). The Hellenistic columns and arches, to which Alexander must have contributed, and the Roman and later remains, stand picturesquely among the trees.

Continue south 26 kilometres (16 miles) on the E24 to Ayvacik, but then take a minor road to the little port of Behramkale. Assos occupies a cone-shaped mass of basalt rock, with the citadel on the flat top and terraced buildings on the seaward slopes.

From the harbour you climb back to the citadel to pick up the E24 for Bergama (Pergamum). Edremit, at the eastern head of the gulf, is the chief town of

Between a Rock
and a Hard Place

On my own childhood, polygamy and its results produced a very ugly and distressing impression. The constant tension in our home made every simple family ceremony seem like a physical pain, and the consciousness of it hardly ever left me.

The rooms of the wives were opposite each other, and my father visited them by turns. When it was Teïzé's turn every one in the house showed a tender sympathy to Abla, while when it was her turn no one heeded the obvious grief of Teïzé. It was she indeed who could conceal her suffering least. She would leave the table with eyes full of tears, and one could be sure of finding her in her room either crying or fainting. Very soon I noticed that father left her alone with her grief.

And father too was suffering in more than one way. As a man of liberal and modern ideas, his marriage was very unfavorably regarded by his friends, especially by Hakky Bey, to whose opinion he attached the greatest importance.

He suffered again from the consciousness of having deceived Abla. He had married her when she was a mere girl, and it now looked as if he had taken advantage of her youth and inexperience. One saw as time went on how patiently and penitently he was trying to make up to her for what he had done.

Among the household too he felt that he had fallen in general esteem, and he cast about for some justification of his conduct which would reinstate him. "It was for Halidé that I married her," he used to say. "If Teïzé had married another man Halidé would have died." And, "It is for the child's sake I have married her father," Teïzé used to say. "She would have died if I had married any one else." Granny took the sensible view. "They wanted to marry each other. What has a little girl to do with their marriage?"

The unhappiness even manifested itself in the relation between granny and Hava Hanum. The latter criticized granny severely for not having put a stop to it before things had gone too far, and granny felt indignant to have the blame thrown upon her by a dependent for an affair she so intensely disliked.

Teïzé, with her superior show of learning and her intellectual character, must have dominated father at first, but with closer contact, the pedantic turn of her mind, which gave her talk a constant didactic tone, must have wearied him. For in the intimate companionship of every-day life nothing bores one more than a pretentious style of talk involving constant intellectual effort. Poor Teïzé's erudition and intelligence were her outstanding qualities, and she used and abused them to a maddening degree. When, after her dull and lonely life, she gave herself, heart and soul, to a man, the disillusionment of finding herself once more uncared for rendered her very bitter; and she either talked continually of her personal pain or else of some high topic, too difficult to be understood by the person she was talking to. Somehow her efforts to dethrone her rival from the heart of her husband lacked the instinctive capacity of the younger woman's, and it was only granny and poor me that sympathized and suffered with her in a grief which did not interest any one else.

The wives never quarreled, and they were always externally polite, but one felt a deep and mutual hatred accumulating in their hearts, to which they gave vent only when each was alone with father. He wore the look of a man who was getting more than his just punishment now. Finally he took to having a separate room, where he usually sat alone. But he could not escape the gathering storm in his new life. Hava Hanum not inaptly likened his marriage to that of Nassireddin Hodja. She told it to us as if she was glad to see father unhappy. The hodja also wanted to taste the blessed state of polygamy, and took to himself a young second wife. Before many months were out his friends found the hodja completely bald, and asked him the reason. "My old wife pulls out all my black hairs so that I may look as old as she; my young wife pulls out my white hairs so that I may look as young as she. Between them I am bald."

Halidé Edib, Memoirs of Halidé Edib

the *vilayet* (provincial government), and its museum has an interesting display of weapons from early times to the present. It is 45 kilometres (28 miles) to Ayvalık, a town situated attractively on a lagoon that is very nearly wholly enclosed, with sandy bathing beaches at Çamlık and Samsaki. Within the lagoon are the Alibey Islands. Cunda, the largest, has a ferry service and is noted for its cheese, honey, fish and wine. The Şeytan Sofrasi (Devil's Dinner Table), on the heights near Ayvalık, offers felicitous views of the gulf, the mountains and the island of Lesbos, all of which you can enjoy while eating. At Dikili, 33 kilometres (20 miles) south of Ayvalik and four kilometres (2.5 miles) off the E24 to the west, is a port from which there is a ferry service to Lesbos during the summer months only. Bergama is 16 kilometres (ten miles) inland from the E24 turnoff to Dikili and then north off the main road for about a kilometre.

Historical Background

To the Byzantines, these were the Princes' Islands, favoured by royalty, and at other times used as a place of exile. Methodius, Patriarch of Constantinople, an icondule supporter, was exiled to the island of Burgaz for several years during the second Iconoclast period when pictures and images were banned from churches.

The great Carthaginian general Hannibal lived as an exile at Gebze and committed suicide there after the Romans defeated the Seleucid, Antiochus III, whom Hannibal had advised, at Manisa in 190 BC.

Mehmet II is said to have died at Hereke, but Constantine I had a preference for the village, set among orchards in the vicinity.

Nicomedia (İzmit today), principal city of Bithynia, was Diocletian's administrative centre for the eastern part of the Roman Empire after he had divided it into two.

İznik was once called Nicaea. Lysimachus, an heir of Alexander, gave it his wife's name after his victory over Antigonus, yet another of the Alexander heirs. Following an earthquake, Hadrian (117–38) rebuilt the city. In the sixth century Justinian restored the walls (on which it is possible to walk for a greater part of their circumference), as did Leo III (717–41), adding aqueducts, baths, a bridge and several churches.

The First Oecumenical Council, convened by Constantine, was held here, resulting in the condemnation of the Arian heresy (adherents of a doctrine which denied the full divinity of Christ) and the promulgation of the Nicene Creed, a formal statement of Christian belief. It was also the initial location for the Seventh Council at which the Iconoclasts (who were against the use of the human form in religious worship) were denounced.

The first Osmanlis (tribe of Osman), about 50,000 under Süleiman, who had entered Anatolia ahead of the advancing Mongols, seem to have settled initially in Armenian territory. As a result of repeated Mongol threats, part of the tribe under Ertogrul (father of Osman) moved westward and took service under the Seljuk Sultan of Konya, a service that was later rewarded by the allocation of land in Bithynia.

Nicaea became the first capital of the Seljuks after their entry into western Anatolia following the battle of Manzikert in 1071. It was recaptured in 1097 during the First Crusade and by agreement given back to the Byzantines. In 1204, after the Latin capture of Constantinople, it became the capital of the Byzantine Empire until Michael VIII's return to Constantinople in 1261.

On the disintegration of the Seljuk Sultanate of Rum after its defeat by the Mongols at the battle of Müghar near Konya in the mid-13th century, its possessions fell to a number of independent emirs, some 48 in all, though many emirates were little larger than the village in which the emir had his residence. The Osmanlis began their expansion by defeating or absorbing those emirates within the vicinity of Söğüt.

Bursa surrendered to Orhan, the son of Osman, in 1326; the news reached Osman on his deathbed. Timur sacked it in 1402, but, since he seldom lingered in the places he had subdued, it was subsequently reoccupied and rebuilt. After the death of Beyazît, whom Timur had defeated, a civil war broke out between the sultan's sons, eventually to be won by Mehmet I Celebi.

Çanakkale was Abydos and, along with Sestos (Eceabat today), controlled all shipping through the Dardanelles and levied dues. It was here, when the straits were the Hellespont, that Leander swam nightly to Hero. Byron swam it in emulation of Leander, and in this century there have been other distinguished crossings, a feat made difficult by the contrary tides of the channel and the strong undertow.

In 480 BC, Xerxes bridged the Hellespont with boats, just to the north of Çanakkale, a crossing Alexander led in reverse a 150 years later when he set out to destroy Persian power.

Schliemann (1822–90) identified Troy and recovered the treasures and jewels he believed had belonged to Priam's royal house. Digging at Schliemann's site in the 1930s, Carl Blegen, an American archaeologist, recorded 46 levels of occupation going back to 3000 BC, and Schliemann himself came to acknowledge that the city of his treasure had existed a thousand years prior to the one he had thought to have been Priam's. Dorpfeld, Schliemann's assistant and successor, established level VI as being the most likely one for Homer's Troy, but subsequently this was amended to VIIA.

Schliemann found his treasure at level II, and Blegen was to find hundreds of gold beads at the time of his excavations. The city of level VI was built by an energetic people who brought the horse into this area. After a long period of stagnation during which living standards fell to an extremely low level, the city was destroyed by an earthquake *circa* 1240 BC. Level VIIA, built over the earthquake ruins, fell victim to assault about a century later.

A most dramatic and tragic episode in the last part of the *Iliad* is where Hector, arriving at the city gate after the other Trojans have gone in, stops and turns towards an insensed Achilles, bounding across the plain of the Scamander towards him. It is as if Hector knows that the coming encounter will be decisive and that it is his destiny to die, yet he resolves to face the challenge manfully. His courage, though, falters, and he runs. Achilles chases him three times round the walls of the city before Hector's courage revives, and he stops at the gate and in the ensuing fight is killed.

Xerxes sacrificed bulls at Troy, and Alexander arrived with a copy of the *Iliad* annotated by Aristotle. Julius Caesar had plans for building, and Constantine set up a gateway as a preliminary to the city he intended. In time the fallen columns, marble blocks and carved metopes were carted away to become incorporated in buildings by Romans, Byzantines and Turks.

Assos has an Aeolic foundation; it was colonized by immigrants from the islands of Lesbos, Chios and elsewhere in the north Aegean region. The Attalids of Pergamum rebuilt it after 190 BC. They were masters at constructing on the steep sides of hills, as will be wonderfully evident at Pergamum. Aristotle spent three years at Assos and, if Strabo's information is correct, was married there.

Pergamum was a fortress in Alexander's time. It was there that Lysimachus, one of his successors, stored a considerable amount of treasure acquired during his conquests. He put Philaeterus, a Paphlagonian, in charge of it. When Lysimachus lost his war against Antiochus (a Seleucid), Philaeterus, who had switched loyalties during the conflict, was confirmed in his role as guardian of the fortress and the treasure. In 263 BC, Philaeterus was succeeded by his adopted son, Eumenes, who opted for independence from the Seleucids, and his successor, Attalus I, made himself king of Pergamum. Attalus allied himself first with Rhodes, then with Rome, and set about expanding his kingdom. Eumenes II was the ally of Rome in its war against the Seleucids, and, on the defeat of the last Seleucid king in 190 BC, Rome, in gratitude, gave Pergamum control of all Seleucid possessions in Asia Minor.

In 133 BC the last Pergamene king, Attalid III, bequeathed his kingdom to Rome, and it became part of the Roman Province of Asia. Marc Anthony gave the Pergamene library to Cleopatra to replace her loss of the contents of the great Library of Alexandria, destroyed by fire, but the Emperor Augustus later restored the books and manuscripts to Pergamum. *Charta pergamene* (parchment), a replacement for Egyptian papyrus, was invented at Pergamum.

Galen (130–200), the first great surgeon and physician, was born at Pergamum and for a time practised there. He wrote treatises and commentaries on Hippocrates and contributed medical documents to the library.

For the Byzantines, Pergamum's importance was strategic rather than civic. In the early eighth century the Arabs sacked it. Leo III (717–41) restored it.

The city held out against the Seljuk Turks but fell eventually to the Ottomans. After Timur's defeat of Sultan Beyazît at Ankara in 1402, the Mongols decimated the population. The Ottomans, in their subsequent reoccupation, ignored the citadel and the city's past in favour of their new town of Bergama.

Sights

The Princes' Islands (Kîzîl Adalar)
Büyük Ada is 13 kilometres (eight miles) in circumference, and among its attractions are imperial-style wooden houses, flower gardens, pine trees and the leisurely pace of its horse-drawn phaetons. In a phaeton a tour of the island takes about one and a half hours.

Burgaz, too, has pines and can offer exceptional views to those who mount to its plateau. The sites of two monasteries and a ninth-century church, St John Prodromos (John the Baptist), are on this island.

Copper was mined on **Heybeli**. Queen Elizabeth appointed Sir Edward Barton as her unpaid ambassador to the court of Sultan Murat III; the ambassador, whose tomb is on Heybeli, died in 1597. The naval school here was a convent founded by Palaeologos, the wife of John VIII. Heybeli can be covered in about an hour.

İzmit
With a history of occupation dating back to 712 BC, İzmit has little to show for it. All that can be seen today are the remains of a Byzantine citadel on the acropolis hill and, from the Ottomans, a mosque designed by Sinan for a vizier of Süleiman I.

İznik
You arrive at the **North** or **Istanbul Gate**, which Vespasian (69–79) may have restored. The **East Gate**, the **Lefke**, probably is Hadrian's, beyond which are the **aqueducts** (restored by Orhan). The **South** or **Yenişehir Gate** has an inscription of Claudius II (268–70). The **West Gate** is under the lake.

To the northwest of the Lefke is the 14th-century **Yeşil Cami** with its green-tiled minarets. Over on the west is an *imaret* (a Moslem soup kitchen) of 1388, one of the first of its kind, now a museum. Two main streets intersect the town, and at the crossroads is Justinian's **Haghia Sophia**, converted to a mosque under the Seljuks and then restored and decorated by the Osmanlis in the 14th century. In the southeast area is the 11th-century **Koimesis Church** (The Dormition of the Virgin). There are several early-style Ottoman mosques: the **Mahmoud Çelebi Cami, Haci Hamza, Haci Özbek** and the **Süleiman Paşa**

Medrese.
    Pliny the Younger, governor here for the Emperor Trajan, reported un-
favourably on the foundations of the **theatre** and was told succinctly to do
something about it. The town is congenial to storks, who have chosen it as a
breeding centre, and the lake has an abundance of fish. Outside the city walls
on the lakeside are the hotels, motels, restaurants and pensions.

Söğüt
Said to be the place where Osman was born, Söğüt has tombs, one claimed to
be that of Ertogrul. Bilecik has a Sinan mosque, the **Orhan Bey**, and there is a
remarkable Sinan bridge of eight arches over the Karasu river. Many Ottoman
and other buildings were destroyed in this area during the 1920–2 Greek–
Turkish War.

Bursa
It is said that Hannibal persuaded the Bithynian king (228–180 BC) who
founded the city to give it his name, Prusias. In 111 Pliny inspected the baths
and agreed with the citizens that a rebuilding was necessary. Justinian built a
palace, as well as another baths.
    The city is built on more than one level, and distances on foot can be longer
than one might expect from looking at a map of the city. The *otogar* (bus station) is in the plain on the north, some two kilometres (1.25 miles) from the
higher level city centre at Heykel where the restored covered market and the
Ulu Cami (Grand Mosque), the largest mosque in the city, can be found.
Alongside of the Ulu Cami on Atatürk Caddesi, and in front of the Koza Han,
are entrances to the covered bazaar and shops under an arcade, among which is
a Tourist Information Office.
    The **Ulu Cami** was begun about 1395 by Beyazit I (1389–1402) but was
not completed until the reign of Mehmet I Celebi (1413–21). It has 20 domes

İznik tiles

Under the Ottomans, İznik's artistic importance was established when
Sultan Selim I imported potters from Tabriz in Persia and set them to
work here. Their tiles subsequently decorated many of the country's
finest mosques and other buildings. Three periods of artistic achievement are recognized: 1490–1525, 1525–55 and 1555–1700. Other potteries were established later at Kutahya (still active) and in the 18th
century in İstanbul.

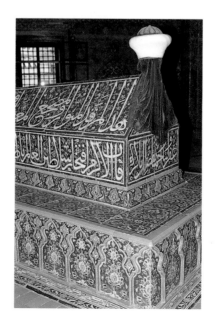

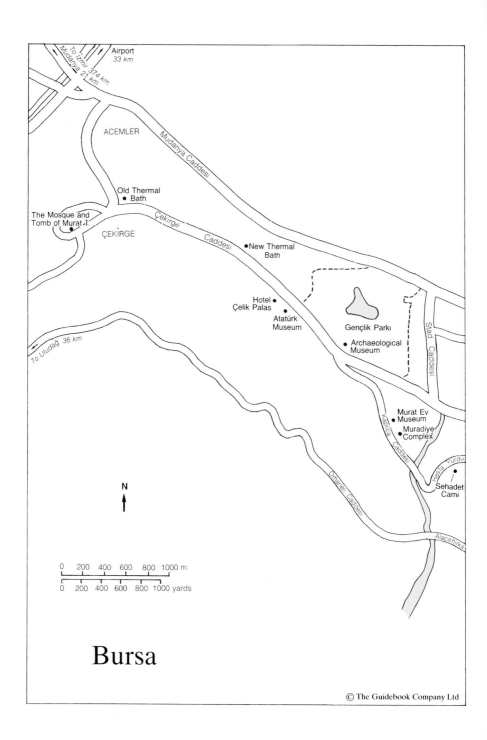

Airport
33 km

To İzmir 374 km
Mudanya 21 km

ACEMLER

Mudanya Caddesi

Old Thermal
● Bath

The Mosque and
Tomb of Murat I.

Çekirge

ÇEKİRGE

Caddesi

● New Thermal
Bath

Hotel ●
Çelik Palas

●
Atatürk
Museum

Gençlik Parkı

To Uludağ 36 km

● Archaeological
Museum

Stad Caddesi

Murat Ev
● Museum
● Muradiye
Complex

Kaplıca Caddesi

N
↑

Orhaneli Caddesi

Hasta Yurdu

●
Sehadet
Cami

Alacahırka

0   200   400   600   800 1000 m

0   200   400   600   800 1000 yards

Bursa

© The Guidebook Company Ltd

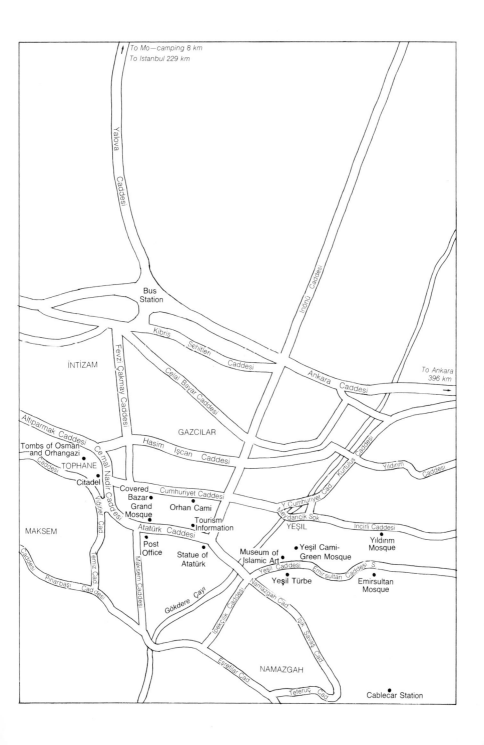

To Mo—camping 8 km
To Istanbul 229 km

Yalova Caddesi

To Ankara 396 km

İHTİZAM

Bus Station

Kıbrıs

Şehitleri Caddesi

Ankara Caddesi

İnönü Caddesi

Fevzi Çakmay Caddesi

Celal Bayar Caddesi

GAZCILAR

Altıparmak Caddesi

Haşim İşcan Caddesi

Tombs of Osman and Orhangazi

Caddesi

TOPHANE

Cemal Nadir Caddesi

Citadel

Covered Bazar

Grand Mosque

Cumhuriyet Caddesi

Orhan Cami

Tourism Information

Vigiler Cad

Y Cumhuriyet Cad

Kurtuluş Caddesi

Yıldırım Caddesi

Meydancık Sok

YEŞİL

İncirli Caddesi

MAKSEM

Atatürk Caddesi

Temiz Cad

Maksem Caddesi

Post Office

Statue of Atatürk

Museum of Islamic Art

Yeşil Cami-Green Mosque

Yıldırım Mosque

Caddesi

Pınarbaşı Caddesi

Yeşil Caddesi

Yeşil Türbe

Emirsultan Caddesi

Emirsultan Mosque

Gökdere Çayı

Namazgah Caddesi

İpekçilik Caddesi

Işık Savaş Cad

Eşrefliler Cad

NAMAZGAH

Teferuç Cad

Cablecar Station

connected by pointed arches on 12 supporting piers, but there was a modification of design after an earthquake in 1855 damaged 18 of the domes. The şadirvan (ablutions fountain) is set in the entrance hall, with an opening in the dome above it. The interior has a grand but austere appearance; decoration is confined to beautiful calligraphic inscriptions on the walls.

To the east is the **Orhan Cami**, built in 1338 on the site of a Byzantine church. An inscription on this mosque is dated 1417 but may refer to a reconstruction. This building suffered damage in the 1855 earthquake and was subsequently repaired.

The rebuilt **covered bazaar** extends behind the Ulu Cami and thc Koza Han. It was damaged in the earthquake and almost totally destroyed by a fire in the 1960s. Bursa is a traditional centre of the silk industry. Cotton towelling, too, is a speciality, and you ought at least to be tempted into buying a bathrobe. Bursa peaches, incidentally, are large and luscious. Besides the fruit, visitors should sample **Iskender** or **Bursa kebab** — beef carved from a rotating upright grill, served on squares of unleavened bread, spread with yoghurt and doused with melted butter.

Going east a kilometre or so from the Ulu Cami, crossing the **Gökdere Çayi** (stream) by a high bridge, and then turning north on Yeşil Caddesi, you reach the **Yeşil Cami**. This mosque is among the first of the structures to achieve a distinct Ottoman style, with an open hall containing the şadirvan, a wide recessed section for the mihrab (niche in a mosque indicating the direction of Mecca) with the mimbar (mosque pulpit) alongside and two domed recesses on either side of the entrance. *Yeşil* means green, and the mosque gets its name from the dark green, dark blue and turquoise tiling. It was begun by Mehmet Celebi between 1422 and 1424.

Over the road from the mosque is the **Yeşil Türbe** (Green Mausoleum), the octagonal tomb of Mehmet I Celebi. The original tiling on this tomb was destroyed in a fire, and the present green tiling dates only from the 19th century. On the south side of the Yeşil Cami is the **Museum of Islamic Art**. To the east is the **Emir Şultan Mosque**, built on an older mosque in the early 19th century. Emir Sultan was the spiritual advisor to Beyazît I.

In the same area, to the north, is the mosque of **Sultan Beyazît Yîldîrîm**. This is believed to date from the late 1390s or a year or two before that sultan's defeat by Timur at Ankara in 1402. Its interior design is similar to that of the Yeşil Cami, for which it may have been the model. Its tiled decoration has been seriously depleted by time and earthquakes.

Back at the Ulu Cami, go west along Altiparmak Caddesi for almost a kilometre. Shortly before you reach the roundabout road junction, a wide high stairway climbs the escarpment on the southern side of the road. Turning right at the top of the stairway, you come to the enclosure within which are the **tombs** of Osman, the dynasty's founder, and Orhan (Orhangazi), who captured

Bursa. On foot, it is a wa. of two or three kilometres (1.25–2 miles) up and then down into a valley to reach the **Muradiye** complex. A bus or a taxi can be taken, however, from the Heykel area. The Muradiye is a large enclosed multi-flowered garden in which, as well as the **Mosque of Murat II** with its distinctive tiling, built between 1424 and 1427, and a *medrese* (school of theology), there are eleven impressive tombs including that of the sultan. His tomb has a decorated, carved wooden canopy. A smaller chamber contains the tombs of four of his sons. An attendant will open these tombs and several others, including that of **Prince Cem** (1494), notable for its rich faience (decorated porcelain) panelling, and that of **Mustafa**, son of Süleiman the Magnificent, with its black and turquoise tiling and an inscribed border of light blue and white on dark blue. In a nearby square is a restored 17th-century house known as the **Murat Ev**.

The **citadel** is in the Hisar area, on a higher level than that of the tombs of Osman and Orhan, which stand close to the **Hisar Kapisi**. There are three other gateways, the **Kaplica Kapisi**, **Zindan** and **Yerkapi**, and sections of original walls among those of Byzantine and Ottoman rebuildings. On the way to the Muradiye from the Osman and Orhan enclosure, you pass the small **Sehadet Cami** and then the city hospital, erected on the foundations of a Byzantine palace.

Çekirge and Uludağ

Near the stairway to the Hisar area and tombs of Osman and Orhan, walk west from the road junction. Another kilometre (.6 mile) on the road to Çekirge will bring you to **Gençlik Parki** (Youth and Culture Park) that spreads on the right down to a lower level and contains restaurants, *pavyons* (nightclubs) and other facilities. The **Archaeological Museum** is located in the park. After passing the roadway entrance to the hotel Çelik Palas, on the left, are the sites of the 16th- and 17th-century **baths**, the **Yenikaplica**, **Karamustafa**, **Kaynarca** and **Eskikaplica** in which some original Byzantine features are incorporated. The hotel, too, has its own baths, constructed on a much earlier structure.

At Çekirage, several kilometres west, the hotels have the curative waters of the spa piped into their bathrooms and washbasins. The **Murad'i Hüdavendigan Türbe** here was commissioned by Nülifer Hanum, the mother of Murat I. Murat was assassinated on the field after his victory over the Serbs at the Battle of Kossovo, 15 June 1389. His son, Beyazit I, avenged his father's death by executing those princes and nobles whom he was holding captive and brought the body of his father back to Bursa for burial. The **Murat I Cami** opposite the tomb dates from the 1360s.

The road up Uludağ (Mount Olympus) starts from Çekirge. Uludağ, 2,328 metres (7,635 feet) high, is a winter sports centre, with alpine-style hotels

among other forms of accommodation. There are ski-lifts and viewing
pavilions on precipitate heights. You can also mount by *téléférique* (cable car);
the station is on the east side of Bursa and well signposted.

Çanakkale

The military cemeteries of the Allied and Turkish dead of the 1915 Gallipoli
campaign are to the south of this town. The fortress, rebuilt by Mehmet II, is in
use by the Turkish military and has a **museum of military ware**. Its companion fortress at Eceabat on the opposite, western side — the waterway is at
its narrowest here — is another Mehmet construction. The **Archaelogical
Museum** has a collection of recoveries from sites in the locality, from pre-Hellenistic times onwards.

Troy

The site is signposted, with arrows indicating a route to be followed. A
Cyclopean-type wall of huge rounded stones, along with a carriage ramp, are
assumed to be of an Mycenaean time (1500–1100 BC). There are the remains
of a **theatre** and a ***bouleuterion*** (council chamber) and remnants of towers and
gateways. Most impressive is a **megaron** (a hall or building of the type Homer
describes), consisting of a large chamber with a central hearth where visitors
were given pride of place.

The plain where the many single combats and battles were fought is under
cultivation, with no obvious evidence of the streams of Scamander and Simois,
locations that were so strategic to the battle. There are mounds near the shore,
though, that might well conceal the charred bones of heroes. Strabo said that
he saw funeral mounds on the shore here at the end of the first century BC.
Mount Ida somehow seems a little too distant for Zeus, or Hera or Athena, to
have been able to keep so constant an eye on the progress of the battle, but
they were after all divine. The island of Tenedos lies just off the coast, to
which the Greeks feigned to retire as part of their deceptive strategy with the
wooden horse, and is now Turkish Boscaada.

Assos

There are many fourth-century BC buildings on the **acropolis**, including the
citadel towers and substantial **city walls**. On the roadway down to Behramkale are the terraced Pergamene stoas and other buildings. The attractive little
harbour, isolated on the northern shore of the Gulf of Edremit, has been
privately and modestly developed, while at the entry to the gulf lies the Greek
island of Lesbos.

Pergamum (Bergama)

The town has one very long main street that ends eventually in the old centre.

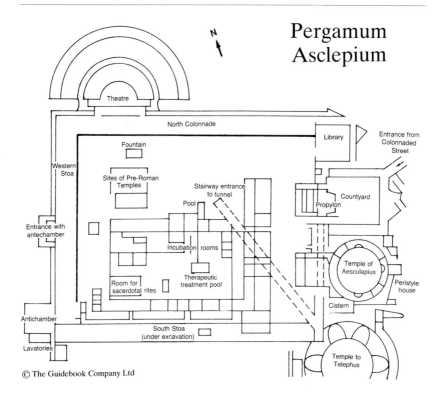

Pergamum
Asclepium

Theatre

North Colonnade

Fountain

Library

Entrance from
Colonnaded
Street

Western
Stoa

Sites of Pre-Roman
Temples

Stairway entrance
to tunnel

Pool

Countyard

Propylon

Entrance with
antechamber

Incubation rooms

Temple of
Aesculapius

Room for
sacerdotal rites

Therapeutic
treatment pool

Peristyle
house

Cistern

Antichamber

South Stoa
(under excavation)

Lavatories

Temple to
Telephus

© The Guidebook Company Ltd

Development has brought new hotels and a number of pensions into existence. The Ministry of Tourism's Information Office is on that main street about one kilometre before the *otogar* or bus station is reached. Continuing on the main road from the bus station, you come to the **museum** on the left where the rise has been landscaped, next to the *belediye* **(town hall)**.

Among its exhibits the museum has models of the **Altar of Zeus** and the **Demeter Temple** and stoa (large colonnaded porch); both sites are on the acropolis. A mosaic floor with a depiction of the Medusa, a **statue of Hadrian**, terracotta statuettes from Myrina and a *kuros* (a young man) from Çandarli are also here. There is an ethnographic section. The museum entrance fee is 5,000TL.

The Asclepium

To reach the Asclepium, continue on from the museum and take a signposted turn to the left (the post office is on the other side of the main road). If you are on foot, the walk is a fair distance from the turn-off. Finally, you follow the

perimeter of a large barracks to reach the carpark and entrance to the site, fee
5,000TL.

The Cult of Healing was brought to Pergamum from Epidaurus in Greece in
the fourth century BC. The **Sanctuary of the Healing-god** was built over an
earlier one to Telephus (a son of Heracles), the founder of the city, and from
the centre of the main temple court a hidden tunnel led to a Temple to
Telephus in which the curative rites were performed. Activity at the sanctuary
reached its highest level during the second century.

From the carpark entrance and paying guichet, you step into a colonnaded
street running in a northeasterly–southwesterly direction. The first section has
lines of square and of round columns, the next section having round columns
with a retaining wall on the right. On the left is a section of wall behind a semi-
circular platform with an olive tree, and next to it a circular structure — site of
a pool or an altar. The centre of the paved way has a covered conduit which
may have brought water to the sacred pool. If this was the **Sacred Way** to the
sanctuary, it could have run from the **stadium**, away to the northwest of the
site, past a **Roman theatre**, then through a gateway, and most likely would
have had shops along it. It leads to a courtyard and the **propylon** (gate),
erected during the reign of Antoninus Pius (130–61). On the left of the stairway to the court are some reconstructed columns and a section of architrave,
backed by a wall. Now you enter a large square, which from the evidence of
column bases, standing columns and steps would have been surrounded by
stoas. On the right of the propylon is the **library**, and the museum's statue of
Hadrian may have occupied a principal niche here. The colonnade running
along that northeast side, some of which was rebuilt after an earthquake of AD
178 brings you to a Greek-style **theatre**, cut out of a steep hill. Over on the left
from the propylon is the **Temple of Aesculapius**, cylindrical in shape and
domed, built about AD 150 and modelled on the Pantheon in Rome. Towards
the centre of the area, in front of the theatre, is a spring and pool and evidence
of shrines. Near the pool is the entrance to a **tunnel** that leads under the site to
emerge at a double-storeyed building in the south corner, beyond the Temple
of Aesculapius. The tunnel leads into a paved outer way that circles the structure, with arched openings into the interior section, and to the hub that is
walled up. This was probably the site of the early **Temple to Telephus**. Between this structure and the Temple of Aesculapius is a **cistern**, and above this
latter shrine is a **peristyle house**. The stoa along the southwestern side of the
main site is at present under excavation. On the rear wall of the enclosure,
there is a stepped columned entrance that was excavated in 1967, and at the
southwestern corner are ancient lavatories, much admired by visitors.

Outside the area of the Asclepium, west of the stadium is a large **amphitheatre** that was used for aquatic entertainments; its water was supplied
through conduits from the nearby Selinus River, or Bergama Çayi. Between it

and the theatre on the Sacred Way is the site of a **Temple to Athena**.

Going by way of the narrow streets of the town's centre, you will find that the acropolis is a fair distance away from the healing sanctuary. On the way to the hill is a large impressive building known as the **Kîz Avlu** (Red Courtyard) because of the colour of the brick; foundation arches of one section span the Selinus River. In origin, this may have been a **Temple to Serapis**, later converted by the Byzantines into a basilica.

The Acropolis

From near the Kîz Avlu, the roadway to the acropolis ascends for nearly six kilometres (four miles) to a parking place on the northeastern side, below the main acropolis buildings —situated on a number of levels. The summit is 440 metres (1,444 feet) above the valley of the Calicus River, or Bakir Çayî.

From the carpark you go up on foot to the **Royal Gate**. From here, moving towards the northwest, you come to the site of the **library**, and further on to the northeast, against the acropolis walls, are the remains of two **palaces**. North of these are Hellenistic houses, followed by a barracks and then an armoury. Northwest of the palaces is a **Temple of Trajan**, at the present time under reconstruction by the excavators. Moving round to the west and south you reach the truly magnificent **theatre** with its auditorium curving down the very steep hillside to a buttressed terrace or promenade where the stage was located. There is a **Temple of Dionysos** on this terrace. Back from the rear of the theatre, a **Temple of Athena** stands on its own terrace to the west of the Royal Gate.

A pathway running down from the Royal Gate reaches a high plinth on which stood Pergamum's most famous monument, the **Altar of Zeus**, with its sculptured frieze of battling gods and titans, built by Eumenes II. German archaeologists first excavated Pergamum and carried out restorations. Important recoveries were taken to Berlin prior to 1945 and are in the Pergamum Museum there. Among its items is a reconstruction of the Altar of Zeus that incorporates sections of the excavated finds, including a wide marble stairway which leads up to a columned stoa-like structure with a winged extension on either side. The great carved frieze runs round below the stylobate (a continuous base supporting a row of columns).

To the east, and on a terrace below that on which the altar stood, is the **upper agora** (market-place). Follow down the pathway, past the *heroon* (shrine) of Pergamene kings, to the level of the **Temple of Demeter**; the setting here is a particular delight. Lower down, to the east, is a **Temple of Hera**, then to the south of this is a three-sectioned, three-levelled **gymnasium** (school), a complex that includes a **palaestra** (exercise ground) and the site of a stadium. Continue on down to arrive at the **lower agora**.

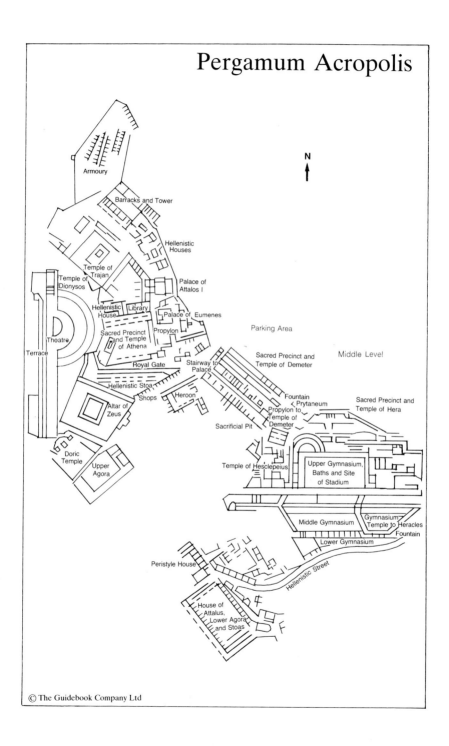

Pergamum Acropolis

N
↑

Armoury

Barracks and Tower

Hellenistic
Houses

Temple of
Trajan

Temple of
Dionysos

Palace of
Attalos I

Hellenistic
House

Library

Palace of Eumenes

Parking Area

Sacred Precinct
and Temple
of Athena

Propylon

Theatre

Terrace

Royal Gate

Stairway to
Palace

Sacred Precinct and
Temple of Demeter

Middle Level

Hellenistic Stoa

Shops

Heroon

Fountain

Prytaneum

Sacred Precinct and
Temple of Hera

Altar of
Zeus

Propylon to
Temple of
Demeter

Sacrificial Pit

Doric
Temple

Upper
Agora

Temple of Hesclepeius

Upper Gymnasium,
Baths and Site
of Stadium

Middle Gymnasium

Gymnasium
Temple to Heracles

Fountain

Lower Gymnasium

Peristyle House

Hellenistic Street

House of
Attalus,
Lower Agora
and Stoas

© The Guidebook Company Ltd

Central Aegean Coast

İzmir, lying at the head of a deep gulf, is Turkey's third city. As Smyrna — its
ancient name — it was destroyed at the conclusion of the Turkish–Greek conflict of 1922. The present city is modern, with a long waterfront and tree-lined
avenues, and pleasant enough to be a base for exploration outside the city. An
International Trade Fair is held here each September in the Youth and Culture
Park, and a visitor without an advanced booking might find difficulty getting a
room, in spite of the increase in accommodation over the past several years. In
general, the hotels, led by the Büyük Efes, Etap İzmir and Kismet, are of a
high standard, and there is a wide choice of medium-range accommodation.
Restaurants are located principally along the harbour and Atatürk Caddesi, the
extended waterfront. The headquarters of NATO's Southeastern Command is
at İzmir, with its display of members' flags in almost perpetual flutter at the
premises on the waterfront. West of İzmir are beaches and archaeological sites,
and at Çeşme there is a 15th-century castle.

Selçuk, the location of one city of Ephesus (for as with Smyrna there were
more than one), has developed as a pleasant tourist centre in its own right and
could be a convenient base for visiting Ephesus as well as other archaeological
sites on this section of the Aegean coast.

An alternative to İzmir or Selçuk as a base for exploring this section of the
Aegean coast is the port of Kuşadasi. Its tourist facilities have been extended
considerably along its coasts to north and south, and as well as an enlarged harbour its amenities include a yacht marina. Throughout the summer there is a
passenger and car ferry service to the Greek island of Samos. To visit the sites
of Priene, Miletus and Didyma from Kuşadasi, allow a minimum of one day,
but two are recommended.

Getting There

Roadways reconstruction on the edge of İzmir has created not so much a
spaghetti junction as a macaroni one, with many underpasses and dual car-
riageways. The *otogar* for long-distance coaches and minibus services is on
this perimeter, and services are frequent. The Adnan Menderes Airport is about
12 kilometres (eight miles) from the bus station.

It is 80 kilometres (50 miles) by road from Konak Square in İzmir to
Çeşme. The town's beach facilities are unexceptional but within easy reach of
hotels, holiday complexes and camping facilities on good sandy beaches.

Leaving İzmir for Selçuk, take the E24 south to Aydin. To visit Ephesus,
take the Kuşadasi road out of Selçuk for about one kilometre, turning left by
the Tusan Motel. After another kilometre, the entrance to the site, lying be-

tween Mount Coressus and Mount Pion, can be reached. You go through the line of the Byzantine walls to reach the carpark. If you are travelling without a car, then a minibus or taxi can be taken from the Selçuk *otogar* which is on the main İzmir-Aydin road.

Kuşadasî is 22 kilometres (14 miles) from Selçuk; the minibus fare is 1,000TL. Visitors to Kuşadasî can take a day trip to Samos, a Greek island. At least three Turkish boats make the two-hour journey at 8.30 am and 3.30 pm, though sailings are less frequent outside the summer months. The single one-way fare is 50,000TL.

While staying in Kuşadasî, you will want to see the sites of Priene, Miletus and Didyma. If you are based in Selçuk, there is a daily tour from the *otogar*, taking in the archaeological sites there and then visiting the three sites named above. The fare is 25,000TL. Again from Selçuk it is possible to take a bus to Didyma, for 7,000TL, and work your way back by minibus to Akköy, near Miletus, and then towards Söke to see Priene. However, the lack of established transport causes difficulty by this route, Miletus being four kilometres (2.5 miles) from Akköy, and Priene, 11 kilometres (seven miles) from a turnoff two kilometres (1.25 miles) out of Söke. The distance from Selçuk to Didyma is 62 kilometres (39 miles); from Miletus to Söke, it is 32 kilometres (20 miles).

If you are driving, two kilometres (1.25 miles) after the road has left Söke going south, take road 525 which branches off southwest for ten kilometres (six miles) to where a roadway runs northwest for one kilometre (.6 mile) to Priene. To see Miletus, go back to the Söke road junction and continue south for 22 kilometres (14 miles) to Akköy; the site of Miletus (or Milet) is four kilometres (2.5 miles) further. Didyma is only a short trip away, in fact, from the gateway at Miletus, the Sacred Way ran for nine kilometres (six miles) to the precincts of the Temple and Oracle of Apollo at Didyma.

Historical Background

The founders of Smyrna were Aeolians, probably from the Aegean Island of Lesbos. By establishing themselves here during the migrations of Greeks from the Greek mainland and archipelago around 1000 BC, they drove the indigenous inhabitants inland. Later the immigrants allowed Ionians from Colophon, an inland town, to settle in Smyrna, and the story has it that the latter took over control on an occasion when the Aeolian residents were out on the hillsides celebrating a Dionysian feast.

Smyrna — like other cities on this section of coast — has had to change its location more than once. Due to the action of the Hermus River, deposits of silt collected at the river mouth, changing the coastline and access to the sea. This also happened with the Maeander and Caister rivers of the region.

Rough Justice

'I am sorry,' said the Pasha, 'that they hung the Koord before your windows. I told them not to hang him before the house of the Persian Plenipotentiary, where there is a gibbet; but to take him to any place where the Koords resorted, and as there are many coffee-houses near you, that is the reason probably why they hung him there. His story is a curious one: I have been looking after him for the last three years; he has robbed and murdered many people, though he was so young a man, but he had always escaped my agents. At last, a few days ago, he stole a horse, in a valley near here, from a man who was travelling, and whom he beat about the head and left for dead. He brought the horse to Erzeroom and offered it for sale, when the owner, who had recovered, saw him selling the horse, and gave him up to the guard. He was brought up for judgment before me, when I said to him, Who are you? After a silence, the man said, "There is fate in this, it cannot be denied. I am **** whom you have been searching for these three years. My fate brought me to Erzeroom, and now I am taken up for stealing one poor horse. I felt when I took that horse that I was fated to die for it. My time is come. It is fate." And he went to be hung without any complaint.'

  I said he deserved it, and hoped others would take warning by his death.

  The Koord above mentioned was hanged in so original a manner that I must shortly describe it, as it took place immediately under my window. What we called at school a cat-gallows was erected close to a bridge over the little stream which ran down the horse-market, between my house and the bottom of the hill of the citadel. The culprit stood under this; the cross-beam was not two feet above his head; a kawass, having tied a rope to one end of the beam, passed a slip-knot round the neck of the Koord, a young and very handsome man, with long black hair; he then drew the rope over the other end of the beam, and pulled away till the poor man's feet were just off the ground, when he tied the rope in a knot, leaving the dead body hanging, supported by two ropes in the form of the letter V. Hardly any one was looking on, and in the afternoon the body was taken down and buried.

In the seventh century BC a new, planned and strong-walled city, oval in shape, was constructed at what is now the district of Bayraklî, four kilometres (2.5 miles) to the north of present-day İzmir. This city was taken and sacked in 600 BC by the Lydian king Alyattes, who had a siege mound constructed to assist in the breaching of the walls. In time this became a hill surmounted by an acropolis, which survives today as Tepekule, at the foot of which is a tomb said to be that of Tantalus, a legendary king of the region. By Alexander's time (fourth century BC) the city was in such a pitiful condition because of silting that Lysimachus ordered a rebuilding; his city was sited on Mount Pagus.

During the time of the Crusades, Smyrna was occupied by the victorious Franks after they defeated its independent Turkish emir. The Crusaders held it for 60 years, until Timur sacked it. After the Mongol's departure it became Ottoman. Even in our present century the silting of the Hermus has threatened İzmir, a city that had become important as an international trading centre, and the river had to be diverted into one of its older beds. In 1920 the invading Greeks made it their principal base in the war against Atatürk's new Turkey. When they were ultimately evicted in 1922, the city of wooden dwellings and buildings was left inexplicably burning.

Ephesus was initiated when Ionian settlers built a city on Mount Pion at the mouth of the Caister River. A century or two later, when Croesus the Lydian king subdued all the Ionian cities except Miletus, the river's silting had rendered the principal harbour useless, so Croesus built a new city on the east side of Mount Pion. Croesus was a generous benefactor, and he contributed largely to the construction of a new Temple to Artemis, the city's patron goddess. He seems to have wanted to emulate, if not surpass in size and magnificence, the Labyrinth, Polycrates's great Temple to Hera on the island of Samos. The new temple was begun in 550 BC but had still not been completed some 14 years later when Croesus lost his throne to Cyrus, the Achaemenid Persian king. There were 127 columns with sculpted pedestals, and a sculpted frieze surrounded the outer portico, running just below the roof. Xerxes paid homage at Ephesus on his way through to his fifth-century BC assault on mainland Greece. In 365 BC, Herostratus, a citizen, set fire to the temple for no explicable reason other than notoriety; it burned to the ground.

The building of a new temple had begun when Alexander arrived. His contribution was to make the Ephesians pay into the building fund those taxes that they would have paid to the unseated Persian satrap. Alexander might even have been willing to donate a sum personally if the citizens had been willing to re-dedicate the edifice to him and not to Artemis, which they were not.

Once again the city fell victim to the Caister, and Lysimachus rebuilt it on the western slopes of Mount Pion; its walls were connected to Mount Coressus, and a new harbour was built on the southwest. The isolated temple now became part of a separate sacred precinct, outside the new city's walls.

Ephesus became the capital of the Roman province of Asia when Attalus III of Pergamum bequeathed them the city in the second century BC. During the first campaign of Mithridates VI of Pontus against Roman domination (88 BC), the Ephesians, siding with the king, butchered the Romans living in the city. On the king's ultimate defeat the privileges attached to Roman citizenship were rescinded. By the third century the city's unending struggle with the Caister concluded in yet another defeat, and its maritime importance ended.

In the sixth century Justinian the Great built a new citadel on a hill to the northwest of the temple precinct and also erected a great church, that of St John Theologos. He used columns from the Artemisium in its construction and also transported other columns to Constantinople for inclusion in the building of St Sophia there. Ephesus became known as Agios Theologos, and the Turkish inhabitants today know it as Ayasoluk.

Miletus resisted Lydian domination, and after the fall of Croesus a deal was struck with Cyrus that enabled it to maintain its comparative independence. In 499 BC after instigating an Ionian revolt against Persian rule resulting in a Persian victory, the city was razed and the majority of its citizens exiled to the Persian Gulf.

When Alexander came, the Persian garrison withdrew into the citadel and hoped to hold out until the Persian fleet could come to its rescue. But Nicanor, Alexander's admiral, forestalled Persian naval intervention by anchoring the

Macedonian ships off the Island of Lade at the entrance to the harbour. The garrison sued for terms of surrender, but as these were unacceptable the Persians defied Alexander and were annihilated; an act their fleet was powerless to prevent. Miletus began its independent life again.

The Maeander, though, as well as the Persians, seemed determined to immobilize Miletus, and the river's silting joined Lade to the mainland and gradually filled the city's four harbours with sand. This, of course, contributed to the decay of its economic prosperity — fine quality wool had been among the principal exports.

Intellectually, Miletus was the leader of the Ionian world, with the philosophers Thales and Anaximander counted among its distinguished sages, as well as Hecataeus the geographer and Hippodamas the architect.

Miletus founded colonies on the north Aegean, Marmara and Black sea coasts, in Syria and at Naucratis on the Nile River delta. It supported Athens in that city's long struggle with Sparta — Pericleos of Athens married Aspasia, a girl from Miletus — and was duly humiliated after Sparta's eventual victory. Miletus became Roman through the legacy of Attalus III of Pergamum. St Paul preached here. Its real decline came under the Byzantines, even though two of its harbours were open still. Following the Seljuk entry into western Anatolia, the city fell to the independent Emir of Menteşe, and later to the Ottomans, by which time silting had not only closed the harbours but also the inlet of the sea that had helped to form the peninsula on which Miletus had been built, and thereby created the inland Lake Bafa.

It has been said that Milesian women and girls do not sit at the table with their men. When the Ionians invaded in the first millennium BC, those who founded Miletus are said to have killed all the males of the territory they occupied and taken by force their wives and daughters, and for this reason the women vowed never to eat with their abusers or ever speak to them.

Seven kilometres (four miles) from the port of Panormos, Didyma was a disembarking point for pilgrims and petitioners. In the ancient world, Didyma's Oracle was second in importance only to that of Delphi, although excavations at Claros, to the south of İzmir, and a re-reading of texts in the light of the discoveries made there, might at least place the Oracle of Apollo at Claros on an equal footing with that of Didyma.

The site had been sacred long before the arrival of the Ionians. An early temple was destroyed, or partially destroyed, when the Persians razed Miletus. At that time the oracle was in the keeping of the Branchidae, a priestly family, who after the Persian victory abandoned Didyma, taking the cult image with them and setting up a Shrine to Apollo at Sogdiana in Persia. Or the Persians may have taken the statue and then invited the Branchidae to set up the shrine. When Alexander came to Didyma, he sacrificed at the temple and ordered a rebuilding, a project that was continued on and off over the next 500 years, and in fact was never wholly completed. When Alexander conquered Darius, the Branchidae were hunted down and killed, and Seleucus, Alexander's general, arranged for the return of Apollo to Didyma. The Goths sacked the temple in AD 256, and in early Byzantine times the adytum, or sacred chamber, was converted to a church.

Sights

İzmir

Konak Square, south of the harbour, is modern İzmir's centre — as it was in the last of Smyrna's ancient cities — with the Town Hall, Opera House, Museum of Modern Art and a landmark in the form of a 19th-century **clock tower** of Moorish design. The **bazaar** occupies a network of streets off the east side of Konak Square, starting on Anafartalar Caddesi. A little to the east of it is the **Archaeological Museum** which contains a rich display of exhibits from excavated sites in this region of the Aegean coast. Among the notable are a statue of Poseidon of the second century, a bronze Demeter of the fourth century BC and sections of the sculpted frieze from the Temple of Aphrodite at Aphrodisias (if this has not been removed to the site museum there, whose curator has claimed it). There are collections of jewels, coins and glassware. Opposite is the **Ethnographic Museum**.

To the north of the museums is the ancient **agora** (market- place), which was rebuilt by Marcus Aurelius in 178 after an earthquake. On the west side is a section of a **portico** with 13 standing columns, all with their capitals. To the left of this is the entrance to a **gallery** which had shops. On the north side are the remains of a basilica-style building on vaulted foundations, supported by substantial columns. The entire site has been landscaped as public gardens. Mosques in the agora area are the Ottoman 16th-century **Hisar** and **Kemeral-ti**, both of which have undergone more than one restoration, as has the 18th-century Şadirvan Mosque with its external ablutions fountain alongside. Mount Pagus, on which an ancient citadel — **Kadifekale** — was built, dominates the city at the southeastern exit. The walls and towers are medieval, added upon substantial remnants of those constructed by Alexander's successor Lysimachus.

The city's main railway station is to the north at Basmane. At Tepecik, two kilometres south of the railway station, on the Melez Çayı where a lake gets its water from several springs, there are the remains of a **Roman baths**, while up river some 300 metres (985 feet) are **aqueducts** of Roman origin, though these were substantially rebuilt by the Byzantines and again subsequently by the Ottomans.

Out of İzmir

The choices for an excursion are manifold, and naturally will depend on time available to the visitor. Bathers, unless they can be content with the pool at the Büyük Efes or another hotel, will be looking for a sandy beach. This is to be found on the peninsula that stretches out westward into the Aegean Sea from south of the city, where sea bathing can be combined with some archaeological exploration. If you are using public transport, take a taxi, minibus or local bus from Konak Square going in the general direction of Çeşme.

Inciralti is a popular beach resort with restaurants, cafés and accommodation. Historically, it is a place of sulphur baths, and, archaeologically, its ancient curative establishment is the Agamemnon Kaplicalari, or **Baths of Agamemnon**, named for the leader of the Greeks during the Trojan War.

From Güzelbahçe, beyond Inciralti, take a road running southward across the peninsula to the site of **Teos**. This was one of 12 Ionian cities that combined together to form a mercantile and naval federation. After the Persian conquest of the sixth century BC, the people of Teos, rather than endure Persian hegemony, removed themselves to Thrace in the north Aegean, where they founded the city of Abdera. Democritus, a pioneer of atomic physics, was born at Abdera. Anacreon, the poet, was a citizen of Teos. The remains of a Hellenistic **Temple to Dionysos** stands near the walls on the west of the lower part of the site, and on the south side of the acropolis hill is a **theatre**. Parts of the original square towers on a section of the **ancient walls** are there still. On the northeast are the ruins of a **gymnasium** and an **odeon** (recital hall). South of Teos, on a rocky peninsula, is Myonessos, another of the Ionian foundations, and to the north at Gümüldür is yet another, Lebedos. These sites repay a visit because of the evidence they offer of the high standard of civilization of small communities.

Cross back over the peninsula to the north and continue westward from Inciralti to Urla. The site of the first city of **Clazomenae** is on a small bay. Its citizens supported a revolt against Persian rule led by Miletus in 499 BC, but on the defeat of the Milesians, and to avoid reprisals, the Clazomenaeans transferred themselves *en bloc* to an island in the Gulf of Smyrna. Clazomenae was noted for its pottery and gave its name to a distinctive style of ceramic decoration. When Alexander defeated Darius, the Clazomenaeans returned to the peninsula and built a new city. There is little to be seen now, though excavators recovered examples of pottery that are on display in the İzmir museum and elsewhere. Anaxagoras, the natural scientist and tutor to Pericleos, the Athenian ruler of the classical period, was from Clazomenae.

West of Urla, a section of the peninsula opens out to the north to form the western arm of the Gulf of İzmir. At İlidir, on a small bay a short distance along the coast, is **Erythrae**, another Ionian site, although there is a claim that this city was founded by victorious Greeks after the conclusion of the Trojan

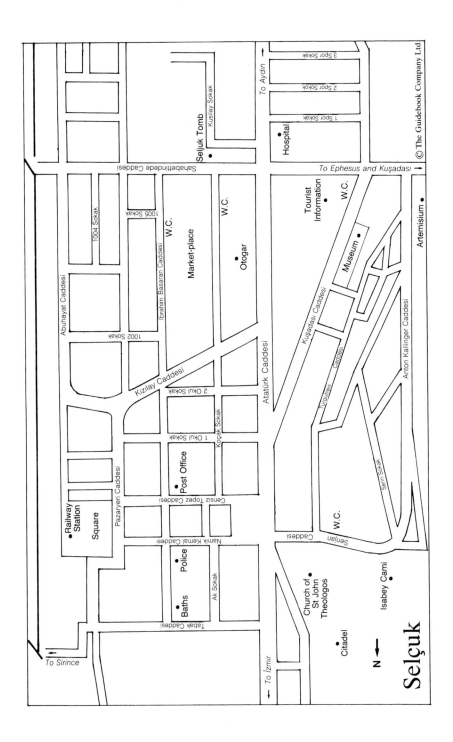

Selçuk

© The Guidebook Company Ltd

To Aydın

3 Spor Sokak

2 Spor Sokak

1 Spor Sokak

Hospital

To Ephesus and Kuşadası

Tourist Information

W.C.

Museum

Artemisium

Kuşadası Caddesi

Anton Kallinger Caddesi

Turgutreis Caddesi

Serin Sokak

Senjan Caddesi

W.C.

Church of St John Theologos

Isabey Cami

Citadel

N

Kusilay Sokak

Seljuk Tomb

Sahabettindede Caddesi

W.C.

Market-place

W.C.

Otogar

1005 Sokak

İbrahim Başaran Caddesi

Atatürk Caddesi

1004 Sokak

Abuhayat Caddesi

1002 Sokak

Kızılay Caddesi

2 Okul Sokak

1 Okul Sokak

Koçak Sokak

Pazaryeri Caddesi

Post Office

Cenisiz Topez Caddesi

Railway Station

Square

Namık Kemal Caddesi

Police

Baths

Ak Sokak

Tabak Caddesi

To Sirince

To İzmir

War. Here is early evidence of town planning. The manufacture and export of millstones was a principal industry of the Erythraeans.

The outstanding feature of the port of Çeşme is its 15th-century **Genoese castle**. The Genoese also had a self-governing colony at Phocaea (Fçca today) on the western arm of the Gulf of Smyrna. The castle was rebuilt by the Ottomans, who added a double wall with towers, a moat and an artillery terrace. Entrance is on the west side, facing the sea, where you cross the moat to a gate in the outer wall, then go left and through the inner wall. The Greek island of Chios lies to the west of Çeşme, only a short boat trip away. Throughout the summer months, regular ferries operate for both passengers and cars; service is less frequent outside the summer season.

Ephesus (Efes)

Selçuk

At Selçuk, there is the **Ephesus Museum** which contains among its mass of interesting exhibits a **statue of Diana** (the Greek goddess Artemis). Unearthed in 1966, it is considered to be the cult image that was buried by temple priests in the fourth century, following an edict of the Emperor Theodosius ordering the destruction of all pagan temples. An angled road runs from the İzmir–Aydin dual-carriageway to the Kuşadasi road, and on this, on the right, is the museum (entrance fee 5,000TL), with the Ministry of Information Office at the end of the left.

The citadel hill is on the right as you enter Selçuk from İzmir. A paved roadway leads up the southern side of the hill, passing the site of a small temple with its ruins and a paved carpark, to reach the impressive towered citadel entrance called — erroneously it seems — the **Persecution Gate**. Entrance fee is 5,000TL. A wide stairway mounts between high walls to the platform or plateau on which the Church of St John Theologos is built. Reconstruction of the church and excavations on the site continue to be carried out by the Turkish Ministry of Culture and Information and the George B. Quatman Foundation of Lima, Ohio.

Much of the city wall has been restored or reconstructed. The excavators are at work on the west side of the hill, and there is evidence of domestic and civic buildings. At the crown of the hill, the fortress walls and towers have reconstructed sections, too. The main entrance is on the west side. On the interior, steps lead up to a sentry walk just below the battlements, and this can be walked on. Within the fortress is a ruined mosque that was a conversion from a Byzantine church, and there is another Byzantine structure. There are some cisterns, also, and what appears to be guard quarters at the main gateway.

Down below is the restored İsabey Mosque, still within the city complex but appearing to stand outside it. Restoration has revealed the building's

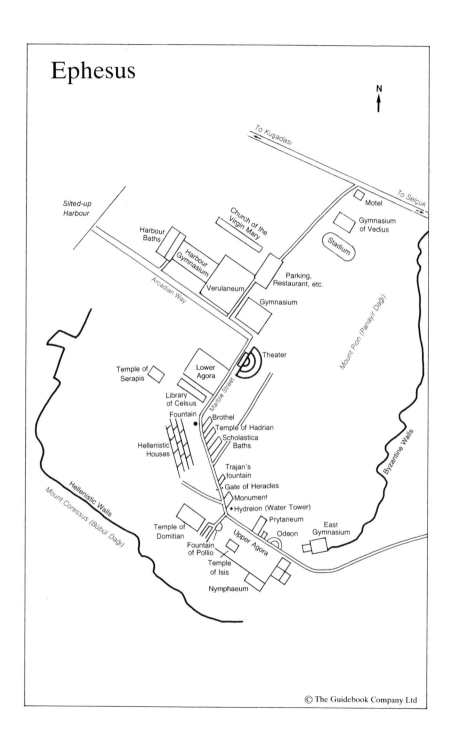

Ephesus

N

To Kuşadası

To Selçuk

Silted-up Harbour

Motel

Gymnasium of Vedius

Church of the Virgin Mary

Harbour Baths

Harbour Gymnasium

Stadium

Arcadian Way

Verulaneum

Parking, Restaurant, etc.

Gymnasium

Mount Pion (Panayir Dağı)

Theater

Temple of Serapis

Lower Agora

Marble Street

Library of Celsus

Fountain

Brothel

Temple of Hadrian

Scholastica Baths

Hellenistic Houses

Byzantine Walls

Trajan's fountain

Gate of Heracles

Monument

Hydreion (Water Tower)

Hellenistic Walls

Mount Coressus (Bübül Dağı)

Temple of Domitian

Prytaneum

East Gymnasium

Odeon

Upper Agora

Fountain of Pollio

Temple of Isis

Nymphaeum

© The Guidebook Company Ltd

Byzantine origin. The high wall of the large rectangular court is particularly impressive. From the walls on that western side of the citadel hill, other Byzantine structures can be noted, and the site of the Artemisium, the great temple, can be observed about two kilometres (1.25 miles) to the southwest.

The tiered and arched entrance of the **Church of St John Theologos** has been restored. On the west side is a chapel with apse, on the east side an apsed chapel with a mosaic floor and an altar. The pivotal interest is the restored **baptistery**, having four entrances, one at each cardinal point of the compass and four arched recesses in the form of a four-leaved clover. At the centre is the font or baptismal pool, permitting total immersion.

By taking a street oppposite the carpark below the Persecution Gate, you can walk down through the old part of the city, wherein many houses have been converted into pensions, and stumble on to a ruined Byzantine church. By this route you can also emerge on the Kuşadasï road and, turning right, take a short parallel road to the **Artemisium** — no entrance fee. The excavators have drained the marsh round the foundations of the great temple, once counted among the seven wonders of the ancient world. Apart from the idea of what was once here, there is little to excite the observer at the present time. However, one column has been re-erected, and the archaeologists may yet uncover interesting finds.

An aqueduct brought water to Justinian's city, and a number of stanchions of this ruined edifice can be seen in the re-vamped market area of the town, near the railway station. In this section of Selçuk, there are some new modest-class hotels and a number of pensions, as well as several restaurants. The streets are closed to traffic at nightfall, allowing visitors to sit out in them and eat and drink.

On the south side of the bus station, a small public garden houses a neat Seljuk cone-topped *türbe*, a Byzantine structure, and there is also an octagonal tomb of a Moslem holy man from Sivas, dated 1455.

Ephesus (Efes): The Early Sites
A thorough exploration could occupy more than one day. Austrian archaeologists, working over many seasons, excavated and restored many of the various sites.

In the area of the entrance guichet (the fee is 5,000TL), there are restaurants, cafés and tourist boutiques. Faced with a number of options, it would be as well to follow an itinerary southward from the entrance.

On the right is an arcaded **Verulaneum**, on the left a **gymnasium** with an arcaded court. Moving further on you reach the **Arcadian Way**, a wide, paved and arcaded road that runs for 500 metres (1,640 feet) east–west from the great theatre to a silt-stolen **harbour**. The Emperor Arcadius (395–408) had it constructed over a former roadway. Statues once stood on the pedestals located along its sides, and many of the columns that supported the covered arcades are in place still. At the western end, and flanking it, are the **harbour gymnasium** and **harbour baths**.

The **theatre** is built into the flank of Mount Pion. It was begun under Claudius (41–54) but completed only in Trajan's time (98–117). St Paul, who preached in it, spent three years in Ephesus, imprisoned for the greater part of that time. The city's silversmiths petitioned the governor for his execution, claiming that his anti-pagan teaching was crippling their trade in Diana-engraved mementoes and votive items for sale to pilgrims. There are enclosed stairways to the upper tiers. The façade was three-tiered in height but has only one tier now with niches in which statues once stood. The structure on the west side could have been a Hellenistic *nymphaeum* (fountain house).

Southwest of the theatre is a spacious Hellenistic **lower agora** with its porticoes and remains of shops. From here a colonnaded street ran west, with a gateway at each end. On the south side of the agora, a stairway leads to a platform or stylobate on which a **Temple of Serapis** stands, the Greek–Egyptian god. This structure with its Corinthian-style columns was converted to a church when pagan worship was abolished by Theodisias I.

On the agora's east side is the stylish, marble-paved '**Marble Street**' which in origin had probably run from the Coressus Gate, situated northwest of the entrance to the site. Statues were set along this, and the medallions of gladiators can be seen still. Holes in the paving were for drainage.

At the southern end of the marble-paved street, on the right, is the **Library of Celsus**. Celsus was a governor of the province in the second century, and his son built the library to his father's memory. The fine two-tiered building has been reconstructed, along with its niches for manuscripts and parchments. In one of the niches is the coffin of Celsus.

A little below the library the marble-paved street connects with the **Street of the Curetes**. This begins at the **gate** where there is a reconstructed **ornamental fountain**. Over from the street, to the right, is a group of Hellenistic houses which probably included those of the *curetes* (temple priests). On the left of the street is the **brothel**, and then comes a reconstructed **Temple of Hadrian**, alongside which is the **Scholastica Baths**, in which much of the conduit piping for heating and drainage can still be seen today.

Beyond the baths, on the left still, and in the following order, are a **Fountain of Trajan**, the **Gate of Heracles**, a **monument** ascribed to Memmius, then a complex of buildings that include a *hydreion* (water tower), after which the area of the **upper agora** is reached. On the northern side is the **prytaneum** (the city prefect's administrative quarters) and a neat reconstructed **odeon** (recital hall) of the second century, seating 1,400 and built by Publius Vedius Antoninus, a prefect and magistrate. Much of the original seating is in place.

Within the upper agora is a **Temple of Isis**. On the western side is the **Fountain of Pollio** and, still on the west, a **Temple to the Emperor Domitian**, erected during his reign (81–96), part of which now houses a **Museum of Inscriptions**.

Outside the area of this itinerary are some other buildings of interest. The House of the Virgin Mary, the **Meryemana** or Panayi Kapülü, east of the upper agora, can also be reached by going seven kilometres (four miles) on a direct roadway from Selçuk. Mary is said to have lived in Ephesus, having arrived there accompanied by the disciple John. Identification is of a comparatively recent date, attributed to the vision of a 19th-century German nun, but more than one Pope has since given credence to the fact by visiting the house at Ephesus. St John may have returned later to Ephesus, to write his gospel and to die there. His bones were later exhumed and reburied in the foundations of Justinian's church on the citadel hill in Selçuk.

There is a **Church of the Virgin Mary** to the west of the main entrance to the site, which is in fact a double building. The first church was erected in the fourth century over a pagan basilica and became the rendezvous for the Third Oecumenical Council of 431. Then in the seventh century a domed church was constructed within the first one. Today both churches harmonize as a single ruin.

One Ephesian legend is that of the **Seven Sleepers**. To avoid persecution in the middle of the second century, a group of young Christian men hid in a cave and fell asleep; later they were rediscovered alive in the time of Theodosias II in the fifth century. On their eventual deaths after a normal life span, this cave became their burial chamber, and a church was constructed which became a place of pilgrimage. A cave associated with the legend was discovered in the 1920s.

North of the site's main entrance, as you approach on the road from Selçuk, a second-century **Gymnasium of Vedius** with its porticoed court is on the lower slope of a hill on the left. Further down on the right is a **Temple to Hera**, and over on the left (near where the Coressus Gate was)

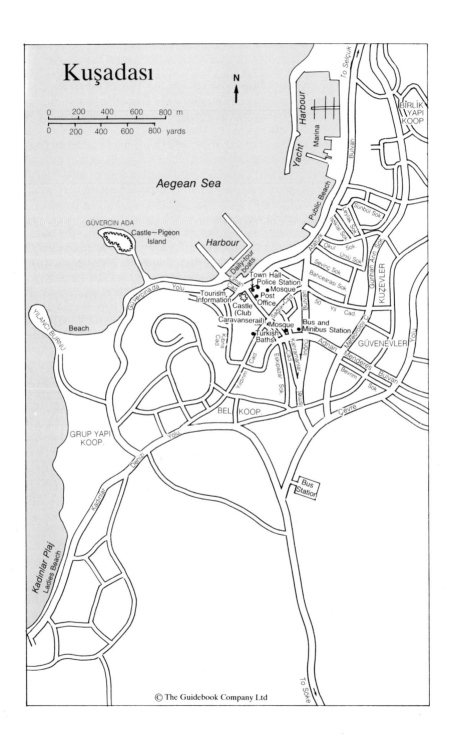

Kuşadası

0   200   400   600   800 m

0   200   400   600   800 yards

N

Aegean Sea

GÜVERCİN ADA

Castle–Pigeon
Island

Harbour

Yacht Harbour

Marina

BİRLİK
YAPI
KOOP

To Selçuk

Bulvarı

Public Beach

Sünbül Sok

Leylak Sok

Işıklar Sok

Okul Sok

Ünlü Sok

Günhan Arın Sok

KUZEVLER

Atatürk

Sevinç Sok

Bahçearası Sok

Daily-tour boats

Liman Cad

Town Hall

Police Station

Mosque

Post
Office

Tourism
Information

Castle
(Club
Caravanserail)

Mosque

Turkish
Baths

Bus and
Minibus Station

Bağlar Cad

Bulvarı

So Yıl Cad

GÜVENEVLER

Meteoroloji

İnönü

Yolu

Adnan

Menderes

Bulvarı

Bevrim
Sok

Güvercinada Yolu

YILANCI BURNU

Beach

Kıbrıs
Cad

Yıldırım Cad

Karamanlı

Eskipazar Sok

İsmet

BEL KOOP.

Yolu

GRUP YAPI
KOOP.

Denizi

Kadınlar

Çevre

Bus
Station

Kadınlar Plaj
Ladies Beach

To Söke

© The Guidebook Company Ltd

is the site of the **stadium**, built in the time of Nero (54–68) with its seating on one side cut out of the hillside.

On the left, before reaching the carpark and entrance, is a Byzantine building that was sited on a Hellenistic or early Roman predecessor. A chamber here has niches for statues along one wall, while another room has an apse-like end wall and may have been a refectory.

Kuşadasi

As with most tourist centres on the Aegean and Mediterranean coasts, Kuşadasi has developed enormously in the past few years. The central streets have become a pedestrian enclave and the old town gate is now almost lost among tourist boutiques selling carpets, leather goods, jewellery and souvenirs. There are good restaurants near the quayside and smaller, less expensive ones in the town. An island in the harbour, Güverçin Ada or Pigeon Island, to which a causeway extends, has a castle that is an Ottoman rebuilding of an earlier Byzantine one. Modifications have been added by the Genoese or perhaps Venetians, since both republics enjoyed trading rights, granted by the sultan in İstanbul.

There are a growing number of hotels, motels, camping sites and pensions on the approach roads from Selçuk, however, the most intense development is on the southern side of town, over the hill on Kadinlar Plaj. The road to Söke mounts this hill, and, after a kilometre or two, it branches off to the *plaj*. There is another road running west from the Kuşadasi harbour that eventually links up with the *plaj* road.

Priene

This fourth-century BC city was designed on a grid pattern by Hippodamas, the town planner of Miletus. It was built on the ascending lower ledges of Mount Mycale, which rises to 400 metres (1,313 feet). Only parts of the walls remain of the citadel on the crest. From the heights the fall to the plain on the side facing towards the coast is almost sheer. Up here the result of the Maeander River's silting activity can be observed; the sea is out of sight some 12 kilometres (eight miles) away, and former beds of the river turn and twist like serpents across the marshland. Priene had more than one harbour and its longshoremen were noted for their professionalism, even though they were often in dispute with those of Miletus over operating rights in the narrows. The harbours are lost somewhere under the silt.

The public buildings and the agora are located in a proximity which would have been most convenient for the citizens, and the principal streets were paved and arcaded. The line of the walls extends for over two kilometres (1.25 miles) along the base and up on the east and west sides to the citadel. The upper sections with their towers are Byzantine.

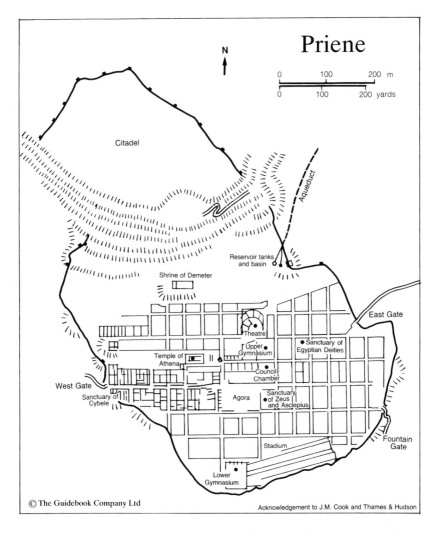

Priene

N

Citadel

Aqueduct

Reservoir tanks
and basis

Shrine of Demeter

East Gate

Theatre

Upper
Gymnasium

Sanctuary of
Egyptian Deities

Temple of
Athena

Council
Chamber

West Gate

Sanctuary of
Cybele

Agora

Sanctuary
of Zeus
and Asclepius

Fountain
Gate

Stadium

Lower
Gymnasium

© The Guidebook Company Ltd

Acknowledgement to J.M. Cook and Thames & Hudson

Enter through the **Fountain Gate** on the southeast. Along the lowest ledge, following the curve of the hill, is the **stadium**, built or reconstructed in the second century BC on an earlier one. It has seating only on the hillside because of the width of the terrace. Its length is 191 metres (627 feet), and the starting line for runners is marked. Adjoining it on the west is the **lower gymnasium** with its colonnaded court, changing rooms and washroom with lion-headed faucets and stone baths. The walls of the room alongside are mottled with name-carvings, ancient graffiti.

Moving directly west from the Fountain Gate, you come to the **Sanctuary of Zeus and Asclepius**. To the west is the **agora** with its public stoas, and, in the southwest corner, the market. Between here and the **West Gate** are the streets of houses, and on the south side of the gate itself a **Sanctuary of Cybele**.

On the terrace above, running along the north side of the agora, is the *bouleuterion* (council chamber) with its banks of seating on three sides and a carved stone altar at the centre. Its accompanying buildings were probably the civic offices. To the west of here, on a high terrace above it, is the Ionic **Temple of Athena** designed by Pytheos of Halicarnassus, and a stoa with Doric columns running along one side. The cult image, towards which Alexander is said to have contributed money, stood on a plinth in the forecourt. It was modelled on the one Phidias sculpted for the Parthenon in Athens. On the next level, and east of the temple, is the **upper gymnasium**, to the east of which is a **Sanctuary of Egyptian Deities**.

From the upper gymnasium, you climb by a steep, stepped street to the **theatre**. Here the seating in the first row at the centre includes throne-like marble seats that were surely installed for distinguished citizens or visitors, and there is a marble altar, too, for ceremonial occasions. There are the changing rooms for performers, each of three having a doorway into the stage or proscenium. The façade is of Doric half-columns, the upper part of the entablature having those niches in which statues stood.

On the hillside above, near the walls on the east, is a **Shrine of Demeter** with, nearby, cisterns and the remains of an aqueduct.

Miletus

The ruins are strewn over a large area that includes the village of Balat, where some houses have made use of fallen items of marble. The **Roman theatre** is by far the most impressive building on site. It was reconstructed under Trajan (98–117) on what in all probability was a Hellenistic rebuilding of an even earlier one. It held 25,000 people, the seating rising to 30 metres (100 feet). The lower tiers are in such good condition still that you might well be tempted to explore in the crevices between the seats for ancient sweet wrappings. The width of the facade is 140 metres (460 feet).

Above, the walls of an eighth-century **Byzantine fort** are merged into the theatre's upper gallery, though a previous fort probably existed here. Columns and blocks from a destroyed pagan temple or a fallen building have been incorporated in the structure, and there is evidence of Turkish rehabilitation subsequent to the Byzantine.

From the theatre's upper tiers the areas of two of the city's former harbours can be identified. To the northeast the **Lions Bay** had sculpted lions to guard it, and these still stand sentinel on the dry sands. On the theatre's east side a rounded plinth was the base for a quayside sculpture erected by Augustus to celebrate a naval victory.

To the south and east of the naval monument is the **northern agora** with its surrounding stoas and shops. On the northeast corner is a **Sanctuary of Apollo**, the **Delphinion**, in which valuable inscriptions on blocks and votive offerings were found. To the north of the Delphinion, on the eastern edge of the former harbour and in a residential area, is a **baths**. Another residential area lay between the northern agora and the theatre.

The northwest corner of the northern agora has a restored **Ionic-columned stoa** standing on a stylobate of six steps, southwest of which is a **Byzantine church** that was probably built over a **Temple to Asclepius**. South of the Delphinion is a **Hellenistic gymnasium**, and to the east of this a **Roman baths** dating from the time of Claudius (41–54). A Roman governor who may have built this could also have been responsible for the Ionic stoa.

Immediately south of the northern agora is the ***bouleuterion***, and still south is the main entrance to the **southern agora**, whose two-tiered, three-arched, columned structure of Diocletian's time has been reconstructed and moved to Berlin. On the top east corner of this agora is a first century ***nymphaeum***, once fed from an **aqueduct** south of the city. On the western side of the agora is a **Temple to Serapis**, and a long building here could have been a warehouse, perhaps for wool.

Return to the theatre and the area of its harbour. On the southernmost edge, 220 metres (720 feet) from the theatre's southern arm, is the large and extensive **Baths of Faustina** — named for the daughter of the Emperor Antoninus Pius and wife of Marcus Aurelius (161–80) — with a **mosaic of the River god** in its main pool. To the west are the remains of the **stadium**.

Northwest of the stadium is the site of a third agora, and on its southwest side is the sixth-century BC **Temple of Athena**, found by German excavators in the 1960s, along with evidence of Mycenaean and Carian occupation. To the east of this, in a courtyard of what could have been a large house, are the remains of a **Temple to Eumenes II** of Pergamum.

From the Baths of Faustina, a street runs southwest to the line of the ancient walls and a **gateway** leading out to the Sacred Way that ran to Didyma. An inscription of AD 100 found here dates a restoration to the time of Trajan. There

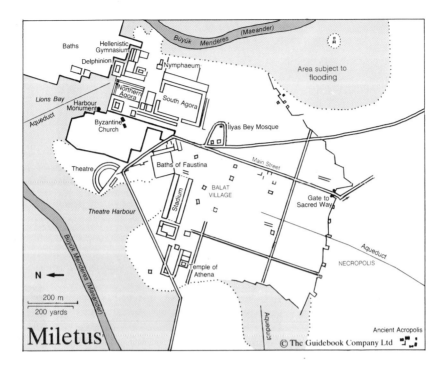

Baths
Hellenistic
Gymnasium
Delphinion
Büyük Menderes (Maeander)
Nymphaeum
Area subject to
flooding
Lions Bay
Harbour
Monument
Northern
Agora
South Agora
Aqueduct
Byzantine
Church
İlyas Bey Mosque
Theatre
Baths of Faustina
Main Street
BALAT
VILLAGE
Stadium
Theatre Harbour
Gate to
Sacred Way
Büyük Menderes (Maeander)
Aqueduct
NECROPOLIS
N ←
Temple of
Athena
200 m
200 yards
Aqueduct
Ancient Acropolis
Miletus
© The Guidebook Company Ltd

are some sections of Hellenistic walls here, and outside the gateway is a
necropolis. On the summit of **Kalabak Tepe**, a hill beyond, was the acropolis
of Miletus prior to 494 BC. South of the hill is a section of that early city's
walls of about 650 BC.

The **Mosque of İlyas Bey** is an early 15th-century structure with a fine
dome. Built during the Emirate of the Mentese, the mosque was constructed
with material incorporated from the Ionian city. Not far from the mosque, on
the street running to the Sacred Way, is the site **museum**.

Didyma

The Sacred Way was colonnaded throughout its length, with shops along it,
and over the last 350 metres (1,150 feet) were marble lions at intervals, alter-
nating with sphinxes and seated figures, all terminating in a sacred wood. One
lion still lies in place within the temple enclosure, near the entrance (fee
2,000TL). Much of the recovered sculpture that was excavated during the mid-
19th century, though, is in the British Museum.

An earthquake in 1456 took a heavy toll on the temple. One column has
been left as it fell, opened up like a pack of cards set for choice of dealer. As
with the temple at Sardis, the column bases have fine and varied carvings.

Only three columns of the temple are standing fully erect, two with their
Ionic capitals supporting a section of carved architrave. From the foot of the

Carts, the best form of transporting produce in Bergama

wide stairway leading up to the stylobate and the columned pronaos, however, there is an impression of a complete temple, since parts of almost all the 122 columns are there, standing at varying truncated heights.

The orientation of the structure is northeast–southwest. At the northeast end, there is a semi-circular terrace dating from a period earlier than the time of the present structure. Within the temple a walled court contained the inner-most sanctum, the adytum. This is set seven metres (23 feet) below a seven-stepped stylobate, and entrance was gained by tunnel-like passageways on either side leading down to the lower level. A wide seven-stepped marble stair-way leads up from the adytum to a columned chamber with an entrance on either side. Probably petitioners were not allowed beyond this chamber, access to the oracle being confined to the priests and initiates. A sacred olive tree stood within the sanctuary, which is surrounded by high walls supported by pilasters on which were gryphon-headed capitals; many of these stand on the floor of the adytum. The oracle section of the shrine is roped off now, contain-ing the circular hole over which the priestess inhaled the vapour from the sacred trance-inducing spring that ran below. A petitioner would have his re-quest transcribed in verse by an official priest, and the reply would be in verse, pronounced in the antechamber and more often than not couched in ambiguous terms, as was Croesus's reply at Delphi. A bronze cult image of the god stood in a separate sacred chamber.

A circular sacrificial **altar** stands in front of the main stairway to the temple, and to the right of this, on the embankment at the entrance, near the lion, is a carved **head of the Medusa**, which was part of an original main frieze. To the right of the altar is a **sacred well**.

Games were held at the shrine, and surrounding it were more than one **gym-nasium**, **baths** and **accommodation**. On the southeast side there are remains of marble seating installed for spectators. The steps along the stylobate have carvings of sectioned circles and squares. It may be that these were a form of dice board whereby waiting petitioners might try to predict the results of their request. To the left of the main stairway, a broken section allows entrance to what appears to be a small chamber, enclosed now by a block inscribed in Greek.

Outside the enclosure, excavation is continuing, as it is within the temple compound. North of the two restaurants, about 500 metres (1,600 feet) along, there appears to be the site a smaller temple, an arched entry with sections of an aqueduct, an agora and an area of private dwellings.

Nine kilometres (six miles) south of the Temple of Apollo is the holiday plage of Altınkum with its fine sandy beaches. Hotels, motels and a marina are situated on this bay at the end of the peninsula. A wide roadway has urban rib-bon development along it, and the *plaj* itself has become one favoured and promoted by West European package tour operators.

Diversions Inland

If İzmir is your chosen base, a two-day journey inland to Manisa and Sardis could be made before moving south. Manisa is set neatly on a mountainside on the edge of a plain. The great plain between Manisa and Sardis, through which the Hermus River flows on its way to the Gulf of İzmir, is an area of orchards and vineyards. Near Sardis the burial tumuli of kings are conspicuous over a wide area.

Pamukkale, and the ruins of Hierapolis, can be found inland from Kuşadası on a plateau 100 metres (330 feet) above the plain. The water from a thermal spring, flowing over the plateau's lip, has formed remarkable travertines, or irregular shelves. Calcareous deposits have contributed a veneer of translucent crystal to the rock down the plateau's side, hence the Turkish appellation of Cotton Castle.

A number of motels and hotels here have channelled the hot spring water into constructed pools on their premises. The oldest of the pools is at the Pamukkale Motel, where you can float over the fluted drums, capitals and sections of architrave. Here at the source of the spring sacred to Apollo, you can be certain of the god's blessing, in water at a temperature of 37°C (98° F).

Although Hierapolis was founded or taken over by the Attalids of Pergamum, the ruins here at Pamukkale are predominantly Roman and Byzantine. If you decide to stay in one of the motels on the ridge, or down in the village, an excursion can be taken to Aphrodisias, as well as to other neighbouring sites.

Other archaeological ruins to be seen in the area include the sites of Laodicea, Nyssa, Tralles and Magnesia on the Maeander.

Getting There

Leaving İzmir for Manisa which is 36 kilometres (22 miles) to the northeast, go out on the Bornova road. To continue on from Manisa to Sardis, take road 250 for 27 kilometres (17 miles) to its junction with the E23. Turn left through Turgutlu to Salihli, another 44 kilometres (27 miles). The site of Sardis, or Sart, is five kilometres (three miles) to the west of Salihli, in fact, the E5 from İzmir intersects the excavations.

A second diversion inland could start from Kuşadası or Selçuk, taking the E24 to Aydın. The road continues along the Maeander valley through Sultanhisar, Nazili and Saraköy to Denizli, 165 kilometres (103 miles) from Selçuk. Pamukkale, 19 kilometres (12 miles) from Denizli, is reached on a main roadway, the Celal Bayer Bulvarı, that runs north from a roundabout at the east end of town. The Denizli *otogar*, for those travelling by bus, is off to the right of the E24, shortly before reaching the roundabout. You will see the *dolmuş* taxis at the side of the road; the minibus fare to Pamukkale is 1,000TL. The village, on the left of the road, is developing now as a tourist centre with its hotels, motels and pensions. Continue on for another kilometre up to the main square of Pamukkale and the ruins of Hierapolis.

The journey to Aphrodisias leaves from below the ridge in Pamukkale village at 10 am and takes approximately two hours, going east on the Isparta road before turning south and then west through Tavas and Karacasu. Nearly three hours are allowed for visiting the sight; the bus departs for Pamukkale at 2.30 pm. The cost is 10,000TL. Another route to Aphrodisias is from Nazili, a town on the E24 road from İzmir. Twelve kilometres (eight miles) east of Nazili, a road turns south for Karacasu.

On returning from Pamukkale to Denizli, the road to Laodicea or Ladik is signposted after nine kilometres (six miles). Nyssa is to the north of Sultanhisar, 25 kilometres (16 miles) west of Nazili. Another 30 kilometres (19 miles) west near Aydin, Tralles is situated on a hill. The E24 passes through the ruins of Magnesia on the Maeander at Tekke, near Ortaklar, 19 kilometres (12 miles) west of Aydin.

Historical Background

At Manisa in 190 BC the Romans defeated Antiochus III and put an end to Seleucid (Hellenistic) rule in Asia Minor. Magnesia was given to Rome's ally, the reigning king of Pergamum.

Mount Sipylus is associated with the mythical Niobe, who was the sister of Pelops and wife of King Amphion of Thebes. Niobe's 14 children were killed on Leto's orders by Artemis and Apollo (her offspring by Zeus), because Niobe had too proudly denigrated the goddess's fecundity by comparison with her own. Niobe wept continuously for her children, and in pity Zeus turned her into insensitive stone, though the tears continued. A natural rock formation above Manisa can be said to resemble a mourning woman. At Akpinar, seven kilometres (four miles) southeast, there is a carved relief, the Taş şuret, also said to be of Niobe, but this is considered a Hittite carving of the Anatolian Mother-goddess, or Cybele, as the Phrygians called her.

Lying as it did on the Royal Road to Susa, Sardis was a key city for the Hittites and a principal one for the Persians later. The Lydians were indigenous to the region, or they had migrated to it from the east at an early date. Their language is considered to have been a mixture of Semitic and Indo-Aryan. Their principal goddess was Cybele, and their symbol of sovereignty was a double-headed axe. They claimed descent from Atys, son of a Phrygian god, Manes; Omphale, one of their queens, consorted with Heracles and thereby inaugurated the Heraclid Dynasty, which came to an end with Candaules.

Gyges, a courtier, was Candaules's best friend. The king, wanting to share with him an appreciation of the queen's undressed beauty, persuaded him to hide in her bedchamber. Offended by what she considered to be an act of indecency, the Queen prevailed on Gyges to murder Candaules and marry her.

Under the Mermnad Dynasty, Lydia attained the acme of its power and civilizing influence. The Lydians probably were instrumental in preventing the Greek colonizers from penetrating too far beyond the coastal areas they occupied, and for a substantial time the Lydians dominated the cities of the coast, except for Miletus. Croesus lost his throne to Cyrus the Achaemenid Persian, ostensibly because he misinterpreted the response of the Delphic Oracle to a question concerning the invincibility of his power. An inconclusive battle was fought in 546 BC at the Halys River, and Croesus, having got the worst of the encounter, retired to Sardis for the winter to reshape his army. Against the unwritten rules of war of the time, Cyrus followed after and took Croesus by surprise. Though Cyrus intended to put the king to death, he changed his mind, and Croesus received courteous and generous treatment until his death in exile.

Hellenistic in origin, the Romans reconstructed and enlarged Aphrodisias. An early sanctuary to Cybele — perhaps earlier to the Anatolian Great Mother, with whom the Babylonian goddess Ishtar may have been associated — became one to Aphrodite (Roman Venus). In Byzantine times, in the fifth century, it was named Stavropolis and was the seat of a bishop. The Seljuks took it in the 12th century, and again in the 13th, after a brief re-occupation under the Byzantine Manuel I (1143–80). After its destruction by Timur, the 15th-century city seems to have been left abandoned.

Sights

Manisa

Apart from the Byzantine walls on Manisa's citadel hill, there is little to show for the occupations from pre-Hellenistic through to Ottoman times. In the town, though, are several notable mosques; the oldest is the **Ulu Cami** on Sandik Tepe. Completed during the 1370s, it was built for Isak Çelebi, an independent Saruhanoğlu emir, whose tomb is within the complex. Material from an earlier Byzantine structure is incorporated in the surrounding portico. On a main crossroads the **Muradiye** of 1583–6 has been fully restored, and the decoration of the mihrab is of interest. In its *medrese* (theological school) is a small archaeological museum. Nearby, the **Sultan Cami**, dating from 1552, was built for the mother of Süleiman the Magnificent. Close to the vilayet (the offices of the *vali*, or governor of the province) on Atatürk Bulvari is the **Hatuniye Cami** of 1485, built by the wife of Beyazit II, whose son Murat (later Murat III) served as governor of this province. The Çesniğer Cami, in the

Sardis

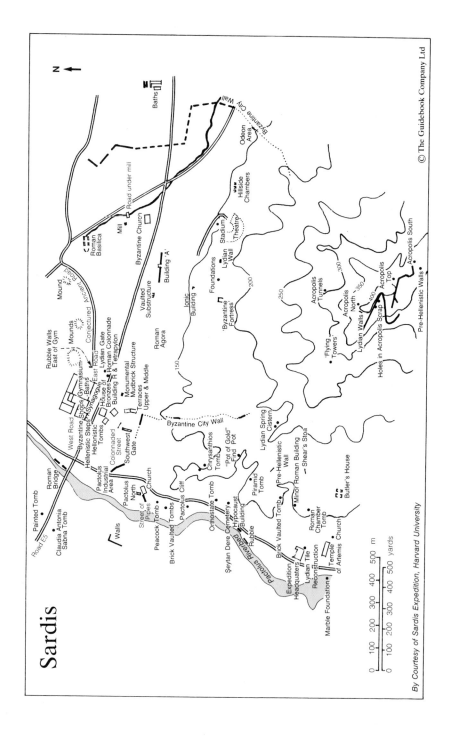

© The Guidebook Company Ltd

By Courtesy of Sardis Expedition, Harvard University

same area, dates from 1475. It is attributed to a slave liberated by Mehemt II, the future sultan, who was a student here.

Sardis

Some of the Lydian burial mounds on the plain between Manisa and Sardis have been excavated and identified, notably that of Alyattes, Croesus's father, and Gyges, the founder of the Mermnad Dynasty of which Croesus was the last representative.

The excavations at Sardis separate into three sections. After the road (E5) has crossed the Pactolus River, on the north side is the first group of buildings. In Roman times a large Jewish community lived here, and an impressive **synagogue** has been excavated and restored by the Sardis Expedition of Harvard University. North of this and adjoining it is a second-century **gymnasium** and **baths**, with its elegantly reconstructed *nymphaeum*. To the west of the synagogue, along the roadside, is a line of shops. Thirty metres (100 feet) east of the synagogue is a **Roman colonnade**, and a little to the east again is a **Lydian gate**.

On the south side of the E5, opposite the above buildings, is a **House of Bronzes**, which may have been a bishop's residence, to the immediate southwest of which are some Hellenistic tombs. South again there is part of a colonnaded street with terraces on its east and west sides, and beyond on the west is the **Southwest Gate**. One hundred metres (330 feet) east of the House of Bronzes stands a **monumental structure** in mudbrick.

Turning south at the E5 crossroads, move down the river where gold was panned and refined. Refineries have been excavated on the banks, and Lydia may have introduced the minting of coins. The temple is about 1,000 metres (3,300 feet) from the turn, or 150 metres (500 feet) beyond the headquarters and site museum of the expedition. Two columns stand against a jagged sandstone outcrop on top of which the now eroded and serrated **acropolis** was located. There are sections of **Byzantine fortifications** on the heights, and a more recent (1985) excavation revealed a **Masonic structure** on a Lydian–Persian spur, probably the base of a sixth-century BC **Lydian building**. Lydian items were also found below a **Roman house** on this same spur.

The **Temple of Artemis** was begun in 550 BC, built over an earlier one to Athena. From the evidence of existing column bases, the carvings and designs throughout were unusual. During the Ionian Revolt, men from Ephesus set fire to the temple, because Sardis was the seat of a Persian satrap. Alexander in his day honoured the citizens of Sardis as non-Greek Hellenes, and as always he encouraged work of reconstruction.

Back at the E5 crossroads, go east 800 metres (2,600 feet) along the road from the synagogue. Off to the north, about 50 metres (165 feet) is a **Byzan-**

tine cruciform church, and 250 metres (820 feet) northwest of it is another in basilica form. East of these two buildings, 700 metres (2,300), is a baths. To the northeast of the gymnasium are burial mounds. On the south side of the E5, 300 metres (1,000 feet) east of the mudbrick monument, is the area of the Roman agora. East again, 150 metres (500 feet), is a vaulted substructure, then 50 metres (165 feet) to the east is another building that is probably Roman. Southeast from here, 200 metres (660 feet), are the stadium and, further south, the theatre and a Byzantine fortress. East of the stadium, 350 metres (1,150 feet), is an odeon. One important find of 1985 was a child's grave of the tenth century BC.

Pamukkale

At the top of the ridge are the ruins of Hierapolis. The minibus stops in an open square, not far from a Roman baths of the first century, dating from the reign of Tiberius when the city was built after an earthquake. Now the museum (entrance fee 5,000TL), the grounds of the baths feature a display of statuary, inscribed stelae and other recovered items. During summer months a mobile bank is likely to be standing near the entrance to the museum, offering foreign exchange facilities.

Along the lower, northeastern end of the square are the premises of the Pamukkale Motel, which includes a restaurant and changing cabins on the right. Behind the motel, on the left, is a *nymphaeum*, and above this on the hillside is the site of the Temple to Apollo. Higher and to the east is the theatre, clearly visible from the square, and a roadway allows tour buses to drive up to the top. Above and to the east of the theatre is a Byzantine church, and above again are sections of the city walls.

On the right of the motel is a ruined Byzantine basilica, and above this, on a line with the nymphaeum, was the entrance to the plutonium, in which the noxious fumes from an underground stream inspired an oracle's prophecies. Above the basilica, on the hill, is the site of the agora, and away to the right of the basilica, continuing in the direction of a colonnaded street, is the South Gate.

On the left or northwestern side of the main square, the remains of the colonnaded street lead northerly to the North Gate of the city. Below this, running from the square, a road leads along the ridge of the plateau to a number of hotels and motels, all of which have their curative water and pools. The road continues for three kilometres to the village of Karahayit. At one point it meets and runs parallel with the colonnaded street where it leads through ruined public buildings and private houses, among which a basilica is conspicuous, before entering a necropolis of many impressive tombs by way of the Arch of Domitian. On the hillside, well above the necropolis, and to the east of it, is the fifth-century Martyrium of St Philip, dedicated to the apostle who died here for his faith in AD 80.

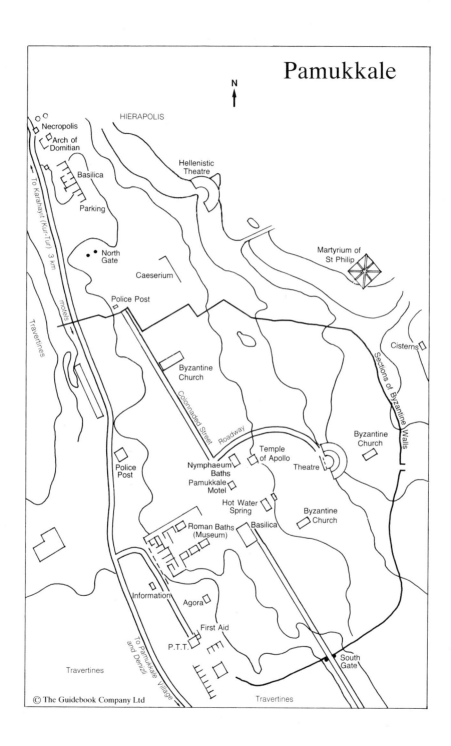

Pamukkale

N
↑

HIERAPOLIS

Necropolis

Arch of Domitian

Basilica

Parking

To Karahayit (Kur-Tur) 3 km

North Gate

Caeserium

Police Post

motels

Travertines

Byzantine Church

Colonnaded Street

Roadway

Police Post

Nymphaeum Baths

Temple of Apollo

Byzantine Church

Pamukkale Motel

Theatre

Hot Water Spring

Byzantine Church

Roman Baths (Museum)

Basilica

Information

Agora

First Aid

P.T.T.

To Pamukkale Village and Denzil

Travertines

South Gate

Martyrium of St Philip

Cisterns

Sections of Byzantine Walls

Byzantine Church

Hellenistic Theatre

Travertines

© The Guidebook Company Ltd

The **Roman agora** is behind the museum and in this area there are other motels with their pools, with the Ministry of Tourism's information office nearby.

Laodicea

The church of this ancient city was one of the biblical Seven Churches of Asia. St Paul's stricture on Laodicean Christianity has provided the English language with the epithet 'laodicean', meaning neither positive nor negative, neither hot nor cold. The city is situated below a hill near the village of Eskihisar, with its citadel on the hilltop. The Roman ruins include a **stadium**, **gymnasium**, **odeon** and **theatre**.

Aphrodisias

Aphrodisias stands on a low plateau under Baba Dağ, the mountain where the marble for its buildings was quarried. The site is under excavation and reconstruction, and many sections are roped off to prevent visitors from entering, nevertheless, there is much of great interest to see. From the carpark and entrance guichet (fee 5,000TL plus 5,000TL for the museum), a short roadway leads into a square that was the village of Geyre until this was demolished and the inhabitants transplanted to a new village of Geyre nearby. On the left of the square is a café and a reconstructed timbered building, and on the right, on the northeast corner, is the **museum**.

Take the path to the left just below the café. A columned structure is next to a Byzantine chapel with a number of sarcophagi. There are many of these stone coffins off the approach road to the square, and perhaps the line of the city's walls was there, with the tombs outside the walls. The pathway skirts the headquarters and workshops of the archaeological expedition to reach the **theatre**. The area is roped, but you can still climb the hill to enter the theatre at the level of its uppermost tiers, and then look down to the columned facade, dressing rooms, proscenium (stage) and orchestra. In front is a paved **court** with a **stoa**, and a **circular altar**, a **gymnasium** and, on the right-hand side, a **columned temple** or **basilica** with an **ornamental gateway**. What could be a second **agora** is there, too. All this makes an impressive view from above.

The area on the right of the theatre, as you descend, is also roped, where a large and lengthy main **agora** is under excavation and reconstruction. You move on round to another **portico**, that of Tiberius, to the area of **Hadrian's Baths**, a complex that includes a **gymnasium**, a **palaestra** (exercise ground) and a **columned pool** or **ornamental fountain**. The tiled court of the palaestra has a number of inscribed tiles in Greek.

Continuing northeasterly, past what could be an extension of the main agora, is the **Bishop's Palace**, to the east of which is an **odeon** (recital hall).

North of the palace and odeon is **Aphrodite's Temple**, along with the remains of the **Byzantine church** that superseded it, making use of the temple's columns, but adding an apse. Restoration work is on hand.

A considerable dusty open space lies between the palace and odeon and the **stadium**, which is situated on the line of the city walls on the north, and incorporated into them. It is a well-preserved stadium, and it is interesting to speculate as to why theatres and stadiums have on the whole survived in better condition than many other structures, particularly the seating, perhaps because the seating is banked, and therefore to an extent reinforced with only the superstructure suffering damage from earthquakes, assault and the erosions of time.

Sections of the **wall** are in good condition, particularly east of the stadium near a section with a **tower** and **gateway**. The location of another gateway over to the west can be noted from the stadium's upper tier.

Following the direction of the walls, again a fair, dusty distance, the **tetrapylon** (ornamental gateway) is under impressive reconstruction. Much of this area was marshy before it was drained, and between the tetrapylon and the entrance square there are several columned buildings under recovery and reconstruction to which entry is at present restricted. Much of the statuary and other excavated recoveries, certainly those of more recent excavations, are in the museum, though the gleanings of earlier excavations are in the museums of İzmir and İstanbul, particularly those of the sculpted friezes. There are many sarcophagi, some with inscriptions, along the exterior paths of the museum and in its garden areas.

Nyssa, Tralles and Magnesia on the Maeander

Nyssa is situated over a ravine of the Thymbrus, a tributary of the Maeander. A Seleucid foundation, its remains are chiefly Roman. Like Aphrodisias it seems to have been abandoned in the wake of Timur's devastations. **Byzantine walls** exist still, as well as a **Roman** *bouleuterion*, a **library**, a **theatre** and a constructed **tunnel** allowing the river to run under the town.

Tralles was inhabited by Carians when Alexander arrived there in 334 BC. Destroyed by an earthquake in 27 BC, Augustus rebuilt it. Anthemius, one of Justinian's architects in the building of Haghia Sophia in Constantinople, came

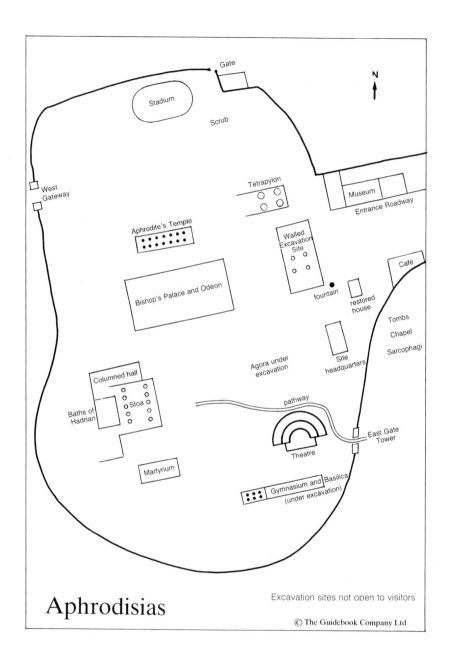

Gate

Stadium

Scrub

N

West
Gateway

Tetrapylon

Museum

Entrance Roadway

Aphrodite's Temple

Walled
Excavation
Site

Café

Bishop's Palace and Odeon

fountain

restored
house

Tombs

Chapel

Sarcophagi

Agora under
excavation

Site
headquarters

Columned hall

Stoa

Baths of
Hadrian

pathway

East Gate
Tower

Theatre

Martyrium

Gymnasium and Basilica
(under excavation)

Aphrodisias

Excavation sites not open to visitors

© The Guidebook Company Ltd

from Talles. In later history the Byzantines lost it to the Seljuks, Manuel I regained it, then lost it to the independent Emir of the Mentese. The Ottomans took it in 1389 but abandoned it after Beyazit's defeat by Timur.

Aydın is the chief city of an agriculture province noted particularly for its figs and grapes. Material from Tralles was used in the building of the 1613 **Bey Cami**. The **Cihanzade Cami** of the 1750s is considered a masterpiece of Ottoman baroque style. Aydın is also a centre of camel fighting, and the locals maintain that a camel's bared teeth are much worse than its bite.

In origin this city may have been one among the very few inland settlements of the Ionians. Magnesia supported Rome in the Mithridatic wars, and the Roman General Sulla on his victory declared it a free city. Earlier, Themistocleos, after being ostracized by his fellow Athenians in 460 BC, acquired this city as a fief from the Persian emperor and is believed to have committed suicide here. French archaeologists excavated the site in the 1840s and found sections of the Amazonian frieze of a Temple to Artemis. There are sections of **Byzantine walls** on either side of the E24 and scant remains of **temples** in the **agora**; a **theatre**, **stadium**, **gymnasium** and parts of ancient walls are on the hillside.

South Aegean Coast

In the heyday of Miletus, Lake Bafa was a sizeable sea inlet. Fishing is good still, and a few small camping and picnic areas exist on the lake's southwestern shore. The site of Heracleia, which is beneath Mount Latmos on the north-eastern side of the lake, may be approached by boat, and it is possible to visit islands with Byzantine religious fortifications. Lat, the eastern Moon-goddess, is said to have had a sanctuary at Heracleia, as did Endymion, the beautiful shepherd who became Lat's — or Selene's — lover. Mount Latmos, named after the goddess, has five peaks (or five fingers, as in the Turkish name, Beş Parmak). Rising to 1,500 metres (4,920 feet), they add to the impressiveness of the site which, more than its ruins, is likely to appeal to the adventurous tourist.

There is a Temple to Zeus among the ruins at Euromos, and another can be found at Milas. If possible, allow time for a visit to the mountain Shrine of Zeus at Labranda, at the source of more than one sacred spring. Before going on southwesterly to Bodrum, swimmers and sunbathers might like to divert for a while to Gülük, a small port on the coast, with its accompanying beaches. If you decide to go straight from Milas to Bodrum, prepare for a climbing, winding road.

Bodrum, with its impressive castle dominating the quay, has become a thriving, international yachting and tourist centre. The hub of the town has narrow streets reminiscent of a Greek island port, and in fact the predominating colour is Aegean blue.

Getting There

After visiting Didyma, travellers on foot will have to return to Söke to catch a bus to Bodrum via Milas. Remember that in Söke the minibus *otopark* and the long-distance coach *otogar* are about 600 metres (2,000 feet) apart.

If you are driving, return to the Söke road, back through Akköy, or take the road that joins the 525 from a junction about a kilometre (.6 mile) south of the Didyma temple. Turn south at the junction to run along the southwestern shore of Lake Bafa. By boarding a boat at the restaurant here, near the Türgüt Motel, you can cross to Heracleia. Or go via the southwestern shore road, a distance of ten kilometres (six miles).

Back at the southwestern side of Lake Bafa, you continue on road 525 to Milas, riding through hilly and spiky mountainous country dominated by olive trees. About 20 kilometres (12 miles) after leaving the lakeside and a ruined castle, a short way off the road on the left is Euromos. Twelve kilometres (eight miles) further on is Milas, and about 15 kilometres (ten miles) to the northeast is Labranda. Güllük is about 20 kilometres (12 miles) from Milas in the opposite direction.

It is 66 kilometres (41 miles) from Milas to Bodrum. Note that an international airport is planned for Bodrum, and this is scheduled to be opened in 1991.

Historical Background

This was Carian country, and Mausolus, the fourth-century BC king, like the Lydian Croesus, was greatly influenced by Hellenistic culture. He employed Pytheos, the Greek architect of the Temple to Athena at Priene, to design his temple and many other fine buildings, not only at Heracleia but elsewhere in his mountainous kingdom. The Romans restored the Carian city and its walls — probably destroyed in an earthquake — and in Byzantine times it became a Christian centre with monasteries, convents and anchorite cells.

Mylasa (Milas) was the seat of a satrap, or governor, during the Persian occupation of this region. Mausolus was born at Mylasa, or perhaps at what is now Peçin Kale, about three kilometres (two miles) away to the south, which was the acropolis of the ancient city.

Labranda is likely to have been a sacred site from a very early time, perhaps for the Dorian colonizers of the tenth century BC, perhaps even earlier, though the cult of Zeus Labrayndus seems to have been a particular one for the Carians.

As Halicarnassus, Bodrum was the birth place of Herodotus, the fifth-century BC Father of History. In the fourth century BC the great wonder of the city was the mausoleum built by Artemisia for her husband Mausolus, of which Pytheos may have been the architect. It was decorated with beautiful reliefs, some of which were of battle scenes. In the 19th century a number of the carved metopes from the ruins of the mausoleum were bought from the sultan by the British Ambassador, Stratford Canning, and are in the British Museum.

Alexander the Great besieged Halicarnassus and almost failed to take it. He may also have offered to marry Artemisia, sole queen at the time of his conquests. This Artemisia is not to be confused with her earlier namesake, whose reputation as a mighty warrior was confirmed at the Battle of Salamis, to which she took a naval contingent of Carians to fight alongside Xerxes.

Sights

Heracleia

Beginning at a stone arch which was the **East Gateway**, there are several **Byzantine buildings** on a protruding section to the south of it, including the remains of a **fort**, a **seminary** (or perhaps the seat of a Bishop) and, down below, some rock tombs. To the west of the gateway is a rock-cut chamber with a columned entrance that was probably a **shrine**, either to Endymion or Lat or perhaps an even earlier divinity. To the north of this, close to the village of Kapıkiri, is the **agora**, with a line of shops on the south side. West of the agora are the remains of a **Temple to Athena**. On the edge of Kapıkiri is the *bouleuterion* (council chamber) and, to the north, a **Roman baths**. East of the baths is a postern entrance in the towered ancient walls, of which a few imposing sections still stand. Now you come to the well-preserved **North Gateway**, in the vicinity of which is another shrine and, west of the gateway, the site of the **theatre**, cut out of a lower slope of the mountain. The remains of the **harbour** and **West Gate** are to the west of the temple.

On the Way to Bodrum

The second-century **Temple of Zeus** at Euromos has 17 of its Corinthian columns upright, supporting substantial portions of architrave. This temple can be a bonus for the traveller by car, set as it is in a small clearing among trees. Fallen column drums, blocks and pedestals, numbered by the archaeologists, are ready for restoration and may well be set up again in the near future. An excavated **altar** dates from a time earlier than that of the Roman temple. To the north of the temple are sections of the city's **Carian walls**, and in the former city's main area there is part of a **columned stoa** in a **Hellenistic agora**, as well as the site of a **theatre**.

Not far south of Milas at Peçin Kale are the ruins of the ancient city of Mylasa. A **Byzantine castle** now stands there, along with evidence of a **pre-Roman temple** and a 13th- or early 14th-century mosque. Modern Milas has an ancient arched gateway, the Baltalı Kapı, whose keystone is shaped like a double-headed axe. This is a Hittite symbol, and a Minoan one, too; one theory holds that the Carians may have migrated from Crete. A **Temple of Zeus** has a single fluted column. The older mosques of Milas were built in the 14th century, under the independent Moslem Emirs of Menteşe, including the **Ulu Cami** and the **Orhan**, both of the early years of that century, and the **Firuz** of 1394.

A paved sacred way once ran from Mylasa to Labranda, a roadway that is easily negotiable by car now. The site at Labranda is on the Batı Menteşe Mountains, and the shrine itself, erected by Mausolus, may have been designed by Pytheos, although this particular architect was not the only Greek artist to be employed by the king or by Artemisia, the king's sister and wife. The ruins are on several terraces, some of them Hellenistic in origin but with Roman additions.

Over on the coast is Güllük, and at Küren is the site of **Iasus**, a Carian city where the principal industry was fishing. It has been excavated by an Italian team, and among the buildings in the main section is a **theatre**. On a small

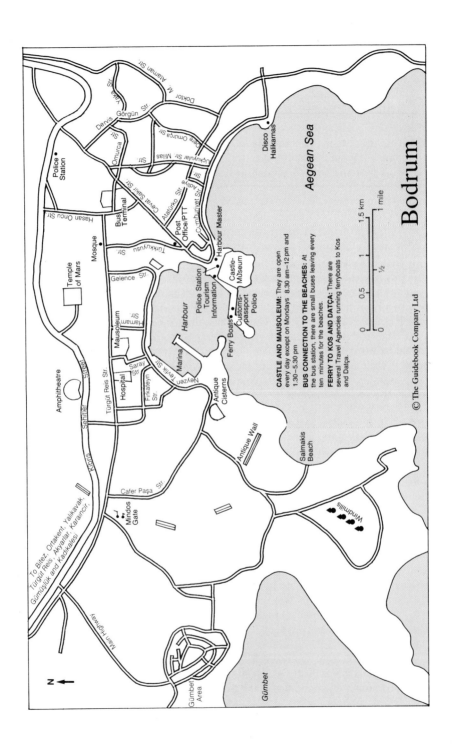

CASTLE AND MAUSOLEUM: They are open every day except on Mondays 8.30 am–12pm and 1.30–5.30 pm

BUS CONNECTION TO THE BEACHES: At the bus station, there are small buses leaving every ten minutes for the beaches.

FERRY TO KOS AND DATÇA: There are several Travel Agencies running ferryboats to Kos and Datça.

© The Guidebook Company Ltd

Bodrum

Aegean Sea

Disco Halikarnas

Police Station

Temple of Mars

Amphitheatre

Mosque

Bus Terminal

Post Office/PTT

Harbour Master

Castle-Museum

Customs-passport Police

Police Station Tourism Information

Ferry Boats

Mausoleum

Hospital

Saray Str.

Marina

Harbour

Antique Cisterns

Antique Wall

Mindos Gate

Salmakis Beach

Windmills

Gümbet Area

Gümbet

To Bitez, Ortakent, Yalikavak, Türgut Reis, Akyarlar, Karamcir, Gümüşlük and Kadikalesi

Main Highway

Sehitler Street

Kibris

Türgüt Reis Str.

Firkateyn Str.

Neyzen Tevfik Str.

Hamam Str.

Gelence Str.

Türkkuyusu Str.

Hasan Oncu Str.

Cevat Sakir Str.

Atatürko Str.

Cumhuriyet Str.

Adliye Str.

Uckuylar Str. Milas

Onurca Str.

Dere Omurca Str.

Görgün Str.

Dervis Str.

Yaka Str.

Doktor M. Alaman Str.

Cafer Paşa Str.

0   0.5   1   1.5 km

0   ½   1 mile

N

peninsula that was an island before silting attached it to the mainland, the remains of fifth century **walls** and a **mausoleum** can be seen. The coast here can be explored by boat out of Güllük.

Bodrum

Bodrum is situated on a large bay with a castle on the extreme part of its eastern arm and a yacht marina on the west. The site of the **mausoleum** (see Historical Background) is on Türgüt Reis Caddesi, above the harbour. Contemporary excavators found what they believe to be the base on which the mausoleum stood. Its underground foundations had corridors that once must have connected it to the tombs of earlier Carian kings. Above this, on the panoramic circular road, is the site of the **theatre**, which must have offered the spectators, at least those in the upper tiers, an uninterrupted view of the harbour, bay and off-shore island that partially encloses the bay.

The **Castle of St Peter** was built on a previous structure by the Knights of Rhodes but has since undergone more than one major modification and reconstruction. The knights have been accused of robbing the mausoleum of material to be used in their construction, but using material from derelict buildings must have been a fairly common practice among builders in those past ages. Archaeological remains are on display in the grounds, and the museum inside has recoveries from ancient wrecks, salvaged by mid-20th-century underwater divers and archaeologists. The knights are commemorated in a restored chapel, and towers have been constructed in Crusader style — English (Plantagenet), medieval French, Italian and German. There is a site of a **Temple of Mars** on a road that runs downhill off the panoramic highway, to the east of the theatre.

There is a bazaar-like activity in the approaches to the harbour, and, for those who prefer a less international flavour, spring or autumn might be more favourable times in which to visit. Beach development is away from the town itself, at Türgüt Reis, Torba, Güllük and other points on the coast, but the many agencies offer daily road or sea excursions to these. There is a daily service with more than one ferry to the Datça Peninsula to the south. The latter sailing takes 90 minutes by sea to Gerince, off the northern coast of the peninsula, where a minibus takes you overland to Datça on the south coast. The inclusive cost of this journey is 15,000TL, and it can be an alternative route to the journey by road back to Milas, then Muğla, on the way to Marmaris and the Mediterranean.

Mediterranean Coast

Approaching Marmaris from Muğla, the views of mountainscape and sea are beguiling, and Gökova has a long, sandy shore with the customary facilities for bathers.

If Bodrum has become internationalized over recent years, Marmaris is becoming super-internationalized. Hotel, motel and holiday complex development has extended round the entire sweep of the bay to the west of the port, a stretch of over ten kilometres (six miles). Its yacht harbour is in three sections and likely to become the largest in the Aegean and eastern Mediterrranean within a year or two. A Yacht Charter Show is held in Marmaris each May.

Datça, to the west, is a holiday centre which has two bays with sandy beaches, plus a harbour and yacht marina. The visitor may like to explore the two nearby Dorian sites of Cnidus.

On the way to Fethiye, rock-cut and sculpted tombs, a feature of the coastal cities of this region, can be seen at Caunus, a Carian city whose harbour is now below the marsh. Turkish archaeologists have excavated the Carian, Roman and Byzantine remains of the city. Nearby are hot sulphur springs, and the lake is noted for its fish and surrounding wildlife and exotic flora.

Fethiye today is a developing modern town and tourist centre, with yacht marina and harbour, good bathing beaches and accompanying holiday extensions along the shore and on the small islands in the bay. If not yet as thriving as Marmaris, it might well be in the future.

Xanthus, Lycia's principal city, and Tlos, a place of rock tombs, are two of the sites on the road going east. At Kalkan, the houses of the town cling like limpets at the base of sheer cliffs stretching above the sea's edge. With an attractive waterfront and its yacht marina, Kalkan is making a fair bid to become an agreeable holiday spot. Kaş has developed as a tourist centre, though at present on a more modest scale, with a less imperative atmosphere than that of Fethiye or Marmaris.

The Church of St Nicholas is in Kale (Demre), an unpretentious place, agreeably Turkish after the internationalized tone of the harbour towns.

Finike, situated on a coastal plain where cotton, citrus and rice are under cultivation, was rebuilt after an earthquake, and there is little of archaeological interest.

Antalya, a principal city of the western coastal region of the Mediterranean, is set on a creek on the innermost curve of the bay. The modern city is on a ridge above the ancient town. Many of the wooden houses of the latter have been reconstructed in traditional style and converted into elegant *pansiyons* (pensions). The old harbour has become a yacht marina; the new harbour is situated ten kilometres (six miles) to the west, where a mercantile and industrial centre is being developed.

Alanya is Seljuk, and the resort is dominated by the high rocky promontory surmounted by a citadel. Beyond Alanya, an arm of the Taurus Mountains makes a dash for the coast and stays there, allowing for the opening here and there of a coastal plain. Castles are a feature of Cilicia, as this coastal region is known. The town of Anamur lies about four kilometres (2.5 miles) inland from a very long shore, backed by a deep fertile valley and enclosed by mountains.

That arm of the Taurus withdraws at Silifke to rejoin its main range, which continues east at a reasonable distance, protecting the northern edge of the great Cilician Plain that stretches to the Amanus Mountains at the eastern extremity of the Mediterranean basin.

At Yümüktepe near Mersin there is evidence of settlements that are among the earliest yet found in Asia Minor. To the east is St Paul's birthplace, Tarsus. Adana is Turkey's fourth-largest city and, as with the other cities of the coast, a growing one. It is a centre of the cotton industry.

Getting There

To continue to Marmaris from Bodrum by road, return to Milas and take road 330 to Yatağan, 36 kilometres (22 miles), and turn south for Muğla, 24 kilometres (15 miles). From Muğla the road south descends to Gökova at the head of the Gökova Gulf. Continue to the junction (with road 400 that runs east to Dalaman airport and Fethiye) and take the route directly south from the junction, starting on a wide road with an avenue of eucalyptus trees alongside and continuing for 30 kilometres (19 miles) through hilly, wooded country to Marmaris.

Visitors can reach Marmaris and other centres in this southwestern corner of Anatolia by flying into Dalaman airport, near Fethiye, 62 kilometres (39 miles) away, from where the package tour companies are transporting their clients by coach to whichever location has been chosen. The *otogar* is on the east of the town, just to the north of the outermost yacht basin.

From Marmaris there is a ferry service to the Greek island of Rhodes, lying just out of sight to the southwest. Three Turkish lines operate this service, with sailings at 9 am and 5 pm each day in the holiday months. As with Bodrum and Kuşadasi, Marmaris is one of the principal ports visited by the cruise ships of Turkish Maritime Lines (Türk Denizyollari).

Road 400 runs westward from Marmaris, along the Datça Peninsula for 75 kilometres (47 miles) to Datça. It can also be reached by ferry boat from Bodrum. The best of the two ancient Cnidus sites is over a poor, mountainous road, 30 kilometres (19 miles) west of Datça.

A minimum of five days should be reckoned for a leisurely journey from Marmaris to Antalya by way of the coastal route, with an extra day if a trip along the peninsula to Datça and Knidus Harbour is intended. Wisdom might suggest yet another day if travel is to be by coach or minibus.

Heading towards Fethiye from the Gökova junction, you take road 400 southeast. After 32 kilometres (20 miles), the road by-passes Köyceğiz, where there is a lake with a sea outlet on the south. To the south and east of Köyceğiz, after 17 kilometres (11 miles), the Dalaman River forms a delta on which, near the village of Dalyan, is the Carian city of Caunus.

Dalaman airport is 14 kilometres (nine miles) southeast of Ortaca, after which the road ascends and drops through wooded, mountain scenery with occasional glimpses of peaceful isolated bays at the foot of cliffs, until it skirts the shore of the Gulf of Fethiye. Fethiye, a port of call for Turkish Maritime Lines, is 135 kilometres (84 miles) from Marmaris.

From Fethiye the road runs for 20 kilometres (12 miles) east towards Kemer, but bypasses that town to turn south above the valley of the Xanthus River, the Koca Çay, on the road to Kaş. The valley opens out on to a plain, and the road continues further south to Eşen, 26 kilometres (16 miles), and to Kînîk, 12 kilometres (eight miles), which is the place to alight for Xanthus.

Patara, at the southernmost end of the Xanthus valley, is 70 kilometres (44 miles) from Fethiye and ten kilometres (six miles) from Xanthus. Letoon, 55 kilometres (34 miles) from Fethiye and five kilometres (three miles) south and west from Xanthus, is near the village of Kümluova.

After leaving Xanthus, rejoin road 400 to continue south, then southeasterly to Kalkan. A further 26 kilometres (16 miles) along is Kaş, another port of call for the ships of Türk Denizyollari. The road from Kaş to Kale (Demre) is at first mountainous, before it descends into an alluvial plain. The distance to Kale, on the delta of the Demre Çayi, is 47 kilometres (30 miles). The cost of the bus journey is 4,000TL.

Finike, 29 kilometres (18 miles) east of Kale, is a large port on the western edge of a gulf; the ships of Turkish Maritime Lines call regularly. The bus journey from Demre to Finike costs 2,000TL. Limyra is ten kilometres (six miles) from Finike, on the edge of the plain to the north, near the small town of Zengerler. From the *otogar* at Finike you can negotiate with a taxi driver to take you there. His charge will be 25,000TL, giving you two hours on site, but if you bargain for a shorter stay on site, say, a 90-minute round trip, he is likely to accept an offer of 15,000TL. Also from Finike, an excursion could be made to Arycanda by taking the inland northern road 35 kilometres (22 miles) on the way to Elmali.

You can get to Antalya by this inland route, continuing north from Elmali to Korkuteli, and so visit the mountain site of Termessos. On the coastal route, the road from Finike continues over the coastal plain east of the town where there is tourist and holiday accommodation on long stretches of the shore. The cost of the bus journey by this route, Finike to Antalya, is 3,500TL.

At Turuncova the road begins to climb into the mountains, and continues at a level above the sea for the rest of the journey, travelling through pine-forested mountain country so that glimpses of the sea below are rare, but there are wonderful mountainscapes as the road rounds the Chelidonian Cape and runs below the majestic peaks of Phoenix, Solyma and Climax on the western arm of the Bay of Antalya.

This new road has made visits to two coastal sites less viable, except by boat from Finike or Antalya. If you happen to be travelling by your own car, at Ulupinar there is a turnoff to Olimpos (Olympos); then three or four kilometres after passing Tekirova is the turnoff to ancient Phaselis.

At Kemer the road from Finike reaches the coast — but does not run along the shoreline. Kemer, 42 kilometres (27 miles) west of Antalya, has been developed as a large international holiday centre with a yacht marina, motels, hotels and holiday villages, as well as *sitesi* (estates) or blocks of flats erected by ministries, banks and commercial and industrial enterprises for the use of their employees or by private speculators. This is a pattern that is prevalent in most coastal holiday centres in western Turkey, and long stretches of coastline are being built up in this way. Beldibi, 25 kilometres (16 miles) west of Antalya, is another such centre.

The bus to Antalya runs past the new harbour area and along Akdeniz Bulvari beside Konyaalti Beach. It turns left on the perimeter road round the city

A Rite of Passage

The Doric peninsula widens out to the group of villages and little anchorage of Datcha, where a road, with a daily bus that takes twelve hours, comes down from Marmaris, and a steamer stops once a fortnight if asked to do so. Here there was a Kaymakam, a hotel and a new school building, and a feeling of prosperity and security very different from the days of Newton, when pirates hung around and money was smuggled 'as if contraband', and people could only negotiate a bill if a mail steamer called. Yet even now it is a local and a small prosperity, not the old sea-going traffic of the ancient capital—whose walls show at the foot of the sea-hills nearby. A few scattered rowing-boats, like worn-out shoes, lay on the edge of the sands; the life was inland, and the Kaymakam offered to take us to see it in Kara Köy, a village where the road ends and the westward track begins. A feast, said he, happened that day to be celebrating the circumcision of twelve little boys.

There was an immediate easiness in the landscape when we left the sea. Carob, oleander and almond, the myrtle whose boughs are tied to the tombstones, and Vallonia oak trees with frilly acorns like ruffs—exported for tanning—filled the shallow valleys; the sharp slopes behind were dark with pines. No panthers are here, they say, but bears and wild boars. An ancient temenos stood by the road that leads to Reshidiye, the main centre of the district, a townlet of thirteen hundred souls. Kara Köy lay to the west, on higher ground. Its up-and-down houses and roofs were crowded with people, and lorry-loads were arriving all the time. Groups of women stood with clean white kerchiefs held over heads and mouths; the young men walked about behind a drum, trumpet and violin; the twelve little boys, the heroes of the day but disregarded, wandered with mixed feelings, and wore embroidered handkerchiefs and tassels stuffed with holy earth to distinguish them from the crowd. Only one of them was rich, spangled with gold coins, but not much happier for that: their moment had not yet come, and we were all intent on feasting.

D.B. sat with the Elders, and I found a circle in a harim where the food came in a more easy-going way but hotter—flaps of unleavened bread, soup, makarna (macaroni), stew, rissoles, beans, yaourt, and rice, and a sweet sticky paste: we dipped it all up from bowls set on the floor. The houses were as clean as the Swiss, their wooden cupboards and stairs were bare and scrubbed; and the people left their shoes as they came in and wiped their feet on a towel at the stair's foot. They were rough folk and mostly plain to look at, with the excellent manners of the Turkish village, the result of a sure and sound tradition handed from generation to generation, which breaks into gaiety when ceremony demands it, as an earth-feeding stream breaks into the sun.

There was a bustle now, the doctor had arrived; his razors wrapped in newspapers were laid on a packing-case; the men all crowded into the largest room as audience. A seat in the front row was placed for D.B. and another for me; the other women remained in their own room, a mother or grandmother stepping out to look round the corner when it was the turn of her child. The rich son of the house, eleven years old, was now seated in the face of all on a chair, frightened but brave; his infantile penis clipped in a sort of pliers; a wipe of disinfectant to the razor, and the moment was over: the child, with a startled look, as if the knowledge that virility has its pains were first breaking upon him, wrung his mouth in his hand to cover his cry, while the men in the room clapped, and someone outside fired a pistol; when the ceremonies were over the child was seated on a bed; visitors as they passed dropped small coins into a handkerchief laid out beside him; and the little creature was out of the harim —a man.

Freya Stark, The Lycian Shore

and enters from the north. The *otogar*, still in its old situation but expanded, is at the north end of Kazim Ozalp Caddesi. If travelling light, you are within a fair walking distance of the clock tower at the hub of the city.

To reach the site of Termessos from Antalya, you go north for six kilometres (four miles) on road 650 to the 350 junction for Korkuteli. At Güllük, 45 kilometres (28 miles), a pathway leads up from beside a café to this 1,050-metre- (3,450-feet-) high city, the mountains folding back in high crests to the north. Another half-day excursion out of Antalya, the site of Perge is 16 kilometres (ten miles) away, or two kilometres (1.25 miles) inland from Aksu. A visit to Perge could take in Aspendos, 26 kilometres (16 miles) east of Asku, since the principle sight there is the theatre. The turnoff to Aspendos is two kilometres (1.25 miles) after leaving Serik, a town on the main road. The road-way to it runs north for four kilometres (2.5 miles) to Belkis. The site of Sillyon, a city of similar foundation date to Perge, signposted four–five kilometres (three miles) beyond the Perge turnoff and eight kilometres (five miles) off the road to the north, could also be included in the itinerary.

The turnoff to Side is 32 kilometres (20 miles) east of the Aspendos junction. Side is situated on a squat peninsula. The road to it turns off the main highway, and seaside development along the coast becomes conspicuous. The road passes into the ruins to reach the parking place and *otogar*, located beside the theatre. Returning to the main road, the town of Manavgat, a large and newly developed one, also caters for tourists on a big scale. Upstream four kilometres (2.5 miles) at Selale on the Manavgat River are the Manavgat Falls, and 11 kilometres (seven miles) further east is the river's *baraj* (dam). The Manavgat River is noted for its trout.

From Manavgat, Alanya is 59 kilometres (37 miles) east. A spur of the Taurus Mountains approaches near to the coast here, leaving only a long and comparatively narrow plain. From Antalya the roadway reaches the coastline at Kizîlcot, 42 kilometres (26 miles) before Alanya, where holiday development may be said to begin. At Okurkalar, there is a section of Byzantine wall; at Alarahan, a Seljuk inn; and at Alara, a fine beach among pines, with holiday accommodation. The road crosses several rivers, and there are holiday villas and hotels at Serapsu, 12 kilometres (eight miles) from Alanya. The bus fare from Antalya to Alanya is 5,000TL.

After leaving Alanya's long shore on the way to Gazipaşa, another 46 kilometres (29 miles) along the coast, there are some attractive rock-patterned coves that are good for bathing, camping or a picnic. After Gazipaşa the road to Anamur, covering 80 kilometres (50 miles), is among the most exciting of mountain drives if you have a preference for looking up to high peaks and down sheer heights to remote, rocky and sandy coves gently washed by sea.

The road from Anamur recommences its mountain journey, mounting and descending through forested slopes of tall pines. From the Kösk River the road

climbs again to descend to bays at Sipahili, Yanisli and Büyükçekeli, where there is a developed *plaj* and camping. Silifke is several kilometres inland north of Taşucu. The *otogar* is on the outskirts of town on a roundabout where all the principal roads converge. Depart from here to visit the site of Uzuncaburç, 30 kilometres (19 miles) in the mountains to the north.

Mersin is 84 kilometres (52 miles) from Silifke. For most of that length the coast has been developed for tourism, to the detriment of at least part of its historical heritage. Some previous remains seem to have disappeared as a consequence of road building and reconstruction, even though the relics may have been transferred from site to museum. Holiday camps, motels, hotels and blocks of holiday flats have impinged irrevocably on the rocky coast with its coves and sandy stretches.

There are several key places, however, where a short stop can be made, particularly if you happen to be travelling by car. This is more difficult if you are making use of public transport, but travel in Turkey in this way is remarkably flexible, and a minibus will set you down at whatever place you have chosen. After you have seen the site, you need only stand by the roadside to hail a passing minibus to carry you to your next chosen stop. The *otogar* in Mersin is about five kilometres (three miles) on the east side of the city, where its hotels and restaurants are located.

To reach Tarsus, continue 30 kilometres (19 miles) east of Mersin. Road 750, the E5, which is the main highway from Ankara through to Antakya, passes through the Cilician Gates of the Taurus Mountains at Dulek, to the north of Tarsus, and reaches the coast five kilometres (three miles) east of Tarsus.

Adana is 37 kilometres (23 miles) east of Tarsus, on a dual carriageway that runs from the west of Mersin.

The E5 crosses the Ceyhan River by a Byzantine bridge, 25 kilometres (16 miles) east of Adana. On the west bank is the village of Misis. By taking a road south from Ceyhan, 24 kilometres (15 miles) after Misis, your journey could include a visit to Yumurtalik.

East of Ceyhan the E5 arrives at Toprakkale, a 12th-century castle of the Armenians. To the east is the barrier of the Amanus Mountains, and here the E5 turns south down the eastern shore of the Mediterranean. At Iskenderun the E5 climbs out by way of the Belen Pass (The Syrian Gates) leading to Antakya. It is another 30 kilometres (20 miles) southwest of Antakya, along the Valley of the Orontes, to the Mediterranean and Samandağ.

Historical Background

Marmaris in ancient times was Physeus, a member of the Rhodian confederacy. The patron goddess of new Cnidus was Aphrodite. Praxiteles, the most famous Greek sculptor of the time, created Aphrodite in all her beauty and voluptuousness; her nakedness stirred up controversy regarding propriety in a goddess. The statue, it seems, had in fact been commissioned by Kos, whose embarrassed elders subsequently, and prudishly, rejected the completed work of art for a clothed statue. Aphrodite's presence at new Cnidus, though, gave a fillip to that city's economy by encouraging tourism among prurient as well as art-loving visitors from all over the ancient world.

A recumbent lion, once the protector of a tomb near the lighthouse, long ago became a resident of the British Museum. When Sir Charles Newton, the 19th-century British archaeologist, dug here, he discovered a cult image of a Demeter of the fourth century BC in a sacred precinct near a cliff. This goddess may have been patroness of a pre-Dorian site, although multiplicity of gods and godesses was the order of the day rather than the exception in those times. Demeter, a seated figure, is in the British Museum.

Eudoxus, the Greek fourth-century BC astronomer and geometer, was from Cnidus. He studied in Egypt. A building in new Cnidus, above the houses, has been designated the site of his observatory, from which he studied the star Canopus.

Fethiye, founded in the fourth-century BC, was ancient Telmessos of Lycia, standing on a bay within a gulf. A fortified island in the bay was inhabited once by the Snake-men of Telmessos, seers of the Hellenistic world. Earthquakes of 1846 and 1957 destroyed almost all the maritime remains of the ancient city.

At the siege of Troy the Lycians were King Priam's most faithful allies; their leader was Sarpedon, the grandson of Bellerophon, a legendary hero. Bellerophon killed his own brother and another young man in Corinth, and King Proetus sent him to Tiryns. At Tiryns the hero rejected the advances of Anteia, the king's wife, and in anger she lied to her husband, putting the guilt on Bellerophon. The king, too cowardly to act, sent Bellerophon to Iobates of Xanthus, father of Anteia, with a sealed message instructing Iobates to have him killed. The king, however, set Bellerophon a number of formidable tasks, one of which was the killing of the dreaded Chimaera. As with Heracles, Bellerophon completed his tasks successfully. After he became king, Bellerophon rode his winged horse Pegasus up to the Oympian Heights where Zeus, angered by this presumption, threw him down and Bellerophon landed in a thorn bush and became lame and blind. Zeus kept Pegasus as a pack-horse to carry his thunderbolts.

Given the quantity of the tombs in these Lycian cities, the inhabitants seem to have had a preoccupation with death. On one occasion the Xanthians chose to commit mass suicide rather than surrender their freedom: when Harpagus the Persian attacked the city in the sixth century BC, the male Xanthians first killed their families and then went out to their own deaths.

Alexander occupied Xanthus, and after his death it came under Seleucus' control. During the Roman civil wars that followed the assassination of Caesar, Brutus recruited Lycians from Xanthus for his army and levied heavy taxes on the citizens, but later he became so dismayed by the self-destructive tendencies of the Xanthians that he sent ambassadors to plead with them to desist from razing their own city. Under Hadrian (117–38) Lycia prospered and continued to do so throughout Byzantine times and until the Arab conquests of the seventh century.

Kale is Demre, Demre was Myra, a Lycian city that enjoyed capital status at one time. In Christian times it became a bishopric. Believed to have been born at Patara, St Nicholas — patron saint of children and sailors — whom legend turned into Santa Klaus (Father Christmas), was a bishop here. He was martyred during a persecution of Diocletian (284–305) and was buried in his church, but in the 11th century his bones were filched by Italian sailors from Bari, an Italian port where an annual festival of St Nicholas is held. His church at Demre (Myra) was rebuilt by the Byzantines.

Olympos was a wealthy city in the second century BC. Above the city on the heights the Chimaera, the fire-breathing dragon whom Bellerophon mastered, had its lair. Its ghost may still haunt the forest: mariners have sworn, even in recent times, that they have seen its flame, however diminished in intensity by age.

In origin a seventh-century BC city, Phaselis had three harbours and was famed for its shipbuilding. Its citizens greeted Alexander with a golden crown, unable maybe to fulfil their boast — unlike the men of Xanthus — of being absolute freedom lovers and thereby fighting to the death rather than submit to an alien conqueror.

Attaleia (Antalya) was founded by the Attalids of Pergamum in the third century BC, but it became Roman in 133 BC when bequeathed to Rome by Attalus III, the last king of Pergamum. The Byzantines strengthened the walls against the Arab attacks of the seventh and subsequent centuries and again in the tenth century under Constantine VII Porphyrogenitus, still it fell to the Seljuk Keyhüsrev in 1207. Taken from an independent emir in 1391, it became the first Ottoman port on the Mediterranean. At the conclusion of the First World War, the Italians, under the Treaty of Sevres, occupied Antalya along with the southwestern region of Anatolia, but relinquished their claim after Atatürk's repudiation of that treaty and his successful establishment of the Turkish Republic.

Though Hellenistic by adoption, the Pisidians of Termessos, a tough mountain people, defied Alexander with such determination that he cancelled his intended siege and departed. In early Byzantine times it was the seat of a bishop, but there is mystery later, with little apparent evidence of occupation after the fifth century, certainly not Arabic, Seljuk, emir or Ottoman. Perge was probably founded by immigrants from the Greek mainland and islands during those early migrations of the first millennium or perhaps even by Achaeans after the Greek victory of Troy. The period of the city's greatest prosperity seems to have been during the time of the Persian occupation, ending with Alexander's conquests in Pamphylia.

The city's elders agreed to accommodate Alexander when he arrived in Aspendos. They gave him horses that were intended for Darius, the Persian ruler, with whom they had a contract for the regular rearing and supply of such. After Alexander went on his way, though, the elders repudiated their agreement and prepared for a siege by strengthening the walls and by bringing into the city all those citizens employed outside it. Characteristically, Alexander was too quick for the schemers and his sudden about-turn found him camped again on the Eurymedon. The elders hardly hesitated over a new capitulation, but this time Alexander took hostages and doubled the amount of levy previously agreed as a contribution to the maintenance of his army. In general, the Aspendians seem to have been unneighbourly as well as perfidious, since Alexander established a court to deal with complaints made by nearby cities, charging that the Aspendians had filched areas of land from them.

The city's founders probably were Ionian or Aeolian, or colonists from Cyme on the Aegean coast, who founded Side further to the east. After the Seleucids (Alexander's successors here), the city along with almost all of Pamphylia became part of the Pergamene kingdom. Eventually, it became part of the Attalid legacy to Rome, though the Romans no doubt would have conquered it as a matter of course. As Byzantine power weakened in Asia Minor, Aspendos lost its status, as did the other cities of this coast.

With Athena as their protector, people from Aeolian Cyme colonized an already settled city at Side about 600 BC. Side is a pre-Aeolian dialect word for pomegranate, and fifth-century BC coins of the region have the helmeted Athena Nike on one side and a pomegranate on the other. Side became a flourishing port but also the main hangout for pirates and a notorious centre of the slave trade. Side stayed prosperous until the arrival of the Seljuk Turks in the 11th century, after which it seems to have lost not only its trade but its inhabitants. In 1895 a new village was established to house Moslem immigrants from Crete.

Alanya was known to the Romans and Byzantines as Coracesium. Antony gave it to Cleopatra. Alaeddin Keykubat (1225), Seljuk Sultan of Konya, chose it as his winter residence and extended and reinforced the Byzantine walls.

A medieval Armenian kingdom existed in Cilicia during the time of the Crusades, and the Armenians, from whom the Crusaders learned much, were accomplished builders. The knights took over existing castles, rebuilding or modifying them, and constructed new ones.

The German Emperor Frederick Barbarossa, a leader in the Third Crusade, was drowned in the Calycadnus River which flows through Silifke in 1130. He fell from his horse in mid-stream, an ominous portent for the success of the Crusade: his vital contingent, depleted by sickness and desertions, foundered before it reached the Holy Land.

The river at Tarsus, the Cydnus, nearly finished Alexander when he impetuously took a dip: the water had been rendered icy by the melting snows of the Taurus Mountains. Justinian rebuilt the bridge that still spans the stream. Romantic legend says that Cleopatra sailed up the river in her royal barge, but experts claim it could never have been so navigable. Silting has done its work well here, for now an extensive forest, wherein the wild boar is hunted in season, stretches away to the south.

A Hittite inscription from Karatepe, northeast of Adana, identifies Adana as the capital of an eighth-century BC Hittite kingdom whose king had suzerainty over other Hittite rulers in Cilicia. Hethoumian kings of the Middle Ages established the Lesser Armenian Kingdom here, with Tarsus, Adana and Mamistra as sister cities. During the Crusades some Frankish leaders chose to stay in Cilicia rather than pursue their spiritual intention of recovering the Holy Land. In 1919 the region, known as the Hatay, came under the French Mandate for Syria but was returned to Turkey by agreement in 1938.

Anazarbus succeeded Tarsus as the principal city of the Cilician Plain when caravan trade switched from an east–west to a south–north direction up the line of the Pyramus (Ceyhan) River. Justinian rebuilt it. Centuries later it became a subject of dispute between the Byzantines and the Armenians, Christian allies against the Saracens, but a compromise solution left it in the hands of the Roupenians. The Armenians supported the Mongol Khan against

Baibars, the Mameluke Sultan of Egypt, and when Baibars overran Cilicia after expunging the Latin Kingdom of Antioch, he took his revenge by sacking the Cilician cities, putting the men to the sword and taking the women and children into slavery.

If the port of Yumurtalik, south of Adana, was Ayas, and the other Ayas to the east of Mersin seems too distant somehow, it became important after the fall of Antioch to the Moslems. Marco Polo was marooned at Ayas while a war raged in Syria, and pirates were active on the seas. Merchants of Venice, Genoa and Pisa had their warehouses at Ayas.

The Plain of Issus is remembered as the site of Alexander's battle with Darius. Some historians claim that the battle was actually fought on the banks of the river at Payas. Payas, too, may have been Ayas. The Ottomans revived Payas in the 16th century, and it became important in the eastern spice trade. After the battle Alexander founded the city of Alexandria by Issus at the head of the present Gulf of İskenderun. Under the French mandate after the end of the First World War, it was called Alexandretta.

Diocletian built the bridge over the Orontes at Antakya (Antioch). This was once the most jovial city in Christendom: the island in the Orontes River was a Coney Island plus Las Vegas in its day, with the Roman Empire's most notorious courtesans having their villas in the hill suburb of Daphne.

Seleucus founded the city, and later Pompey acquired it for Rome, declaring it a free city. The earliest Christian community (or church) is thought to have been started here by St Peter. St Paul later directed the community when he and Barnabus went there, and in the early centuries of Christianity its patriarch was a rival to those of Alexandria and Constantinople. Heraclius recaptured Antioch from the Persians in the seventh century, though it fell to the Arabs soon afterwards. It came into Christian hands again with the Latin Crusaders of the 12th century, remaining Christian then for 175 years. In 1516 Selim I took Syria and Egypt, and the Ottomans then held Antioch until Turkey's defeat in the First World War. When the French mandate was relinquished by agreement in 1938, Antioch (along with the Hatay region) became Turkish again.

Legend has it that when Seleucus was sacrificing to Zeus on the site under Mount Cassius that he had chosen for his city, an eagle swooped down, snatched up the sacrificial animal and dropped it on the northern tip; Seleucus saw this as a sign to build his city there. Later, a successor decided that Antioch's site was by far the better one for a city, and Samandağ became its port. This was the last place from which the Latins were able to make their escape as Baibars overran the Latin Kingdom.

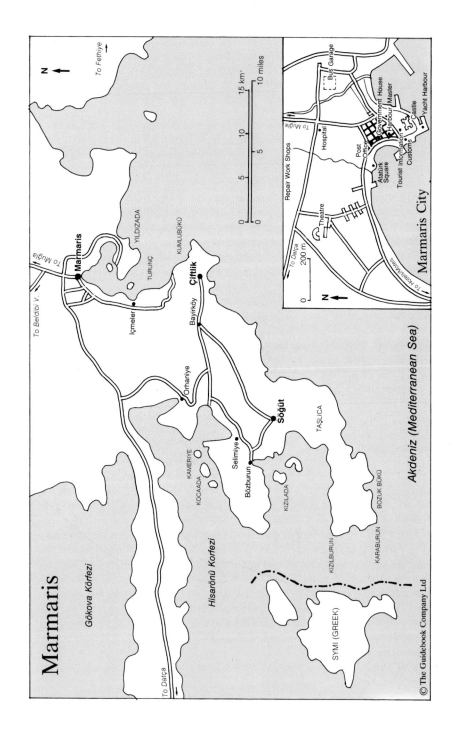

Marmaris

Gökova Körfezi

Hisarönü Körfezi

To Datça

To Beldibi V.

To Muğla

To Fethiye

Marmaris

İçmeler

TURUNÇ

YILDIZADA

KUMLUBÜKÜ

Bayırköy

Çiftlik

Orhaniye

KAMERIYE

KOCAADA

Selimiye

Bözburun

Söğüt

TAŞLICA

KIZILADA

KIZILBURUN

KARABURUN

BOZUK BÜKÜ

SYMI (GREEK)

Akdeniz (Mediterranean Sea)

0 5 10 15 km

0 5 10 miles

Marmaris City

Repair Work Shops

Bus Garage

To Muğla

Hospital

Theatre

To Datça

Atatürk Square

Post Office

Tourist Information

Customs

Government House

Harbour Master

Castle

Yacht Harbour

To Holmasköis

0 200 m

N

N

Sights

Around Marmaris

As Mobolla, Muğla was the principal residence of the Menteşe emirs. Its oldest mosque is the 14th-century **Uç Erenler**.

The **castle** at the centre of Marmaris dates from the time of Süleiman the Magnificent in the 16th century. It has been restored and refurbished, and it is now the town **museum**. The area around it, the old market, is a pedestrian precinct, with restaurants in the bazaar arcades, streets of boutiques — leather and suede goods are a speciality — and narrow walkways with beer houses and discos. The Ministry of Tourism Information Office is close to the old quay.

Besides climbing to the remains of the acropolis situated on a hill north of the town, you may like to take a boat to ancient sites in the area. On the Bözburun peninsula that stretches into the Hisarönü Gulf towards the Greek island of Symi (Sömbeki in Turkish) there are sites at **Kumlukübü** and the small port of Bözburun. On the tip of the latter are the ruins of Loryma with its ancient harbour and castle. Another excursion starts by road to Gökova on the Gökova Gulf, and then continues by boat to Sedir Island, known now for romantic reasons as Cleopatra's Island. Here is ancient Cedrai with its **walls**, **theatre** and **temples**.

There are some small hotels and a legion of pensions in Datça, and *tatil köyü* (holiday villages) are along the shore towards Petya on the town's east side, where considerable new development is taking place. In the Petya area, a kilometre (.6 mile) from the present centre of Datça, is the first of the two Dorian sites of Cnidus; a later settlement is located at present-day Knidus Harbour on the extreme west end of this peninsula.

There is little of old Cnidus left to see at Petya, except substantial sections of seawalls, some sections of land walls, a few filled-in experimental archaeological shafts, scattered pottery sherds and a light-house on a rocky islet.

New Cnidus, at Knidus Harbour, has much more to offer. **Aphrodite's Temple** is circular in shape; the cult image itself has not been found. Among the other remains are a well-preserved **theatre** and an **odeon**. An extensive **necropolis** of free-standing tombs is outside the walls and along the approach road to the city. The Ministry of Culture's Information Office in Datça organizes a daily trip to Knidus Harbour, starting at 9 am and returning at 5 pm each day. The cost of the trip is 30,000TL.

Fethiye

Telmessos was established here in the fourth century BC. The elaborately carved **tombs** and sarcophagi (massive stone coffins with heavy lids) can be

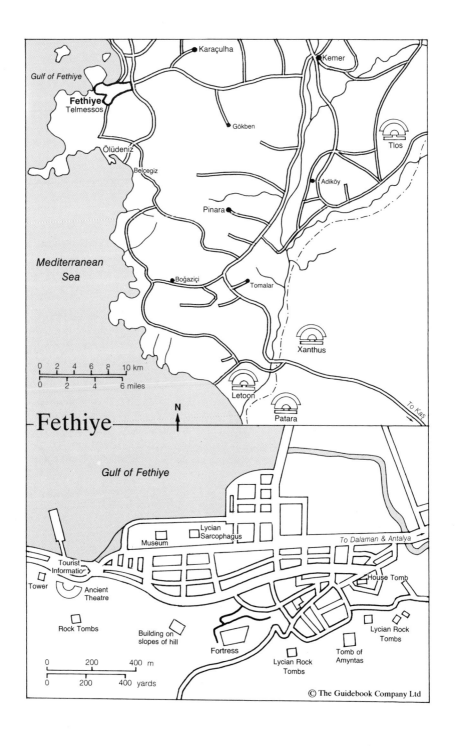

Karaçulha

Kemer

Gulf of Fethiye

Fethiye
Telmessos

Gökben

Ölüdeniz

Tlos

Belcegiz

Adiköy

Pinara

Mediterranean
Sea

Boğaziçi

Tomalar

Xanthus

0 2 4 6 8   10 km
0   2   4   6 miles

Letoon

To Kaş

N

Patara

Fethiye

Gulf of Fethiye

Lycian
Sarcophagus

Museum

To Dalaman & Antalya

Tourist
Information

House Tomb

Tower

Ancient
Theatre

Rock Tombs

Lycian Rock
Tombs

Building on
slopes of hill

Fortress

Tomb of
Amyntas

0   200   400 m
0   200   400 yards

Lycian Rock
Tombs

seen in the cliff-face at the rear of the town. Take Eski Mezarlik Sokak, a road going inland from the waterfront about one kilometre (.6 mile) from the Ministry of Tourism's Information Office, leading to Amyntas Yolu which winds up along the rocky escarpment. The tombs were carved out of the rockface, and three main ones have had steps cut up to them. The inscribed **Amyntas Tomb**, the most impressive, had its entrance carved in the Ionic order, while its gateway, doorways and chamber were modelled on a timbered Lycian building. Not far from these tombs is a **fortress** which dates perhaps from the fourth century BC but may have been occupied and modified during the Crusades. There are many **column tombs** in its neighbourhood.

Following the roadway back to the centre, you will see a typical small **Lycian tomb** standing in the roadway, and below this the ruins of others and then what may have been the **town's wall**. In the centre of town are something like 16 sacrophagi, 15 of the Roman period, but near the post office is a **Lycian tomb** of the fourth century BC, with carvings of city life and battle scenes.

Çalış beach, four kilometres (2.5 miles) to the west, with its accommodation, camping and restaurants, and the island of Sovalye opposite are good for bathing. Motor-boat transport is available. A mountain road can take you to Belceğiz Bay, to the south. There are mountain guesthouses on the way and camping facilities on the shores of the bay, with the lagoon-like water of Ölüdeniz particularly attractive.

With Fethiye as a centre, excursions can be made to the historical sites of Xanthus, 60 kilometres (37 miles) away, Letoon, 55 kilometres (34 miles), and Patara, 70 kilometres (44 miles). The local offices of principal travel agencies are able to arrange for daily tours to one or more of these.

Xanthus and Tlos

A tomb at Tlos, near the village of Doğer beneath Mount Akdağ, 45 kilometres (28 miles) from Fethiye, has a carving of Bellerophon on Pegasus attacking a wild beast, and the tomb is believed to belong to the hero. Among the Roman ruins of Tlos, there are an **agora**, **baths** and a **fort**. Tlos gets a mention in Hittite records, and the Hittites might well have been here: the symbol of the moon appears on both Hittite and Lycian coins.

Xanthus's archaeological treasures, the recoveries of an expedition of 1842, are in the British Museum. A French team excavated here in the 1950s, uncovering among other items a number of **pillar tombs**, a form of burial almost exclusive to this city. The **Harpies Tomb** has elaborate carvings and is so called because of the subject matter of the main relief. On top of another pillar stands a second structure, a hypogea or temple-like building, perhaps set there after the first tomb had become almost totally buried by earth. Plaster reproductions of particular carved metopès have been set up *in situ* to replace the originals.

The pillar tombs are to the west of a **Roman theatre** of Hadrian's day. North of the theatre is the **Roman agora**, built over an earlier one. At the northeast corner a pillar or obelisk tomb has a Lycjan inscription; the carved frieze from it is in the Archaeological Museum in Istanbul. The acropolis hill, south of the theatre, has the remains of a **palace** and ruins of a **temple**, with a cistern below it. At the southwest corner a terrace overlooks the river valley. Many cut-out tombs exist on the **necropolis**, outside the city walls to the northeast, and west of the burial ground is a **Byzantine monastery** and another temple site.

The **Nereid Monument**, so called because of its carvings, stands in the south of the city; its sculpted decoration is in the British Museum. A **Roman arch**, near the **South Gate**, has a dedication to Vespasian (69–78). The parking area for the site is here, and near the theatre, east of the parking area, is a second **agora**, and east again a **Byzantine church** in basilica form.

Patara and Letoon

Patara was the port for Xanthus. On the roadway into the site from Ovagelmiş is a triple-arched **Roman gate** and, off to the left, a **baths**. Further along the track is a basilica-style church and then the **Baths of Vespasian**. West towards the shore is the **theatre**, and on top of the hill into which the theatre is built is a large cistern. North of the theatre, between the trackway and the former **harbour**, is the **Roman temple** of Hadrian's time, and alongside the harbour is a **Roman granary**.

Letoon has a **Leto Sanctuary** and **temples** to Artemis and Apollo, Leto's children. The site is under excavation.

Kaş

Kaş was Lycian Antiphellus, harbour of Phellus. It is situated on a bay at the base of a mountain, within a narrow gulf. If you have arrived by bus, go down about 500 metres (1,600 feet) to the waterfront and turn right to follow along Hastane Caddesi where there is a section of the **city wall** of the Hellenistic period. On the waterfront side there are old houses along the line of the walls that have been converted into pensions. Over a kilometre (.6 mile) along, above the roadway on the right is a sixth-century BC Greek-style **Theatre of Psellus**. A Lycian structure, modified in later Hellenistic and Roman times, it has been partly reconstructed. The **agora** was alongside the theatre. There is now only one structure among present-day houses that may stand as evidence of it. North of the theatre is a **tomb** known as the Doric because of its facade. It has a passageway surrounding the interior; its carved relief is of maidens dancing.

Turning right on the waterfront, after moving down from the *otogar*, you come to the harbour, which has a **Lycian tomb** on the quayside. There are other rock-cut tombs in the rockface above the harbour. The Greek island of Castelorizo, the most easterly of Greek possessions, lies offshore here and can be visited. An agency on the waterfront, beyond the restaurants, has a one-day excursion that includes visits to Patara, the island of Kekova (the sunken city), Letoon and Xanthus, starting at 9.30 am and returning at 6.30 pm; the cost is 15,000TL.

Kekova Island, an elongated island whose sound is a perfect haven for yachtsmen, is off the coast to the southeast. Its ancient name was Cistene-Dolochiste, and the submerged town of Tersane is a good place for swimming. On the mainland, opposite the town of Kekova, is the walled town of Aperlae, whose castle, houses and necropolis are seen to best advantage from the sea.

Demre (Myra)

Walk back from the *otogar* towards a square and take the turning on the left. There are some pensions in and near the square. Along the street there are small simple restaurants, and further on, about 500 metres (1,600 feet), is the **Church of St Nicholas**; entrance costs 5,000TL. It is a substantial and imposing Byzantine structure as befits such a renowned and well-remembered saint and benefactor. It is in a good state of preservation, has undergone some rebuilding and may have been put to use as a *han* (inn) at one period.

The ruins of Myra are two kilometres (1.25 miles) away. From the street with the church, turn left in the square and continue on that road. A taxi will take you to Myra for 2,500TL, and for 4,000TL will wait while you visit the site and bring you back. At present there is no entrance fee. You take a path beside some tourist boutiques to the **theatre**, again a remarkably well-preserved building of Roman design, with part of its erect façade and its arched side entrances to the proscenium. There is a double stairway to the **upper gallery**, and on a plaque behind the upper tier of seating is a carved figure with an inscription in Greek.

The cliff above the theatre has its quota of burial niches and tombs, and on its summit are the remains of Byzantine fortifications, including a castle wall and, below it, a section of the outer wall. Tombs on another part of the cliff are the **Painted Tomb** and the **Lion Tomb**, notable for their carvings. On the left of the road back to Kale (Demre) is a vaulted **Byzantine structure** with arched sections.

If you have decided on a short stay at Demre, there are beaches in the vicinity such as **Sülüklü Plaj**, two kilometres (1.25 miles) away, **Taşdibi**, seven kilometres (four miles) east, **Çayağzi Plaj**, 3.5 kilometres (two miles) south, and **Kum İskelesi Plaj**, three kilometres (less than two miles) southeast.

Finike and Limyra

The Alakir Çayî flows into the sea at Finike, and if you stroll into town from the *otogar*, past an interesting mosque, you are almost bound to run into Akil Kildir, an insurance agent and tourist shop proprietor. He was helpful to John Marriner, who sailed here 20 years ago and wrote *Journey Into The Sunrise*, a book about this southwestern region of the Mediterranean coast.

In Limyra, the **theatre** is off the road to the left as you enter the site area. Dated 141, it is another structure in a good state of preservation, with the upper gallery intact, though the façade has gone. It was built by a wealthy citizen, Opramoas, who made similar donations in more than one city of this coast. Close to the theatre is the site of a **temple** and a well. Above the theatre, on the escarpment, was the **acropolis**, with many **Lycian-style tombs** outside the walls on the hillside. Two notable tombs of Limyra are those of Catabura of the fourth century BC and Tabersele of an earlier date. On the main site is the *Heroon* (shrine) **of Pericleos**, a local ruler and not the famous one of Athens. The reliefs from this high-walled structure are in the Antalya Museum.

Go on beyond the theatre to arrive at the main site, on the right of the road. Flowing through this site is a cool stream, turning among rushes and past areas of fresh-looking grass. On a hot day you can take shelter beside it under a shady tree. A German archaeological team is at work excavating and reconstructing a **temple** in the area of the **agora**. There are many remains of Byzantine buildings, as well as substantial sections of the city walls. Among the structures is a **Roman baths**, and another **baths** here may be early Ottoman.

Fifth-century BC Arycanda is located in forested and mountainous country, and water for the **baths** came from a nearby waterfall. East of the baths is a **gymnasium** and, as with all Lycian sites, there are the tombs. Excavations are being accomplished by a Turkish archaeological team from İstanbul.

Olimpos (Olympos) has a **Genoese harbour**, a ruined **Byzantine bridge** and Genoese and Byzantine **fortresses**. A **temple** on the heights is dedicated to Haephaestos.

Antalya

On the ridge there are sections of the city wall still and Hadrian's Gate, the entry into the old town. The most conspicuous monument within the walls is the **Yivli Minare**, the ribbed or fluted minaret, built by Seljuk Sultan Alaeddin Keykubat (1219–36) when he converted an accompanying church to a mosque. Near this minaret is the **Karatay Medrese**, a theological school of Seljuk construction (1250) with geometrical decoration and a restored doorway in traditional stalactite pattern. This stands above the harbour on a paved terrace with trees, along with the Atatürk Memorial to the west. Down some

Farming at Incirkay, Fethiye

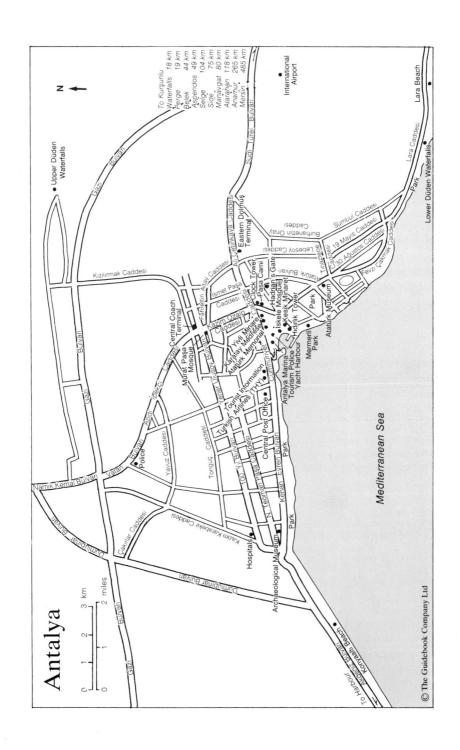

Antalya

0 1 2 3 km
0 1 2 miles

N

© The Guidebook Company Ltd

Mediterranean Sea

Upper Düden
Waterfalls

To Kurşunlu
Waterfalls   18 km
Perge   19 km
Belek   44 km
Aspendos   49 km
Selge   104 km
Side   75 km
Manavgat   80 km
Alarahan   118 km
Anamur   265 km
Mersin   485 km

International
Airport

Lara Beach

Lara Caddesi

Park

Lower Düden Waterfalls

Gazi Bulvarı

Sütlü Turel Bulvarı

Kızılırmak Caddesi

Ali Çetinkaya Caddesi

Eastern Dolmuş
Terminal

Burhanettin Onay
Caddesi

Sümbül Caddesi

19 Mayıs Caddesi

30 Ağustos Caddesi

Lebesoy Caddesi

Fevzi Çakmak Caddesi

Atatürk Bulvarı

Tınaztepe

İsmet Paşa Caddesi

Paşa Cami

Hadrian's Gate

Kesik Minaret

Hıdırlık Tower

İskele Mosque

Park

Atatürk Museum

Clock Tower

Kazım Özalp Caddesi

Yivli Minare

Karatay Medresesi

Atatürk Memorial

Mermerli
Park

Antalya Marina
Tourism Police
Yacht Harbour

Cumhuriyet

Fahrettin Altay Caddesi

Central Coach
Terminal

Murat Paşa
Mosque

Yenal Ulusoy Bulvarı

Tourist Information

Turkish Airlines (THY)

Central Post Office

İpekçi Caddesi

Abdi

Gazi
Bulvarı

Bulvarı

Police

Yavuz Caddesi

Tonguç Caddesi

100 Yıl Bulvarı

N Teoman Paşa Caddesi

Kenan Evren Bulvarı

Park

Namik Kemal Bulvarı
Vatan

Kazım Karabekir Caddesi

Çakırlar Caddesi

Archaeological Museum

Hospitals

Dumlupınar Bulvarı

Gazi Bulvarı

To Konyaaltı Beach

To Harbour

steps near the memorial is a park, in which the Ministry of Tourism Office is located.

On the south of the old town the **Kesik Minaret** is attached to a fifth-century converted church which was built on the site of a Roman temple. The minaret lost its top in a storm of 1851, but reconstruction work seems to be replacing the lost crown. On the southernmost height of the old town is the **Hildirlik Kulesi**, a tower of an early but unknown date. It may have been constructed as a lighthouse.

From the main crossroads just east of the **clock tower**, a broad avenue, Atatürk Caddesi, with a double line of palm trees on its centre spine, starts off southerly and then curves round to the east. About 50 metres (165 feet) from the crossroads is **Hadrian's Gate**, with towered bastions on either side, one tower on the north and two on the south. The three arches of the gate have companion columns with their capitals. The area on the interior of the gate has been refashioned as a pedestrian enclave. Besides this main entrance to the old town, it can also be entered by taking a downward street on the corner opposite the clock tower, where the **Paşa Cami** is situated. There are sections of old walls along Atatürk Caddesi, and where it turns east is the main entrance to Mermerli Park (formerly İnönü Park) on the west side. By walking down the main avenue of the park, you reach a southern terrace from where there is an unrestricted view of Antalya Bay and, on a clear cool day, the great mountains on its western arm.

On the left of the entrance to Mermerli Park is the **Atatürk Museum**. The **Archaeological Museum** is on Kenan Evren Bulvari, about a kilometre (.6 mile) along. This is a wide avenue that runs westward from the clock tower and eventually connects with the coastal Akdeniz Bulvari. The museum has a fine collection of recoveries from sites in the vicinity.

By going south from the paved square at the park entrance, past the modern stadium, you make your way to Lara Beach, a bathing and holiday centre, 12 kilometres (eight miles) out of town. About a quarter of the way there, the Lower Düden Falls spill into the sea; the Upper Falls are 14 kilometres (nine miles) to the northeast. The minibus *otopark* for continuing a journey eastward is near a roundabout at the east end of Cumhuriyet Caddesi (on which the clock tower stands) and the beginning of Ali Çetinkaya Caddesi.

There are two mosques of interest, the 16th-century **Murat Paşa Cami**, close to the *otogar*, and the earlier İskele Cami on the harbour quay.

For hotels there is the five-star luxury-class Talya, and there are several in the lower categories, such as the three-star Büyük Oteli (Grand Hotel) on the terrace just to the east of the Atatürk Memorial. Besides the pensions in the old town, there are good, if less ostentatious, ones, such as the White House, in an area of narrow streets on the east side of Kazim Ozalp Cadesi, south of the *otogar*.

Termessos

This Pisidian site in the mountains to the west of Antalya can be visited on a
one-day or half-day excursion. The climb up the path is a long one and sometimes breathtaking. Semi-nomads make use of the site in summer months, and
herds of goats are pastured here.

The remains of the city's outer walls, which run up and down the slopes,
and the **Roman gateway** are a climbing distance still from a central **agora** of
Arcadian aspect. The site's principal buildings are signposted and identified,
even if the various land levels and entangling undergrowth make it difficult to
approach some buildings— the **baths**, **gymnasium**, **temple** and **theatre**.
Carved metopes of bird, beast and fish are among the fallen stones in the agora
due, one day, to be set up or perhaps removed to Antalya's museum.

The Pisidians seem to have been as tomb-conscious as their Lycian neighbours: the necropolis has giant sarcophagi, and the high northern cliff is rid-
dled with burial chambers. A wall encloses the valley at its high, narrow point,
and on a cliff wall on the left side is a sentry walk.

Perge

There is a lower town in the plain and a walled acropolis. On entering the site,
the first major building is a Greek-style **theatre** on the west side. Set into the
flank of a hill, it held 15,000 people and served as yet another rendezvous for
St Paul, who preached here. The Emperor Trajan (98–117) has the credit for
restoring it. A little to the north of the theatre is the **stadium**, where the vaulted
foundations and the area for the shops are in good condition still, particularly
on the east side. An arched gallery runs behind the topmost seating.

A long, paved and **colonnaded street** traverses the site from the **south
entrance**, running through the walls to a **Hellenistic gateway** between ruined
towers and on to the **acropolis gateway**. This street is crossed at its northern
end by another, also paved, on which there were shops. The **agora**, to the right
of the first gateway with the towers, had a columned **portico** or **stoa** surrounding it. Just to the left, before this towered gateway, is a **baths**.

On the approach road, outside the lower line of the walls, is a **necropolis**,
but there are clusters of tombs elsewhere in and around the town. The **temple**
site on the acropolis may have been a Byzantine church, a conversion of a
Roman Artemisium perhaps. East of the crossing are sites of a **gymnasium**
and a **palaestra** (exercise court), the latter having survived in better shape than
the former; it bears an inscription to the Emperor Claudius (41–54) dated AD
50.

The extent of the town in and outside the lower walls suggests that the city
enjoyed a long period of peace and security, seeming to have undergone
heavier fortification only after the passage of Alexander. Excavated recoveries

from Perge can be seen in the Antalya Museum.

Aspendos

Aspendos is on the banks of the Eurymedon River, which in Alexander's time
was navigable as far as the city. The arches of a very fine **Seljuk bridge** grace
the river crossing and account for the stream's name of Bridge River. Kimon,
the Athenian admiral, won a double victory here, by sea and by land, against
Xerxes.

The **theatre** was constructed by a local architect in the second century and
was dedicated to the Roman gods and Marcus Aurelius (161–80). It has survived as the best preserved theatre of its kind, being very nearly intact, except
for depredations on the proscenium and façade. The building underwent
modification when a Seljuk sultan turned it into a *han* (inn). A festival of
drama and music is held here annually.

The theatre backs up to the two hills of the former **acropolis**, where the
steep inclines called only for ramparts, without a need for reinforced walls.
Remains are few: there is a section of a ***nymphaeum***, a building housing a
sacred spring under the protection of nymphs. Its walls have the niches in
which statues were placed. There are the remains of a ***bouleuterion*** (council
chamber) and behind the **south gate** — the city had four —a **gymnasium** and
baths. North of the theatre is the **stadium**, and north of the town are sections
of an aqueduct. One section, astride the valley, has the remains of two towers
that had been constructed to raise the water by reverse gravity to the level of
the conduits.

The **acropolis** at Sillyon is a high one, partially destroyed in a 1969
landslide. Its **theatre** is in almost as sheer a position as the one in Pergamum.
In an extensive site there is a **towered gateway**, **Hellenistic buildings**, a **Seljuk fort** and underground cisterns.

Side

Today's ruins are mainly Roman, or rebuildings of Hellenistic structures, or
Byzantine additions. The principal streets were colonnaded, and off them there
were private houses with mosaic-tiled courtyards, garden ornaments, decorative fountains and frescoed interiors. The Greek-style **theatre**, erected or restored in the second century BC, is among the largest in Asia Minor; the cavea
(semi-circle of seats) is 120 metres (400 feet) in diameter. The upper tiers and
their structural supports were added later and increased seating to 20,000.
Entrance was between shops via a portico from the **agora**, the large rectangular area northeast of the theatre, then through a passageway to an inner arcade, with other passages leading into the orchestra. There are the remains of
the **stoa** that surrounded the agora, and in the southern area are the foundations

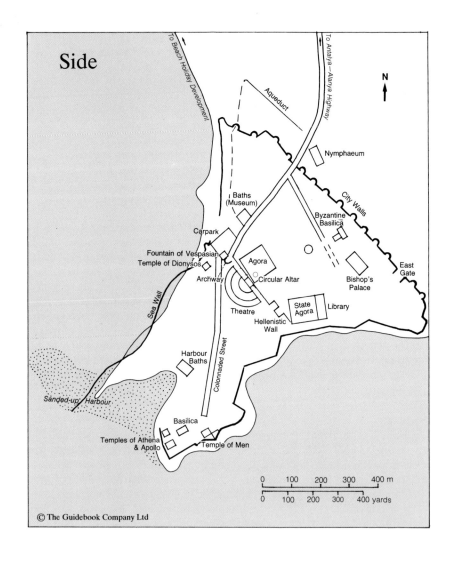

Side

To Beach Holiday Development

To Antalya–Alanya Highway

Aqueduct

N

Nymphaeum

City Walls

Baths
(Museum)

Byzantine
Basilica

Carpark

Fountain of Vespasian
Temple of Dionysos

Agora

East
Gate

Archway

Circular Altar

Bishop's
Palace

Theatre

State
Agora

Library

Hellenistic
Wall

Sea Wall

Harbour
Baths

Colonnaded Street

Sanded-up Harbour

Basilica

Temples of Athena
& Apollo

Temple of Men

| 0 | 100 | 200 | 300 | 400 m |

| 0 | 100 | 200 | 300 | 400 yards |

© The Guidebook Company Ltd

of a circular **altar**, which may have been where the slaves were sold. Off the northern end of the agora, below the *otogar*, a former **baths** has been restored. Its various rooms have been identified, and it is now a museum. A colonnaded street ran diagonally from the area of the present *otogar* out to the temples on the southeastern tip of the peninsula. Here on the headland alongside a silted-up harbour are **Athena's Temple**, a **Temple of Apollo** and, east of these, a **Temple of Men**, the Phrygian Moon-god, and the remains of a **Byzantine basilica**.

The roadway into the site has the ruins of private houses on either side as it approaches the agora. There are sections of **Roman walls** here, and a **triumphal arch**, along with a **Fountain of Vespasian** (69–79) and a **Temple of Dionysos**, flanking the theatre on its western side.

Back at the entrance to the site, the Byzantine walls, that incorporate sections of earlier ones, can be followed round to the **East Gate**. Within the line of the walls, to the west, is a **Byzantine basilica** in a complex that includes the **Bishop's Palace**. South and east of the palace is a second or state agora with, on its east side, an imposing ruin set about a court that may have been the **library**, though a statue of Nemesis in one of its niches suggests the building may have been used as a law court. Other sculpted figures from this building are in the museum. The city's administrative buildings are likely to have been located in this agora.

Alanya

The town and beach expansion begins four or five kilometres (three miles) before reaching the old centre. The main coastal highway continues as Atatürk Caddesi and then for several kilometres as Keykubat Caddesi, both with countless hotels and motels and the long sandy shore. The *otogar*, on the outskirts, is over a kilometre (.6 mile) from where the Ministry of Tourism's Information Centre is located, opposite the museum, beside the Atatürk Park. The road where these are found leads down to the old town and the harbour.

The red crenellated walls, towers and bastions of the **citadel** zigzag down the steep slopes to a **gateway** of Norman-like durability up on the southwest side and to the old town and harbour on the east. The old town is no longer tucked in under the east face of the promontory but has an enlarged harbour with a yacht marina and a wide esplanade and *plaj* which curves round to the east. The restored **Kîzîlkule** (Red Tower) on the quayside is an Alaeddin defence work. Under the rock beyond the southern extent of the harbour are the vaulted galleries of a **Seljuk boatyard**. This is reached now by a roadway from the esplanade that runs in front of the tower. A pedestrian route up to the citadel heights, signposted to Kale, leads off just above the harbour near the Blue Sky Bayîrlî Hotel. The way up to the gateway by car starts opposite the taxi rank at the roundabout, back from the harbour. The cost of a taxi is 5,000TL.

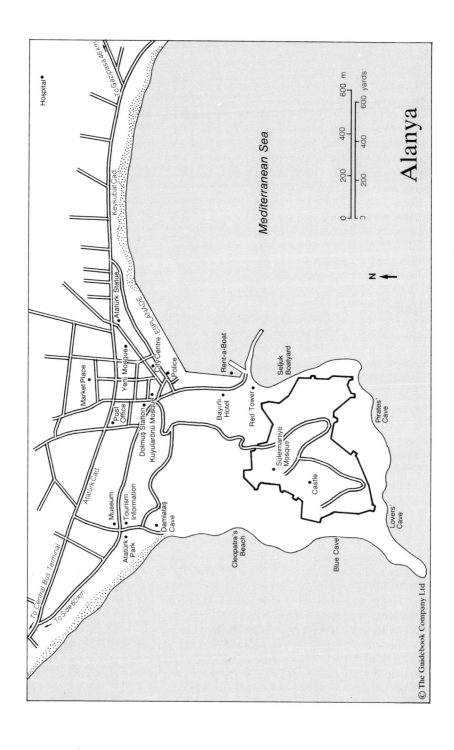

Alanya

Mediterranean Sea

N

0   200   400   600 m
0   200   400   600 yards

Hospital

To Gazipaşa 46 Km

Keykubat Cad

Atatürk Statue

ESPLANADE

City Centre

Police

Rent-a-Boat

Selçuk Boatyard

Yeni Mosque

Market Place

Post Office

Dolmuş Station

Kuyularönü Mosque

Bayırlı Hotel

Red Tower

Süleimaniye Mosque

Pirates' Cave

Castle

Museum

Tourism Information

Atatürk Park

Damlataş Cave

Cleopatra's Beach

Lovers' Cave

Blue Cave

AtatürkCad

To Central Bus Terminal

To Side 60 km

© The Guidebook Company Ltd

On the western side of the promontory is a deep stalactite-stalagmite cave, the **Damlataş Maǧara**, widely acclaimed for its ability to cure bronchial and asthmatic disorders. Boat trips can be taken to other sea caves — the **Pirates'**, the **Lovers'** and the **Phosphorus** —or to **Cleopatra's Beach** in a cove on the western extent of the rock.

The pedestrian climb to the citadel, 120 metres (400 feet) high, is strenuous but pleasant after you have passed the new housing on the lower slopes and have reached the olive and citrus groves. From the bastions there are splendid panoramic views. Among the ruined buildings are an early mosque and some tombs. There are also a number of cisterns. In the neighbourhood of the towered gateway are the former **bazaar** and the ruins of a **Byzantine church**.

For accommodation, the old town has its spate of pensions and some new lower-rated hotels; the new town has an almost unlimited choice of motels, hotels and pensions.

Anamur

Bananas and groundnuts are among the principal products of the area, which is certainly a lush one. The town itself has only a few central streets and one or two modest hotels round the main square. The *otogar* is less than a kilometre (.6 mile) from the square, and there is a local bus service. A taxi driver will offer to take you to town for 2,500TL or to the İskele on the shore, where there are several motels, some pensions, restaurants, bars and discos, for 4,000TL. However, there is a minibus service from the town's square which goes to the İskele for 500TL. The İskele is the harbour, but there is no harbour, only a long pier on which the citizens stroll in the evening, and there is no yacht marina; the locals proudly claim that their sea is the cleanest in the whole Mediterranean basin, and certainly its appearance is of champagne quality.

Anamur's **castle**, and there are several in this region of Cilicia, is on the sands at the eastern end of the shore. The walls, towers and turrets of its three wards are in prime condition, and its sea wall is lapped by waves. You can mount by stairways to the battlements.

Anemurium, the ancient city, is on the western extremity of the shore. Though it is mentioned by Tacitus in the first century, an earthquake destroyed the city, and its present ruins date mainly from the third and fourth centuries. The buildings, in an ash-coloured stone, are crenellated, with the **citadel** above on a craggy hill. There are **baths**, a *nymphaeum* with mosaic decorations, a **palaestra**, **gymnasia**, a **theatre** and a well-preserved **odeon**. A wall separates the city from its **necropolis**, situated on the upper slopes, with something like 350 free-standing constructed tombs. Marble and mosaic materials were imported from Cyprus. A lighthouse stands on a headland that is the most southerly point of Anatolia. Though there is evidence of seventh-century occupation of Anemurium, archaeologists believe the city was abandoned shortly after that as a consequence of Arab attacks from the sea.

Ten kilometres (six miles) to the north of Anamur is the **Küsikbükümastim Mağarasi**, the Trofstein Cave. There is also a cafeteria here.

Approaching Silifke

The castle of **Softa** stands on its pointed hill on the right of Bözyazi with, further on, some extensive ruins the castle must once have controlled. There are bays at Tekeli (Akkaya), Yenikas, which has an intensive hothouse industry, and Aydincík, an expanding town from where a road runs north to Gülnar, a distance of 40 kilometres (25 miles). Excavations there in 1971 unearthed Meydancik Kalesi, a **Persian palace** of the Achaemenid period (546–334 BC), believed to be such because of the resemblance of carvings recovered there to those at Persepolis.

Ovacik's bay is backed by a coastal plain, and then the road crosses the Yasildam valley to climb again and descend to Bağsak, with its bay, beach, holiday facilities, river and **castle** that keeps guard on a second bay, with its offshore island.

Not so many years ago, Taşucu was a neglected, soporific harbour, perhaps with one motel on its outskirts, but today it is a large and active port catering for ocean-going ships and tankers, albeit with holiday centres on its nearby beaches.

Three kilometres (two miles) before reaching Silifke, a road branches off to Ayatekla. Aghia Tekla was the first female saint, converted to Christianity, it was said, by St Paul. Her angry, rejected pagan fiance had her put to the lions, an ordeal she survived to become an anchorite or religious recluse. The Emperor Zeno (474–91), a native of the region just to the north, erected a church in her honour; her cave had become a place of pilgrimage. Only an apse of his **church** remains, but the sacred cave, to be found among the remains of churches and monasteries, is visited still.

Silifke

Silifke was Seleucia on the Calycadnus; the site of the ancient city is six kilometres (four miles) distant from the modern, expanding town. The Calycadnus River still flows here, crossed by a fine Roman bridge. The **castle**, Byzantine with Armenian modifications, stands 200 metres (600 feet) above and away from the town. In 1210 the Armenian king gave the castle to the Knights Hospitallers in exchange for military assistance, and it became known as Camardesium. The horseshoe-shaped towers are a Crusader feature, designed for better observation of an attacking force. The **necropolis** lies below the castle's walls.

Fragile Beauty

There are no roads here; so by a lane that would shame the roughest in Ireland, came the Sultan's married daughter,—married to Aali Ghalib Pasha, the son of Reschid Pasha. Edmund helped Lady Robinson into some brambles on the steep bank; I was already safely wedged in the roots of an old fig-tree; and thus we quietly awaited the passing of the Asiatic beauties.... We could not see much of the lady (who is said to be very lovely), the Negroes keeping close to the windows, as they splashed up the mud all over their uniforms; besides which, her yashmak was thickly folded. I could only see plainly her beautiful fan of snow-white feathers, the handle glittering with emeralds.

The lady on the opposite seat (there were three in the carriage) was more thinly veiled, very young, and very pretty. I saw her face plainly, and her feridjee being a little off her shoulders, I threw an envious glance on a violet-coloured velvet jacket embroidered with gold, and fastened at the throat with a large jewelled clasp, which gleamed through the gauzy veil. As to beauty of mere dress and ease of attitude, nothing that I have seen in life or in pictures can give the slightest idea of the wonderful grace, the extreme delicacy, and bird-of-paradise-like uselessness of the Turkish belle. Women of rank look like hothouse flowers, and are really cultivated to the highest perfection of physical beauty, having no other employment but to make their skins as snow-white and their eyebrows as jet-black as possible. When young, their skin is literally as white as their veils, with the faintest tinge of pink on the cheek, like that in the side of a shell, which blends exquisitely with the tender apple-leaf green, and soft violet colours, of which they are so fond.

The reverse of the picture is, that after the first bloom of youth is past, the skin becomes yellow and sickly-looking, and you long to give the yashmak a pull and admit a fresh breeze to brighten up the fine features.

Lady Hornby, Constantinople During The Crimean War, *1863*

From Silifke, an excursion can be made to Uzuncaburç. This was a city-state under the control of priest-kings. An **Oracle of Zeus Olbius** existed here in the third century BC. This city became Diocaesarea for the Romans and Byzantines.

On a north–south line the city is crossed by a colonnaded street running east–west, and the standing columns of the **temple** and **sanctuary** are to the right, before the crossing is reached. The temple was converted to a church by the Byzantines. South of it is a two-storey second-century **building**, columned on the upper floor. West of the crossing is a first-century BC **Temple to Tyche**, goddess of Fortune. At the northern end of the street, above the crossing, is a **Roman gateway**, to the east of which, along a **Sacred Way**, is the village of Ura which, as today, was the site of Olba's residential quarter. As well as the remains of private houses, there are sections of an **aqueduct** and a *nymphaeum*. A second-century BC **tower** stands to the north of the Roman gateway. Gauged by the number of ruins of Byzantine churches, Olba would seem to have been as significant for Christian as it had been for pagan pilgrims. Its necropolis has a number of **hypogea**, Roman temple-like tombs.

On the Road to Mersin

From Silifke, after crossing the plain through Atayurt and Kapisli, the great holiday build-up begins at Susanoğlu, after which Narlıkuyu is the first of the coves along the road. A colourful floor mosaic known as the Three Graces, lodged in a small museum here, is all that remains of a fourth-century Roman baths.

Twenty-five kilometres (16 miles) from Silifke, two kilometres (1.25 miles) inland — well signposted — are two natural pits known as Cennet and Cehennem (Heaven and Hell). In fact, 'Heaven' is the easier to descend! At the bottom is an Armenian 11th-century **chapel**, with a spring under an arched rock, which is likely to have been a pagan grotto. A descent and ascent of Cennet takes about an hour. Cehennem, believed to have been an acknowledged entrance to the Underworld, is less negotiable without the help of an expert speleologist (cave explorer).

Between the mosaic at Narlıkuyu and the pits are the ruins of Paperon, a Roman-Byzantine city. Inland from the road is a necropolis in which there are tombs modelled out of rock, more than one having an imprint of hands at its entrance; one tomb has the portrait of a lady, and another has the insignia of an Order of Knights. There are underground columned cisterns among Paperon's ruins.

Further on the road at Sebaste, the landward side has a low, arched bridge near a Byzantine chapel among ruined buildings with, further inland, a section of an aqueduct.

The road arrives at Corycos with its two maiden castles, one on shore, the other on an island 100 metres (330 feet) out in the bay. The two castles were once connected by a sea wall and causeway. In 1361 the last Armenian king of Cilicia gave Corycos to Peter of Cyprus, the last Frankish king in the Near East. Peter's possession was shortlived, since Cilicia soon afterwards was overrun by the Mameluke Sultan Baibars. The land castle has the insignia of the Knights of Cyprus over the main gateway. The area is a popular bathing resort with camping and holiday accommodation.

To the east of Corycos is Ayas, whose ruins reveal it to have been a principal city of this Roman province, over which Cicero was governor from 52 to 50 BC. Among the ruins is a **Byzantine basilica**. There are ancient houses on the hillside, and going over the hill are many Roman hypogeal tombs, one with a sarcophagus on top of it. Many marble sarcophagi with carvings are standing on both sides of what was probably a **Sacred Way**. Here, too, there is a section of aqueduct, another section of which stands at Sebaste. New construction exists among the ruins at Ayas. There is an organized beach here. At Yemiskümü, further on, there is a long beach that is over-developed with holiday flats.

Kanlidivane is inland a kilometre from the road at Kumkuyu. Here is a large square-shaped pit that is wider and much shallower than either Cennet or Cehennem. On the south wall is a carving of a family group, and on the west side is a single Roman soldier. North of the pit is an abandoned town whose houses are half-buried but can be entered, where semi-nomadic Yuruks spend the winter months, moving to upland pastures in the spring. Yuruk women weave attractive **kilims** (pileless, double-sided carpets) for floors, wall hangings or bed covers. Near Kanlidivane is a section of an aqueduct astride a narrow valley.

After Kanlidivane and before the main road leaves the shoreline, there are holiday centres at Tirtar, Limanoğlu —the latter having a ruined castle — and Kocahasanli. A large camping site leads to the market town of Erdemli. Eighteen kilometres (11 miles) beyond Erdemli at Mezitli, a turning on the right leads to Viranşehir which was **Pompeiopolis**. Here a columned street runs some 500 metres (1,600 feet) to a former harbour, now a sandy beach Twenty columns with Corinthian capitals are standing erect. The city was in origin Soli. When Alexander arrived sick after plunging into the icy waters of the Cydnus at Tarsus, he vented his anger on the citizens by imposing a fine of 200 talents of silver on them for giving their support to Darius, and he castigated them on their atrocious Greek, hence 'solecism'.

The harbour was an important haven for pirates until Pompey cleared them from the eastern sea, but then, to compensate them for their loss of income and employment, he allocated accommodation to them in his new city, whose acropolis mound now has a military post on its summit.

Mersin

This modern port, with its large harbour and ancillary services of an oil refinery, storage tanks, grain silos and docks, has developed into a megalopolis. On its coastlines, east and west, are conglomerates of construction — industrial and holiday. The old centre of Mersin has a palm-lined esplanade with gardens, hotels and seafood restaurants. From Mersin you may take a boat to Famagusta in Cyprus and destinations further east.

The ancient city is inland several kilometres at Yümüktepe. Thirty-two excavated levels take occupation back to the fifth millennium BC. Walls and fortifications are of several epochs, including Hittite. Many recoveries are in the Archaeological Museum in Adana, and others can be seen at the museum in Ankara.

Tarsus

St Paul was born here, but there is little now of that Roman period other than an **archway** known as St Paul's Gate. Gözlültepe is ancient Tarsus, an excavated mound on the south side. As at Yümüktepe, the archaeological discoveries go back to the fifth millennium BC. Minoan artifacts, Hittite seals and Mycenaean pottery have been found here, along with Assyrian clay tablets that

have revealed a connection with Assyrian kings such as Sennacharib, Sardanapulus and Shalmanazar III.

The reputed Tomb of Sardanapulus, whose claim was that he built Tarsus and Anchialis in one day, is the Donak Taş at Gözlükule, southeast of the town. This monarch abjured those who might read his valedictory to live every moment of life to the full, since personal power was of little more value than a handclap.

Castle lovers could visit Lampron at Namrun, by taking the road to Çamliyayla, 44 kilometres (27 miles) out of Tarsus. The impressive stronghold was the seat of Hethoumian kings but was later held by the Crusaders.

Adana

The city stands on the Şeyhan River (the Sarus), which is no longer navigable. The river is spanned by a **Roman bridge** built by Hadrian and rebuilt by Justinian. Of its 23 arches, 14 of the original are still in place. A new bridge was built upstream of the old one in the 1960s. The city's **Archaeological Museum** (see Mersin above) is on the riverside, close to the new bridge.

Of the Adana mosques, the 16th-century **Ulu Cami**, behind its high wall, has a Syrian-style minaret with black-tiled courses, a *medrese* and a tomb within its complex. It was built by an independent Ramazanoğlu emir. The **clock tower** in the central market place is an installation of 1882.

Karataş, at the mouth of the Şeyhan River (the Pyramus) and a busy port in Roman times, is 50 kilometres (31 miles) directly south of Adana. It offers the closest beaches and bathing facilities to the city. For boating and water-skiing, go to the Şeyhan Baraji, eight kilometres (five miles) to the north of Adana. The dam is set fjord-like among the Taurus foothills.

A one-day excursion can take in three castles to the northeast of Adana and include the site of Karatepe. A short distance east of the Şeyhan River, a road turns northeast for Kozan, 72 kilometres (45 miles) away. **Tümlü** is the first of the castles, 46 kilometres (29 miles) along the way, standing on a spur in the plain. It has only its walls now — archaic, Roman, Byzantine, Roupenian and Crusader. A line of such strongpoints stretched northwards across the Cilician Plain into the Taurus Mountains, protecting Asia Minor's southern flank. From Tümlü's battlements the citadel of **Anazarbus** can be seen to the north.

Anavarsa, the village next to the ruins of Anazarbus, is separated from it by a Roman three-arched **monumental gateway**. The **citadel** is up on an elongated spur, narrowing about the middle where the walls of a **keep** are thick and the bastions substantial. Beyond the keep, on that section of the spur least accessible, is the **burial place** of Roupenian kings. There is a **chapel** here, too, with a frescoed apse.

In the lower town, double walls on the north side are separated by a deep fosse. Byzantine workmanship can be admired in the brickwork of a **baths**. Along a **colonnaded street** many column bases are in position, their fallen drums scattered. The **theatre** and **stadium** are situated in isolation from the public buildings of the **agora** and the citizen's houses. At the village end of the site you can climb to the spur by a stairway.

Kozan, on the banks of the Pyramus, was Sis, the Roupenian capital. The **Byzantine citadel**, modified by the Armenians, was constructed on an earlier fort. In the 13th century the Genoese were granted a permit to reside and trade here. Beyond Kozan the road continues to Vahka, in the Taurus foothills, yet another of the line of Cilician strongpoints.

Near Kadirli, which is 36 kilometres (22 miles) to the southeast of Kozan, Karatepe is a Hittite site situated among wooded hills. In 1946 bilingual texts in Hittite and Phoenician that were found here led to the deciphering of Hittite hieroglyphic. Basalt sculptures and inscriptions were also unearthed, including one to Asitawandas, a king and vassal of the Hittite king whose capital was Adana. Though most of the recoveries are in the Hittite Museum in Ankara, some carved blocks with inscriptions have been left *in situ*.

Misis and Yumurtalik

This was the site of Mopsueste, or Mamistra, one of three Cilician sister cities; Tarsus and Adana complete the trio. A **Roman bridge** crossed the river a little way upstream from the Byzantine one, and its piers are in place still. A **colonnaded street** ran from this bridge to the city's **acropolis**. Ruins of buildings stand on either side of the river, with some sections of the city walls on the eastern side. In the village is the house that was used as a hostel and workplace by the members of the expedition who dug here, its walls inscribed with their names. The yard still harbours evidence of their work. Down river, near Yakapinar, is a carving of a Hittite River-god on a rock overhanging the water.

Misis as a separate excursion could extend to include **Yilankale** (Snake Castle), standing on a high rock above the Şeyhan River, a little off the E5, yet seeming to dominate it. The castle's name is derived from a serpent in the armorial bearing above the **double gateway** to the inner ward. There are chambers off the courtyard of the outer ward, and a **postern gate** offers vertiginous command of the countryside.

As at Corycos, there are two castles here, the one on land having only a few stones now, along with a disused harbour, but the other castle on an island out in the bay has its walls still. Yumurtalik has become a holiday centre of the neighbourhood.

The Plain of Issus

With massive walls and rounded towers, **Toprakkale** stands sentinel above a narrow defile that leads into the plain where, in 333 BC, Alexander fought Darius and routed him in the decisive battle of his campaign. The sea has receded here because of silting, and it is difficult to visualize the restricted confines within which the battle was fought. But a diligent visitor might still find arrowheads or other remnants of that conflict.

Beyond Issus, on the marshland to the right of the road, are the ruins of **Epiphania**, with a section of **aqueduct** prominent. There is a turnoff here to **Payas** where some of the buildings have been attributed to Sinan, but the **castle** is Venetian.

İskenderun

İskenderun is a modern and developing port situated picturesquely under the Amanus mountains, with an attractive waterfront.

Belen is built on twin hills above a deep gorge, and a building of interest is an Ottoman *han* erected under Selim I (1512–20), with Sinan as the probable architect. Down below, on the east, is the Plain of Amik where, alongside the Lake of Amik, is the excavated Hittite city of Alalakh, which revealed early Egyptian and Sumerian connections. The **Castle of Baǧras** dominates the Belen Pass, the watchdog of Antioch. Saladin succeeded in storming its formidable defences. Later it came into the possession of the Knights Templars.

Antakya

Byzantine walls exist still on the hills to the east, but the most interesting exhibits of the past are in the **museum**, close to the bridge. Along with recoveries from Alalakh and elsewhere, and a fine numismatic (coin) section, the museum has the greatest collection of secular mosaics to be found anywhere; the exhibits are a remarkable testimony to the art of the mosaicist.

In the town the **Habibnacar Cami** originated as a Roman Temple to Apollo. Daphne, eight kilometres (five miles) out of town, is in the wooded suburb of Harbiye. There is an **aqueduct** here built by Hadrian, as well as the source of a sacred spring. Apollo lusted after the nymph Daphne, and because she rejected his importunate advances, he turned her into a laurel bush — *daphne laureolus*.

Samandaǧ

The ruins of the former port are on the northern edge of the wide shore at the river mouth. On the opposite southern edge is sacred Mount Cassius. Still to be seen are the remains of Vespasian's water system that controlled the flow of water in and out of the harbour, although now the site is sanded up almost completely.

The Crusader **Castle of Cursat** is near the village of Sofular, close to Antakya. **Trapesac** of the Knights Templars is just to the north. **Civlan** is perched 1,000 metres (3,282 feet) high to the northeast, and the renowned **Krak des Chevaliers** is just across the border in Syria. Near the village of Islahiye on the railway line to Aleppo in northern Syria is the excavated site of the 14th-century BC Hittite city of Zinjirli.

Central Anatolia

Ankara, on the central plateau standing at a height of 855 metres (2,800 feet), is set in a bowl surrounded by hills. It is a city in a desert, though reafforestation and planned cultivation, apparent as elsewhere in western Turkey, is helping to change the landscape and the environment. Climatic temperatures, however, are extreme between summer heat and winter frosts. From Ankara, a two- or three-day trip can include the Hittite sites of Alaca Hüyük, Hattusas and Yazilikaya. A visit to Gordium, the Phrygian capital, can be a day trip from Ankara.

Caesarea (Kayseri) was the capital city of the extensive Roman province of Cappadocia. Today it is largely modern, but Byzantine walls still surround the central medieval city, particularly in its northern section. The monuments are mainly Seljuk, with a Danişmend memory or two and Ottoman touches.

A minimum of three days is recommended for a visit to the rock-hewn churches, monasteries and other sights of this region. The most fascinating monuments of Cappadocia are concentrated within the triangle of Nevşehir–Kayseri–Niğde.

Konya's location is a strategic one, lying as it does on the southern edge of the central plateau and commanding the passes down through the Taurus Mountains into the region of Cilicia. It is the centre, too, of the great wheat-growing area of the Konya Plain, a reason, perhaps, for the existence of shrines to the Anatolian Great Earth Mother, to Phrygian Cybele and, in the time of Hadrian, a sanctuary to Roman Demeter. Southeast of Konya is the site of Çatal Hüyük, *circa* 7000 BC; recoveries can be seen at the Archaeological Museum in Ankara.

Getting There

One long thoroughfare runs from Ulus at the north end of central Ankara to the crown of Cankaya Hill at its southern end, intersecting the city. From Ulus Meydani (Ulus Square) with its equestrian statue of Atatürk, the road running south is Atatürk Bulvari, and it goes through the city centre at Kizilay, then up the long steep hill to the Presidential Palace on the top. At Bakanliklar, a little way up Kizilay, the Parliament and other government buildings can be found, and on the ascent from here are almost all the accredited foreign embassies, except for those of the USA (out beyond Kavaklidere) and the USSR (at Maltepe).

To take an excursion to the Hittite sites, go out east on the E23 for 120 kilometres (75 miles) through Elmadağ and Kirikkale to a road junction six kilometres (four miles) south of Delice. From this junction continue another 56 kilometres (35 miles) northeast to Sungurlu and eight kilometres (five miles) beyond to the turnoff for Boğazkale. A further 13 kilometres (eight miles) southeast, Boğazkale is where you will find the site of Hattusas, and three or four kilometres (two miles) to the east is a unique Hittite sanctuary, Yazîlikaya. To visit Alaca Hüyük, go east of Sungurlu towards Alaca.

To visit Gordium, go to Polatli, 76 kilometres (47 miles) southwest of Ankara on road E23. Polatli is a kilometre (.6 mile) off the road to the north, and in the 1960s workmen, while digging foundations for new houses there, unearthed the top level of a site that subsequently was discovered to go down through many levels to the neolithic. Continuing on the E23, 17 kilometres (ten miles) further west, a road turns north for 12 kilometres (eight miles) to Yassîhüyük and the site of Gordium.

Turkish Airlines has flights to Kayseri, which is also on the main railway line from Ankara to the east of the country. Key places in the area can be reached by public transport in combination with the minibus services. As with visits to the Hittite sites and Gordium, there are organized tours to Cappadocia available from established tour agencies in Ankara.

Going south from Ankara on the main E5 highway, you turn off some ten kilometres (six miles) past Gölbasi, at Ogülbey, to join road 66 to Kirşehir, 147 kilometres (91 miles) away. On this route the road crosses the Kîzîlîrmak River over a fine Seljuk bridge. Road 41 forks south 29 kilometres (18 miles) beyond Kirşehir. You can choose between going on southeast to Kayseri, another 137 kilometres (85 miles), and begin your Cappadocian tour from there, or going the 67 kilometres (42 miles) south to Nevşehir where the first 'fairy' cones can be seen and investigated.

From Nevşehir take road 73 eastward. Five kilometres (three miles) along this road is the entrance to the Göreme valley, the principal visiting centre of the region. At the northern head of the valley, Ürgüp is 21 kilometres (13 miles) east of Nevşehir.

Kaymaklî is 20 kilometres (12 miles) south of Nevşehir on the road to Niğde, and Derinküyü is ten kilometres (six miles) further. The Soğanli valley, east of Derinküyü, is a rich replica of the Göreme valley, if less accessible. A similar settlement exists at Özkonak, 20 kilometres (12 miles) northwest of Avanos.

To reach the area of Îhlara, go southwest out of Nevşehir on road 300 to Aksaray, along which are three Seljuk inns. In particular the restored Ağzikara, just before a turnoff running southeast to the Mamazin Dam, or eight kilometres (five miles) before Aksaray, will repay a visit. A right fork, 23 kilometres (14 miles) along the abovementioned turnoff, leads to Îhlara, another 11 kilometres (seven miles) away.

Niğde is 84 kilometres (52 miles) south of Nevşehir. From Niğde to Kayseri, the 128 kilometre (80 mile) road skirts the magnificent Mount Erciyes, 3,916 metres (12,850 feet) high. The Mount Argaeus of antiquity, its peak is perpetually under snow. The site at Kültepe is 20 kilometres (12 miles) northeast of Kayseri on the Sivas road.

For a hurrying traveller, Konya could be a one-day excursion from Ankara. The distance by road is 220 kilometres (137 miles) through the wide Konya Plain. There are Turkish Airlines' flights to Konya, and the coach and minibus services are as convenient as in most areas of Turkey.

For the traveller along the Mediterranean coast, Konya can be reached from Silifke by bus. The road climbs above the valley of the Göksu River through the Taurus Mountains to the plateau by way of Mut and Karaman. This is a recommended journey, to be taken in late afternoon with the light softening mountain peaks and captivating rock formations. After Mut, the feathery green of the Mediterranean pine gives way to the deeper reassuring green of the spruce. Much reafforestation has taken place on these mountain slopes, as elsewhere in Turkey's mountainous regions. The road system in Konya has undergone reconstruction, and the *otogar* is about three kilometres (two miles) northwest of the city centre.

The site of Çatal Hüyük can be found 34 kilometres (21 miles) southeast of Konya near the town of Cumra. Twin mounds are located on a track to Küçükköy, ten kilometres (six miles) from the town.

A suggested trip for the motorist is to venture from Konya to Denizli via İsparta. The cost by coach is 14,000TL. The route takes you west to Beyşehir, to run northwest along the length of the Lake of Beyşehir before diverting through mountainous terrain and afterwards turning southwest to reach and skirt the eastern shore of Lake Eğridir. The town of Eğridir on the lakeside is an attractive holiday resort, having its quota of pensions and hotels, lakeside restaurants, a castle and a causeway out to Yeşilköy, or Green Island. After reaching İsparta, the road runs north to Dinar, then turns southwesterly for a longish haul to Denizli, from where Pamukkale and Aphrodisias can be visited.

Historical Background

In 1923 Kemal Atatürk made Ankara the capital of the Turkish Republic that he had founded. The Anatolians of the plateau had supported him in his rejection of the Treaty of Sevres made between the Western allies and the sultan at the conclusion of the First World War, and they had provided his military strength against the Greek incursion of 1920–2. Therefore, his preference was for Ankara rather than İstanbul, whose cosmopolite citizens he had reason to distrust.

The name of the city could derive from Ankuwash of Hittite texts. It became Phrygian when the Phrygians destroyed Hittite power in Central

Anatolia. The Persians held it before Alexander arrived in 334 BC. In the third century BC it was in the hands of Galatians, invading tribes who had terrorized western Asia Minor before the Attalids drove them east. By St Paul's day Ancyra, or Angora, was the capital of the Roman Province of Galatia; the former savage tribes seem to have settled by this time to an urban way of life, with Christian converts, since St Paul addressed an epistle to their church. The Arabs sacked and occupied it in the seventh and eighth centuries and, after the Byzantines had strengthened the defences, again in the tenth. The Seljuk Turks occupied it following their victory at Manzikert, before moving on to make Nikaia (İznik) their capital. Timur (Tamerlane) defeated the Ottoman Sultan Beyazıt I at Ankara in 1401 and might have put an end to Ottoman power had he stayed in the west, but the Mongol Khan returned east and died in 1405.

Under later Ottoman sultans, Ankara declined in importance.

Clay tablets in cuneiform script were found at Boğazkale, indicating that in the 18th century this city was Hattusas, capital of the Land of Hatti. Under the Hittites, their Indo-Aryan overlords, the Hattians may have retained their indigenous customs. Later, the Hurrians, another Indo-Aryan people, moved here from the vicinity of Lake Van, and another connected people, the Mitanni, moved southeast as far as Babylon. These four peoples combined to create a Hittite culture.

An early Hittite Kingdom, whose script was in cuneiform, came to an end about the 16th century BC, but it was succeeded by an Hittite Empire, in which the script was hieroglyphic. This period concluded in the 12th century

BC when Phrygia became the dominant power in western Anatolia. A late-flowering of Hittite culture came about with the establishment of a number of independent Hittite kingdoms in northern Syria and Cilicia, the last of which, centred on Carchemish on the Euphrates, was overrun by the Assyrians in 724 BC.

The Phrygians are thought to have immigrated into Asia Minor from Thrace, west of the Bosphorus, or even further west from the Rhodope Mountains and the North Aegean. In time they overturned the Hittites in western and central Anatolia and took over as principal power.

Midas is said to have been their king when the Phrygians, in their turn, were overpowered by wild Cimmerian tribes coming across the Black Sea from Crimea. Midas is said to have committed suicide by drinking bull's blood (as Themistocleos, the fifth-century Greek victor of Salamis, is also said to have done, ending his ostracism and exile in Lampsacus). Midas, though, may well have been an eponymous title for king, as Augustus and Caesar became for Roman emperors.

Gyges, founder of the Lydian Mermnad dynasty at Sardis, fought and expelled the Cimmerians and extended his kingdom and control throughout Phrygia, but by Alexander's time Gordium was no longer a major city, having been reduced in importance under Persian rule following Cyrus's defeat of Croesus.

Prior to his death Gordios, the patriarchal founder of Gordium, had tied the yoke of his wagon — symbol of his peasant origins — to the shaft with an injunction that whoever should untie it would make himself master of all Asia. Alexander cut through the knot with a sword stroke and became master of Asia.

Kayseri was probably Mazaca for the Hittites. Under Trajan it became Caesarea, capital of Cappadocia. The Persians occupied it after their defeat of the Emperor Valerian (253–60) on the Euphrates. Eusebius (264–340), the historian of early Christianity, was a distinguished bishop here. Influential early Fathers of the Church born in this city were Basil of Caesarea, Gregory of Nyssa and the latter's younger brother, Gregory Nazianzus.

In the sixth century Justinian, after extensive reconquests in the east, rebuilt the walls, and for a time it was known as Eusebia. After the Seljuk arrival in Anatolia in the 11th century, Kayseri became the city of a Danişmend independent emirate. After this followed Seljuk reoccupation, Mongol violation, Karamanoğlu possession and Mameluke residence until Sultan Selim I made it Ottoman in 1513.

Konya is said to have been Kuwanna to the Hittites, Kowania to the Phrygians — who believed it was the only city to survive Noah's flood — Eikonion to the early Greeks, Iconium to the Romans (for a short time Claudiconium) and Ikonion to the Byzantines. St Paul preached to a nascent Christian community at Konya.

From the seventh to the tenth centuries the Byzantine city became a target of the religious and military expansionist aims of the Arabs, but its status was changed appreciably when the Seljuks, after losing Nikaia (İznik) to the Knights of the First Crusade, made Konya the capital of their Sultanate of Rum. For the Seljuks it was a sacred city, later to become the centre of the mystical cult of the Mevlana. The Seljuk architectural achievement took place here between the late 11th and the 13th centuries, though almost nothing of the earliest part of that period has survived. Today's monuments date mainly from the time of Sultan Alaeddin Keykubat I (1220–37).

Sights

Ankara

North of Ulus Meydanı, Atatürk Bulvarı becomes Çankırı Caddesi, and along this on the left is the site of a third-century **Roman baths** with a **palaestra**. To the right of Ulus Meydanı and Çankırı Caddesi is the **citadel hill**. From the square, take Hisarparkı Caddesi to go up to the Hisar Kapısı (Castle Gate) in the outer wall of the citadel. Or take Anafartalar Caddesi and mount by way of the narrow market streets. You then go through the medieval area between the walls. Parmat Kapısı is the **gateway** through the inner walls that were reinforced under Heraclius in the seventh century. The outer walls and those of the citadel were strengthened against Arab attacks by the Byzantines in the eighth and ninth centuries, and one of the towers, the **Şark Kulesi**, was refurbished as a strongpoint. Later, some Seljuk defence modifications were added.

The Archaeological Museum

This occupies a restored *bedesten* (covered bazaar) of the 15th century, along with a companion *han* of an earlier date. It is situated on a garden terrace down from the Hisar Kapısı. There are exhibits of early Anatolian civilizations and from the neolithic sites of Çatal Hüyük (near Konya, see page 208), Hacılar (near Burdur) and Yumuktepe (at Mersin), as well as from later Roman, Byzantine and Turkish periods. The outstanding sections are those containing the Hittite sculptures in high and in low relief, the engraved seals, the worked-iron and bronze medallions and the jewellery, all an astonishing revelation concerning a people who have become known in greater detail only in this present century.

Monuments

Off the right-hand side of Çankırı Caddesi, not far from Ulus Meydanı, is a short street leading to Hükümet Meydanı, a square in which there is a **Column**

of Julian, erected for that emperor's visit in 362. In the next square, a little to the northeast, is the 15th-century **Haci Bayram Cami**, which has some very attractive tiling. Along the east side of this square are the remains of a **Temple to Rome and Augustus**, constructed on the original site of a Temple to Cybele; this latter temple had been built over a Shrine to Men, the Phrygian Moon-god. In the pronaos (body of a temple) an engraved text once recorded the achievements of Augustus, but only a few Latin characters of this text can now be deciphered. There is evidence of the **Byzantine church** to which this temple was adapted.

Mosques
Within the citadel is the Seljuk **Alaettin Cami** (Alaeddin) of 1178. To the southwest of the museum is the **Arslanhane Cami** of the 13th century, so called because of a stone lion in the forecourt. It has wooden columns, and a **mihrab** in enamelled faience; its carved **mimber** is in walnut wood and is dated 1290. The late 14th-century **Ahi Elvan Cami** is in a street a little lower down and has Roman columns incorporated in its structure; the **mimber** is dated 1413. The **Yeni Cami**, 400 metres (1,300 feet) east of the Arslanhane Cami, was erected in the 16th century in the time of Süleiman the Magnificent.

Anıt Kabir — The Atatürk Mausoleum
This monument is on a hill on the outskirts west of the city. It can be reached by going out on İsmet İnönü Bulvarı from Bakanlıklar. An impressive monument to a great man, it is set in landscaped grounds with a marble-paved access roadway. Flanking pavilions have sculptured reliefs, and a wide stairway leads up to the columned **mausoleum** in which is the marble sarcophagus. Within the complex is a museum containing exhibits of Atatürk's personal belongings.

Atatürk Orman Çiftliği
A legacy of Atatürk exists to the north of Anıt Kabir and is a memorial to his far-sightedness. The Atatürk Orman Çiftliği is a model farm which he pioneered. Its dairy products can be sampled at a restaurant there. In the grounds are two constructed lakes, an aquarium and a small zoo.

National Theatre and Opera House
Ankara's National Theatre and Opera House is on Atatürk Bulvarı, between Ulus Meydanı and Kızılay. Behind the Opera House is the Youth Park (Gençlik Parkı) where there is a boating lake, restaurants, cafés and fun-fair pavilions.

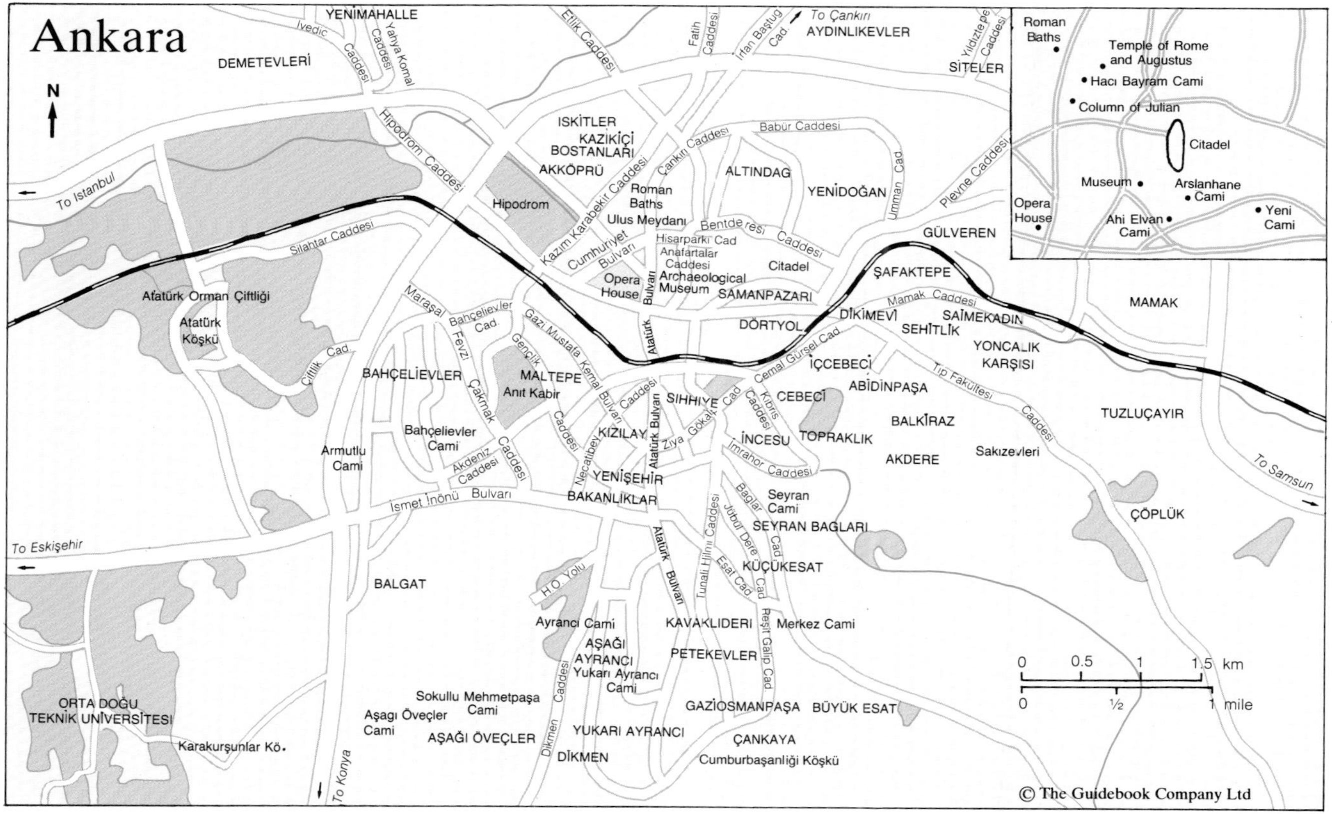
Ankara
N
DEMETEVLERİ
YENİMAHALLE
Ivedic Caddesi
Yahya Komal Caddesi
Etlik Caddesi
Fatih Caddesi
Irfan Baştuğ Cad.
To Çankırı
AYDINLIKEVLER
Yıldıztepe Caddesi
SİTELER
To Istanbul
Hipodrom Caddesi
Hipodrom
ISKİTLER
KAZIKİÇİ BOSTANLARI
AKKÖPRÜ
Kazım Karabekir Caddesi
Çankırı Caddesi
Babür Caddesi
ALTINDAG
YENİDOĞAN
Umman Cad.
Plevne Caddesi
Roman Baths
Ulus Meydanı
Bentderesi Caddesi
Hisarparkı Cad
Anafartalar Caddesi
Cumhuriyet Bulvarı
Opera House
Archaeological Museum
Citadel
SAMANPAZARI
GÜLVEREN
ŞAFAKTEPE
Silahtar Caddesi
Atatürk Orman Çiftliği
Atatürk Köşkü
Çiftlik Cad.
Maraşal Fevzi Çakmak Caddesi
Bahçelievler Cad.
Gazi Mustafa Kemal Bulvarı
Gençlik Caddesi
BAHÇELİEVLER
MALTEPE
Anıt Kabir
Atatürk Bulvarı
DÖRTYOL
DİKİMEVİ
Mamak Caddesi
SAİMEKADIN
SEHİTLİK
MAMAK
YONCALIK KARŞISI
Cemal Gürsel Cad
İÇCEBECİ
CEBECİ
ABİDİNPAŞA
Tıp Fakültesi Caddesi
TUZLUÇAYIR
SIHHIYE
Kıbrıs Caddesi
Gökkak Cad
Ziya
KIZILAY
Necatibey Caddesi
İNCESU
TOPRAKLIK
BALKİRAZ
AKDERE
Sakızevleri
İmrahor Caddesi
To Samsun
Bahçelievler Cami
Akdeniz Caddesi
Armutlu Cami
YENİŞEHİR
BAKANLIKLAR
Ismet İnönü Bulvarı
Seyran Cami
SEYRAN BAGLARI
Bağlar Cad
Jübül Dere Cad
Tunalı Hilmi Caddesi
Esat Cad
KÜÇÜKESAT
ÇÖPLÜK
To Eskişehir
BALGAT
H.O. Yolu
Ayrancı Cami
AŞAĞI AYRANCI
Yukarı Ayrancı Cami
KAVAKLIDERI
PETEKEVLER
Reşit Galip Cad
Merkez Cami
GAZİOSMANPAŞA
BÜYÜK ESAT
ÇANKAYA
Cumburbaşanliği Köşkü
YUKARI AYRANCI
DİKMEN
Dikmen Caddesi
Sokullu Mehmetpaşa Cami
Aşagı Öveçler Cami
AŞAĞI ÖVEÇLER
ORTA DOĞU TEKNİK ÜNİVERSİTESI
Karakurşunlar Kö.
To Konya
0 0.5 1 1.5 km
0 ½ 1 mile
Roman Baths
Temple of Rome and Augustus
Hacı Bayram Cami
Column of Julian
Citadel
Museum
Arslanhane Cami
Opera House
Ahi Elvan Cami
Yeni Cami
© The Guidebook Company Ltd

Fishing, boating and winter sports

The Çübük Dam, out on the airport road, is good for a picnic, for fishing and boating, as is Gölbasi Lake, 22 kilometres (14 miles) south of the city. El-madağ, the mountain range to the east, is popular for winter sports.

An excursion to the Hittite sites

Hattusas, at Boğazkale, or Boğazköy, stands on an irregular outcrop cut by deep ravines and buttressed by spurs. Its walls are remarkably strong still, especially the bastions on the south and east.

Mounting a pathway from the plain, you pass the ruined **palace** in which, among other buildings, is the **archives** where the clay tablets were found. There are kilns here in which they were fired, and the evidence suggests that the entire building was destroyed by fire.

Moving round the spur you reach the **King's Gate**. A sculpture of a Warrior-god was found here and is in the Ankara Museum. He has a beaked nose and is wearing a kilt-like skirt with a heavy belt and a helmet with ear guards. His weapons are an axe, a sword and a belted dagger and, as with most Hittite figures, he appears to be on the march. Within the walls of the city are the sites of four **temples**. A **tunnel**, too, leads down to a **postern gate** in the outer wall. The next principal entry along the line of the walls is the **Gate of the Sphinxes**; the carving of one of the sphinxes is in the İstanbul Archaeological Museum, and the other one is in Berlin. A third entry, the **Lion Gate**, has a rampant lion with its mouth open in a roar on each jamb of the main portal.

Below the spur on its north side, the principal **temple** is in the plain. It stands on an elevated shelf of land, and its court is paved in black basalt. The peristyle has massive square-shaped columns in a double tier, while the inner sanctum is perhaps less accessible than Apollo's at Didyma. Here the deity would have been the Great Mother of Anatolia, or the Sun-goddess, seated in that formal austerity of Egyptian deities: her appeasement may have called for the sacrifice of a prisoner-of-war, a disgraced soldier or a runaway slave. The city's administrative offices probably were within the temple complex, with the market-place adjoining it. A **Sacred Way** led from the gate in the lower city's walls to the temple's entrance, and here a large stone receptacle no doubt served for ritual ablutions. Boğazköy, the village, is outside the gate, and the quarters of the Assyrian merchants may well have been located there.

Entrance to Yazilikaya, in the same vicinity, is through a fissure in a rock outcrop. On the walls on either side of a lower chamber is a line of carved deities converging on a panel on the end wall. On the panel, a marriage is depicted between Arinna, the Mother-goddess, and Sharma, the Weather-god. A gryphon guards the short stairway to an upper chamber. The main relief here is of Sharma, in an attitude of genuflection, with a smaller figure of a king between his knees, as though under the god's protection. The god's symbol of divinity is a high conical-shaped hat. The carving is assigned to the reign of Tudhaliyas IV, *circa* 1250 BC. Another carving in this chamber is of a Sword-god, and there is also a panel, a similar one appearing in the lower chamber as well, of twelve figures who seem to be hurrying, each carrying a sickle-shaped object.

Alaca Hüyük is 30 kilometres (19 miles) to the northeast of Boğazköy and Yazîlikaya, situated outside the town of Alaca. Sections of the outer walls are there, as well as a gateway with sphinx carvings on either jamb, in which both creatures seem to be leaning or projecting out of the stone. On another block is a double-headed eagle — with a goddess above its head — holding a hare between its talons. Other less definable carvings are in the same line of the walls. Among the widespread excavations is a **palace**. Also, there is an oval-shaped early **altar**. Tombs of kings, some dating to Hittite times, have yielded weapons, bronze standards and pottery. Many recoveries are housed in the museum in Alaca, alongside the headquarters and hostel of the Turkish team that dug here. Exhibits include a selection of decorated pottery of several periods, weapons, artifacts and reconstructed tombs and burial urns. The garden has a Hittite lion, along with examples of Byzantine carved sarcophagi and inscribed stelae.

Gordium

There is a **palace** dating from about 700 BC among the excavated buildings. Much Phrygian pottery is colourful and highly decorated, but also at Gordium some huge metallic-tinted **amphorae** (two-handled narrow-necked jars) were found, with at least one bearing an inscription in Lydian. As at Polatli, the excavated shafts descend through many formerly occupied layers. Although most recoveries have gone to the museum at Ankara and elsewhere, there is a display in the former workshops of the American expedition that dug here. Phrygia had a reputation for its ivory artifacts, faience beads, gold filigree and items in terracotta.

Away from the excavated city is the **Burial Place of the Kings** where funeral mounds have been opened. A corridor — ingeniously concealed — leads down through the mound to the hardwood-panelled burial chamber. Finely carved wooden screens surrounded the tomb. This country had been heavily forested in Phrygian times, and timber was used extensively in construction. A model for houses of later times, a typical Phrygian house was a half-timbered structure on two floors, with an upper wooden balcony and balustrade overlooking a central courtyard.

The Sakarya River flows on the eastern side of the site excavations. Here the Greek expeditionary force of 1920–2, in its conflict with Turkey, was halted and retreated eventually. The lines of the former trenches are discernible still, along the banks of the river.

Cappadocia

On the route to Nevşehir, a stop can be made at Hacibektaş where a neat complex includes a **monastery**, a **library**, a small museum and the **Tomb of Haci Bektaş**. Haci Bektaş founded an Order of Dervishes, the Bektaşi, whose precepts incorporated Shia, Sunni and Christian tenets. Member of this order were appointed teachers in İstanbul to boys recruited or abducted into the Corps of Janissaries. The grounds of the monastery complex are well maintained and offer a favourable place in which to pause.

Nevşehir is at the base of a hill that is honeycombed with caves and crowned by an **Ottoman citadel**. The first cones can be seen on the right of the road as you approach the city, and you can go into some and explore them.

The Göreme Valley

More than 350 rupestrian churches have been carved out of the volcanic tufa in the valley. Most have elaborate architectural features, and many are

Hittite Theology

Professor John Garstang, who excavated Yümüktepe at Mersin and worked elsewhere in Turkey, is a fascinating interpreter of Hittite theology. He believes that the gods and goddesses of the peoples who contributed to Hittite culture were brought together at Yazilikaya to witness a marriage that would synthesize the various conflicting religious beliefs; quantity had led to duplications of the divine services for which each deity was responsible. At Yazilikaya, too, there was the attempt to establish protocol among the higher echelon of divinity, as well as in the lower echelon, such as the deities in procession on either wall of the lower chamber.

In the Wedding Panel, the principal gods and goddesses of the Hittite and Hurrian pantheons are represented. Arinna is the Sun-goddess, and in origin this shrine may have been hers. Sharma, the Weather-god of Anatolia, is her son and consort. In the Hurrian or Hurrite pantheon, the Queen of Heaven was Hebat, her son and consort was Teshub. On the panel, Hepatu is depicted as the Mother-goddess, with Teshub as her consort, while Sharma, a figure smaller in size than Teshub, is standing on the back of a lion to the rear of Hepatu. It should be remembered though that, in such a wall carving, size could denote distance or eleva-'ion rather than importance. Sharma carries a double-headed axe, which a Hittite symbol, while Teshub stands astride the shoulders of Namni and Hazzi, who were either minor deities or superceded or demoted

decorated with geometric or pictorial frescoes. A local publication providing detailed information is available at the entrance. A guide can be hired here.

Of particular interest are the restored frescoes of **Elmalı Kilise**, a church opposite a monastery, on the left. Its rooms are carved out on more than one level and include a chapel, refectory and kitchen area. The **Karanlık Kilise**, **Yılanlı** and the **Tokatlı** should also be visited. A number of places have been signposted for the convenience of visitors, but personal exploration is possible still and recommended.

Ürgüp

This town has developed into a large tourist centre with its hotels, pensions, boutiques and restaurants — the wine of the district is also most potable. Many of the cones in the vicinity are fitted out as well-appointed dwellings. Avcılar, too, has cones and converted rock dwellings. Uç Hisar has a carved edifice consisting of three castles, and Ortahisar's castle dominates a needle-pointed

gods. Elsewhere in Hittite depictions, Namni and Hazzi are personalized mountains, and in others they represent Night and Day. In yet other carvings, Teshub as the Weather-god is depicted in a chariot drawn by two bulls, Sari and Hurri, and again in others the Bull-gods seem also to represent Night and Day. In the Wedding Panel, each bull is a separate entity; one is associated with Teshub, the other with Hepatu.

To the rear of Hepatu and Sharma, two goddesses share a two-headed eagle which holds a lyre between its claws. These two goddesses are the daughter and the granddaughter of Arinna. At the back of Teshub is Telepinu, a god of Vegetation, and third in line in the hierarchy of Young-gods. A Young-god such as Teshub — as with such gods in other religions, ie Adonis, Tammuz, Osiris, Baal — is the god who must die, be sacrificed or be hidden away during the summer drought, later to be reborn, revived or found again in the spring through the agency of the Mother-goddess, and he becomes her consort. In some Hittite texts, Telepinu is the Young-god, and he, as with Teshub in others, is the protagonist in a fight with the dragon Illuyankas in which, at first, the dragon gets the upper hand but is finally killed by the Hero-god through the favourable intervention of the Mother-goddess or one of her agents.

Professor Garstang believes that an annual ceremony was conducted at Yazılikaya in which a marriage was enacted and consummated between the reigning king in the role of Teshub and a priestess of the sanctuary in that of the Mother-goddess.

mass of carved-out dwellings, with churches and monasteries in its neighbour-hood. Çavuş In is a village at the base of a semi-circular cliff that harbours a legion of caves — note here the **Church of St John Prodromos** (John the Baptist). At Avanos, on the north bank of the Kizilirmak River, the potteries make use of the district's red earth; objects in onyx are also manufactured. Nearby Zelve has the entrance to yet another valley of conic shapes and con-cealed ecclesiastical structures. Sari Han, near Avanos, has a Seljuk *han* with a fine gateway and courtyard.

Kaymakli and Derinküyü

Entry to these two many-storeyed underground cities is by tunnel. Chimne·'-style shafts or ducts supplied air to the thousands of villagers and town-dwellers who took refuge in them from the frequent and anarchic depredations of marauding armies from the seventh to the 15th centuries.

In the neighbouring valley of Cemil, among other structures is the **Monastery of the Archangelos**, a feature of which is the large arcaded **refec-tory**. At Girgoli the **Aghiasma of St Luke** is on the site of an ancient sacred spring, where there are several accompanying chapels. Near it, at Sinasos, is a **Chapel of the Virgin Mary**. Damsa, another village close by, has a Seljuk mosque.

Niğde

Niğde has a claim to Hittite origin, but its standing monuments are mainly Sel-juk. A ruined **castle**, probably Byzantine, stands on the hill above the town. The Seljuk **citadel**, with its polygonal keep, dates from the 11th century, but it was restored under the Ottomans in the 15th century when a wall with bastions was built round the citadel's mound. South of the citadel is a triple-domed **mosque** of 1203. Later restored by Sultan Ala et Tin, it bears his name. Below the mosque is the long, arched covered market. The Mongol 14th-century mosque opposite the market is the **Süngür Bey Cami**. By a **town gate** in the citadel walls is the **Eskiçiler Çeşmesi**, a fountain of 1421, behind which is the **Şah Meşcit**, a small mosque of the 15th century with Byzantine columns incor-porated in its structure. Near the Süngür Bey Cami, the **Ak Medrese** (theologi-cal school) has a modest archaeological museum. The building is a Karamanoğlu one of 1402 (the Karamanoğlu became the heirs of the Sultanate of Rum following its disintegration). The **Diş Cami** is Ottoman of the 16th cen-tury. The largest of three **tombs**, the **Hüdavent Türbesi** of 1312, is that of a princess; the two other tombs are of a later date.

İhlara and the Peristrema Gorge

With extra time, a visit could be made to the Peristrema Gorge in the foothills

to the west and south of Nevşehir. In the İhlara valley, churches and
monasteries are as legion as at Göreme, only here there are constructed buildings and not only structures carved out of the tufa. In the gorge itself, it is
usual to ford the Melendiz River, or cross by footbridge if the river is in spate.
Churches to be seen for their colourful and dramatic frescoes are the **Eğri Taş
Kilise**, the **Kökar** and the **Pürenli Şeki**; there is abstract decor at the **Ağaçili
Kilise**, which has steps up to it formed from tree trunks.

Kayseri

The **Byzantine fort** within the citadel was strengthened by the Seljuks in 1224
and again under the Osmanlis. The latter reinforced the walls and their 19
square or rectangular defence towers. The Seljuk lions at the gate keep watch
on the **covered bazaar** over the way. The **gateway** is double, and there is an inscription over the inner gate relating to Mehmet II, the Conqueror, who added
the small **mosque** and **fountain** within the walls. Stairways lead up to the accessible sentry walk.

The Ulu Cami near the bazaar is a Danişmend twin-domed structure begun
in 1135 but completed later under the Seljuk reoccupation. The **Huant Hatun
Cami** dates from 1237. Huant Hatun was the Georgian wife of Sultan
Keykubat; her octagonal-shaped tomb is in the mosque complex. There is also
a *medrese*, now the Ethnological Museum.

Behind the park the double building of 1205, the **Çifte Medrese**, has a fine
entrance and was founded by Sultan Keyhusrev. One building (the **Giyasiye**)
was designed as a medical school, one of the first of its kind; the other (the
Şifahiye) was a hospital. The **Sahibiye Medrese** dates from 1267, and this
also has a fine entrance. The restored interior houses a collection of Seljuk
stone carvings. The **Hacı Kılıç Cami and Medrese** on Cumhuriyet Bulvarı is
of 1249 origin. The **Güllük Cami**, although 1210 in origin, was rebuilt about a
century later by the Seljuk Güllük Şamşeddin; it has a fine mihrab of floral
tiles and a carved cornice. An Ottoman mosque in the park, the restored
Kurşunlu, is believed to have been designed by Sinan in 1518.

A *kümbet* is a mausoleum, and there are several outstanding ones in the city.
The **Döner Kümbet** (Revolving Mausoleum), an ornate Seljuk construction of
1275, is decorated with leaf-patterned carvings, arabesques and feline creatures. Its tower is cylinder-shaped on a square foundation and topped by a conical roof. Close by is the **Sırçalı Kümbet** — Faience Tower —though here
much of the tiling that gave it its name has gone.

The **Archaeological Museum** on Atatürk Bulvarı includes Hittite finds
from the site at Kültepe.

Homes carved from pinnacles of sandstone (left); church interior, Cappadocia (right)

Kültepe

The clay tablets in cuneiform that record the transactions of Assyrian merchants were found at Kültepe, the Hittite city of Kanesh, and were key elements in the deciphering of Hittite texts. Assyrians, who traded throughout Anatolia, lived in established quarters outside a major city, forming a *karum* or a bazaar consisting of a group of traders, that could also include workers in metal. As well as Hittite, the site revealed evidence of Akkadian occupation in the days of Sargon (*circa* 2500 BC) and of a later Anatolian coalition that was formed against Naram Singh, Sargon's grandson. Pre-Hittite pottery known as Cappadocian ware, decorated with geometrical and symbolic motifs, originated at Kanesh. Levels of two Phrygian cities of the ninth and fifth centuries BC were also identified.

Konya

Most of Konya's development has happened west of the old city. Nearly all the monuments of Konya are situated on or a near an east-west axis, running for about 1.5 kilometre (one mile) between the square where the Mevlana Monastery is situated and the central park with the Alaeddin Mosque on its hill. The Seljuk citadel was erected on the ancient mound that has provided excavators with information on the site's earlier, and earliest, occupiers, and it is now incorporated in Alaeddin Park at the western extremity of that central axis.

From the crossroads and roundabout near the *otogar*, take a minibus indicating its destination as Uçler, or ask for Mevlana. If you arrive after dark, you will have no difficulty recognizing your stop: floodlighting then illuminates the monastery with the conspicuous green cone, as well as the Selimiye Mosque close by.

Starting from the **Mevlana Tekke**, or monastery, now a museum (entrance fee 5,000TL), you enter into a fountained court with the entrance to the principle rooms leading off one side and the cells of the dervishes, or monks, off the other three sides. On the left of the main entrance into the complex, two cells have been reconstructed and fitted out: one as though occupied by a dervish and the other as though occupied by the head dervish, or abbot. There is a display of fine prayer rugs in the arcade of this section.

One of the principal rooms has the coffins of the abbots, including Mevlana's marble sarcophagus. The walls of this section are hung with fine drapery, and Mevlana's tomb is covered by a brocade which was donated by Sultan Abdul Hamit II in the 19th century. A newel post at the head of each coffin has the turban of the occupant wound about it; the number of turns of the cloth, it has been said, indicates the degree of sanctity obtained by the tomb's occupant. At the rear of this chamber is the chapel. The second room is the one in which the ritual dance of the order took place. In it there is a display of fine

Konya

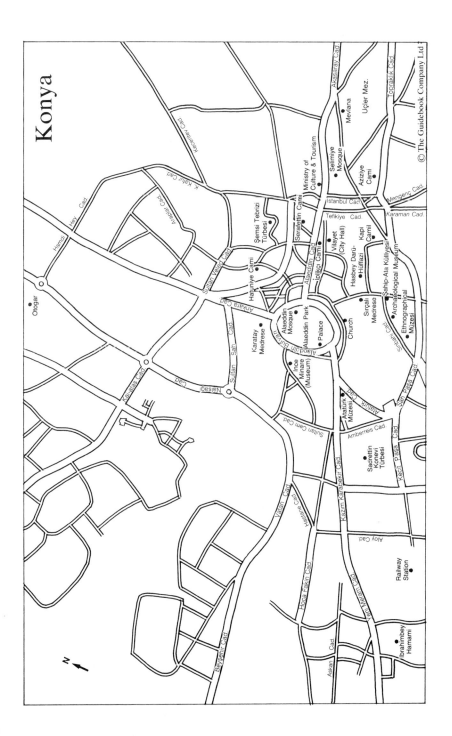

N

Otogar

Hamdi Hey. Cad.

Keçeciler Cad.

K. Kafur Cad.

Atabtar Cad.

Sultan Veled Cad.

Şemsi Tebrizi Türbesi

Hatuniye Cami

Ankara Cad.

Karatay Medrese

Alaeddin Mosque

Alaeddin Park

Palace

Ince Minare (Museum)

Sultan Şah Cad.

Nalçacı Cad.

Karakaş Cad.

Serafettin Cami

Ministry of Culture & Tourism

Akasaray Cad.

Selimiye Mosque

Mevlana

Üçler Mez.

Aziziye Cami

Toprakiık Cad.

İstanbul Cad.

Tefikiye Cad.

Mengenç Cad.

Karaman Cad.

Vilayet (City Hall)

İplikçi Cami

Alaeddin Cad.

Kapi Camii

Hasbey Darü-Hüffazı

Sahip-Ata Külliyesi

Archaeological Museum

Church

Sırçalı Medrese

Sırçalı Cad.

Ethnographical Müzesi

Atatürk Müzesi

Atatürk Cad.

Şah Paşa Cad.

Amberreis Cad.

Sultan Cem Cad.

Hastane Cad.

Vatan Cad.

Kazim Karabekir Cad.

Sadrettin Konevi Türbesi

Keçi Paşa Cad.

Aloy Cad.

Railway Station

Beyşehir Cad.

Hoca Fakin Cad.

Fetih Mekam Cad.

Askan Cad.

İbrahimbey Hamamı

© The Guidebook Company Ltd.

manuscripts, including the Koran and the works of Celâleddin Rumi Mevlana (1207–73), the order's founder. Other cases hold exquisitely woven prayer rugs, and there is one case containing the musical instruments used by the musicians in the ritual dance.

Outside, the green conical dome of the monastery rises above a wide-ribbed drum of glazed turquoise tiles. The top of the drum is encircled by a blue kufic-scripped band. This section of the complex is Seljuk of the 13th century; the other part is 16th-century Ottoman. Each former cell has a leaded dome over it, and there is a single minaret.

The **Selimiye Mosque**, next door, was begun in 1558 by Selim II while he was governor of Konya, but it was not completed until he became sultan in 1566. Sinan is said to have had a hand in the construction. Substantial columns rise to a high dome; windows round the base let in the light to an open interior.

Moving west along Alaeddin Caddesi, you will find the Ministry of Tourism's Information Office on the right. Some little way further on, in an opening to the right, is the **Şerafettin Cami**, an open style mosque with side chapels and a central domed area. A Seljuk building modified in Ottoman times, it was ultimately restored in the 19th century after having been damaged in a fire.

Some distance down past the local bus stops and a small garden area, you eventually reach the large, circular Alaeddin Tepesi (Alaeddin Hill or Park). The **Alaeddin Mosque**, the central monument on the park's mound or hill, is temporarily closed to visitors while under restoration. Within a walled section of the complex, which has a Seljuk façade built over a Byzantine structure, are the tombs of Mesult I (1156), Kîlîç Arslan II (1192), Rukneddin Süleiman II (1204), Giyaseddin Keyhüsrev II (1246), Kîlîç Arslan IV (1266) and Giyaseddin Keyhüsrev III (1283), as well as those of royal sons and other princes.

Walking clockwise on Alaeddin Bulvarî, the road that encircles the park, starts from Alaeddin Caddesi, opposite a *çay bahçe* (tea garden) and Ordu Evi (barracks) inside the park. On the left of the bulvarî is the **İnce Minare and Medrese** with its decorated entrance and turquoise-ribbed minaret which, struck by lightning once, is minus its top. The *medrese* is now a **Museum of Stone and Wood Carvings**. Further round and on the same side is the **Karatay Medrese** of 1251, with a dome decorated in blue tiles with gold embellishments. The tall entrance has a carved stalactite pattern and an entwined rope motif. A calligraphic frieze, incorporating the names of the first four caliphs, runs round the base of the dome. The *medrese* now houses a **Tile Museum**. Going further round, inside the park, are the remains of a **Seljuk palace**, which may have been built over a Byzantine one. What is there is being protected by an arched concrete structure.

By taking a street running south from the park, you come to the **Sîrçalî Medrese** of 1242, now a **Museum of Carved Tombstones**. In a street running

east from just below the Sîrçalî Medrese is the **Hasbey Darül-Hüffazi** of 1421, a School of Koranic Studies founded under the Karamanoğlu. A little further south of the Sîrçalî Medrese, and to the right, is the **Şahip-Ata Külliyesi** with its mosque and the **Tomb of Fahrettin Ali**. Fahrettin Ali was a grand vizier who held office from 1269, in the reign of Giraseddin Keyhüsrev III, until 1288 in the reign of the latter's successor. Near the tomb are the **Archaeological Museum** and, a little to the west, the **Ethnographical Museum**.

Returning then along Alaeddin Caddesi before reaching the area of Serafettin Cami, you approach the imposing stone building of the **Vilayet**, or offices of the governor of the province. Near it is the **İplikçi Cami**, built in the late 12th century and since restored. Back towards the Mevlana Square, on a street leading to a market area, is the **Aziziye Cami**. This is a baroque mosque of 1641 with a very high decorated marble doorway and a columned portico. It has interesting twin minarets, each with an ornamented cupola. In an area to the north of Alaeddin Caddesi is the site of the **Hatuniye Cami** of 1213, which, alas, has only its minaret left standing on its octagonal base. West of it in another street is the **Şemsi Tebrizi Türbesi**. Sems was the tutor and spiritual guide of Mevlana.

As a community, Konya is proud to be the repository of the fundamentals of Islamic faith, although that general aspect has become modified in recent years, and if women as yet have little chance of spiritual elevation, their presence in the city has become less veiled. Perhaps this is due to the influence of Western backpackers with their less conventional gear, however, modesty is required of female visitors at Moslem shrines, and cotton skirts are loaned at the Mevlana.

Çatal Hüyük

The site of Çatal Hüyük was excavated in the 1960s by James Melkaart of the British Archaeological Institute in Ankara. The finds are neolithic *circa* 7000 BC, and the artifacts unearthed are of a level of culture beyond anything that could have been expected of such a period. Wall paintings are on plaster, not on the bare rock. Recoveries are in the Ankara Museum and include a reconstruction of a neolithic settlement based on the excavator's findings.

Southeastern Anatolia

Among the mainly Moslem inhabitants in Gaziantep, there are some Christian-Turkish families, some Syrians and some Kurds. This population make-up is repeated to an extent in the towns and cities along Turkey's southern frontier with Syria.

Called Antep by the citizens, Gaziantep was awarded the prefix *Gazi* (the title for a distinguished general) after the city's stubborn resistance to occupation by the French during Atatürk's War of Independence. Today Gaziantep is known for its pre-eminent copperwork and the profitable cultivation of pistachio nuts. Many large orchards extend to the south and southeast of the city. With a day or perhaps two days to spare, a diversion to Nemrut Daǧ, the mountain-top tomb of Antiochus I Commagene, can be undertaken northeast of Gaziantep.

The Hittite site of Carchemish can be seen by diverting to the south for an hour or two from Nizip. Crossing the Euphrates River at Birecik on the way to Şanlıurfa, you enter Mesopotamia, between the Euphrates and the Tigris. Besides the site of Edessa at Şanlıurfa, another site can be seen by again diverting to the south. The site of Harran is alongside a village of beehive-style houses, a form of domestic construction common throughout northern Syria.

Along this former Garden of Eden, the frontier route from Şanlıurfa to Mardin runs through the Plain of the Jezireh, dotted with mounds that are an indication of the extent to which it was populated before the dikes that once controlled the Mesopotamian waterways were destroyed by the Mongol invaders of the 13th century.

Diyarbakır stands above the Tigris; the black basalt outer walls and towers of the ancient city look impressive from whichever direction you approach them. The river flows round the base of the hill on which the city stands and out through a ravine on the east side. In the early part of this century the Tigris was navigable by raft from here to Baghdad (a journey of several days), but this is no longer possible.

Getting There

A journey into this border region could start at Adana or from Antakya. Although the E5 turns south at Toprakkale, the E24 continues east through the Amanus Mountains to Gaziantep, 136 kilometres (85 miles) away.

To reach Nemut Daǧ from Gaziantep, take the Kahramanmaraş, or simply Maraş, road 53 kilometres (33 miles) to Narlı, then go northeast to Gölbaşı, 73 kilometres (45 miles) away. Gölbaşı is on the railway from Gaziantep, Maraş or Narlı. From here take the Adıyaman road, and after 12 kilometres (eight miles) turn southeast onto a road to Besni, from where the really strenuous part of the trip begins. Go east for 45 kilometres (28 miles) to Eski Kâhta on the Kâhta Çayi (Nymphaeon River), followed by a climb which can be accomplished by minibus.

If you wish to see Carchemish, turn off the E24 at Nizip, 36 kilometres (22 miles) from Gaziantep. Take a road running south 30 kilometres (19 miles) to Barak. You are on the frontier with Syria here, and should ask at the military barracks for permission to proceed to Carchemish (Kargamiş), a kilometre (.6 mile) further. Near the site is a railway bridge across the Euphrates; it carries the line to Aleppo in Syria.

Back on the road 15 kilometres (nine miles) east of Nizip, you cross the Euphrates River by a long bridge at Birecik, a pleasant-looking town that slopes up from the river's bank to a citadel. In Seljuk times there had been a bridge of boats on this river. Şanlıurfa is 83 kilometres (52 miles) from here.

Like Carchemish, Harran is close to the Turkish–Syrian frontier. You go out of Tanlıurfa on road 885 running south to Akçakale, and after 32 kilometres

The Mevlevi: The Whirling Dervishes

At the completion of a series of spiritual exercises, the novitiates of this Order of Dervishes attained their ultimate state of mystical perception in a formal dance. Revolving to the accompaniment of drum, flute and stringed instruments, the novitiate wore a white, flared, ankle-length robe and white jacket. As the dancer rotated, right arm held up in prayer, the left downwards, the skirt spun out in a whorl. A white conical-shaped hat resembling a high-crowned fez was worn. Symbolically, the hat represented a tombstone, while the jacket and skirt represented the tomb and shroud respectively. The white jacket would be discarded at the beginning of the dance, thereby implying that earthly connections had been discarded.

Celâleddin Rumi Mevlana was a Persian citizen born in 1207 at Balkh in what is now Afghanistan. His father was a distinguished theologian, and the family, displaced because of Mongolian rampaging, was eventually invited to Konya by the Seljuk Sultan Alaeddin Keykubat. Celâleddin was a lyrical poet; his spiritual mentor, Şems, was a mystic Persian philosopher and unorthodox teacher, whose death Celâleddin mourned in a sequence of poems. Celâleddin was an Islamic counterpart of a St John of the Cross, and his religious philosophy, based on a concept of universal and non-sectarian divine love, was a compound of Islamic, Christian and Zoroastrian precepts. He was also

(20 miles) take a turning for Altınbaşak, 12 kilometres (eight miles) east. The site itself is beside the village.

The distance from Şanlıurfa to Mardin is 185 kilometres (115 miles). There are ruins on the outskirts of Viranşehir which a truly inquisitive traveller might find time to explore. At Kızıltepe the high mountain barrier to the north moves dramatically closer; it stretches up almost sheer from the plain to where Mardin stands perched on the edge. One kilometre (.6 mile) beyond Kızıltepe you take a turn to the left, and after 11 kilometres (seven miles) begin to climb to Mardin, a further nine kilometres (six miles).

Leaving Mardin on the east side, road 955 descends southeasterly to join the E24 on the Jezireh Plain again. At Nusaybin, 30 kilometres (19 miles) east of the road junction, is a main frontier crossing into Syria and the last Turkish station on the railway to Baghdad. From the 955 road junction with the E24, the main road continues to Cizre, 131 kilometres (81 miles) east, where the E26 runs southeasterly through Silopi to the frontier and crosses 46 kilometres (29 miles) into Iraq.

---

an exponent of religious tolerance. His poetry earned him the title of Mevlana, the equivalent of a British Order of Merit, and he was appointed court advisor on religious questions. Subsequent abbots of the order served in this capacity with later Seljuk and Ottoman sultans. The Rumi in Mevlana's title refers to the Seljuk name Rum, for Rome. His poetry, his beliefs and his teachings have come to be associated with Sufism.

Atatürk's reforms at the time of the establishment of the Turkish Republic included the closing of all religious houses and Islamic schools. His intention seems to have been to end what he considered to be the narrow, anachronistic influence of the imams (Muslim leaders) on the daily life of the ordinary people in Turkey's towns and villages, and the wearing in public of all forms of religious garb, of any denomination, was banned.

The Mevlana monastery, among others, was closed, and its rituals ended. Today, however, a festival of the Mevlana is held on each anniversary of Celâleddin's death, 17 December 1273, during which a performance of the dance is given. The exemplars are recruited not only from within Turkey but also from volunteers, young men who consider themselves converts and exponents of Sufism, in other countries. The traditional garb is worn, and musicians play on instruments applicable to that past age. Authorized performances have also been given outside Konya, at folklore festivals in other parts of the country and abroad.

Going northwest from Mardin through mountain and wooded country, the journey then becomes pastoral and riverine. About two kilometres (1.25 miles) southeast of Diyarbakïr, a Roman bridge with ten irregular arches spans the river. Diyarbakïr can be reached as well from Şanlïurfa, a distance of 186 kilometres (116 miles), although the more felicitous approach is from Mardin.

Historical Background

At the time of the First Crusade, Gaziantep, along with Maraş, 82 kilometres (51 miles) to its northeast, became part of the Latin County of Edessa. As Gurgun, Maraş was the centre of a 12th-century BC Hittite kingdom that used hieroglyphic script; it was referred to in Assyrian texts as Markasi.

In the first century Gaziantep was Roman Germanicea. The Arabs took it from the Byzantines in the early seventh century, and from then until its occupation by the Seljuks in the 11th century, it changed hands between Arabs and Byzantines as the fortunes of war favoured this empire or that one, until the Crusaders arrived. For a period after that it became part of the Kingdom of Cilicia that Baibars overran. Selim I (1512–20) took it for the Ottoman Empire, and its citadel is as the Ottomans rebuilt it.

Mithridates Callinicus founded his kingdom in the first century BC: it stretched north from Gaziantep to Adïyaman, a distance of 150 kilometres (93 miles). When an alliance was formed with Rome, the country became a buffer state between Rome and Persia. Antiochus claimed to be related to Alexander through his mother and Darius through his father, therefore, his ambitions were large and his achievement small, though his tomb is spectacular.

Edessa (at Şanlïurfa) dates back to the 16th century BC, when Egypt was in control but allowed its Phoenician–Syrian occupants a degree of independence. Later there was Hurrite–Mitanni (Hittite) occupation that spread throughout northern Mesopotamia. Alexander's Macedonians named it Edessa after his birthplace. At one time Edessa had 11 successive Aramaic rulers, the Abgars, who held power for 400 years from the second century BC. One Abgar prince claimed that a cloth bearing the imprint of Christ's face, the Mandillion, had been given to him by Jesus. John Curcuas, a successful general under Romanus Lecapenus, took the Mandillion back to Constantinople after his tenth-century victory over the Arabs. Yet another Byzantine general, George Maniaces, reoccupying Edessa, took back to Constantinople yet another sacred relic, a letter purported to have been written by Jesus to that Abgar prince to whom the Mandillion had been given. Another Abgar prince (179–214) was the inspiration and promoter of Christian-Aramaic literature. Edessa became Ottoman in 1536, though its territory was not incorporated into the empire until 1637.

The site at Harran was Roman Carrhae, important as a stronghold on the military road from the Mediterranean to the Upper Tigris. Here, on 28 May 53, besides the 20,000 men who were killed and another 10,000 who were taken as prisoners, the Roman general Crassus lost the Imperial Eagles to the Parthian King Oroder I. In 1104 Bohemond and Tancred, the Norman–Franks of Sicily, lost a battle to the Saracens and thereby ended their hope of extending their territory as far as Mosul, as well as putting a seal on the fate of the Latin County of Edessa. Tradition has it that Abraham spent several years at Harran on his journey to Canaan.

Sadly, a 19th-century Ottoman sultan settled numbers of dispossessed Circassians on the land approaching Mardin, but though they worked with a will they were unable to discard the habits or the clothing of their Caucasian homeland, and many succumbed to physical exhaustion while others were decimated in an outbreak of cholera.

Mardin was Marde when Justinian and Chosroes the Persian fought for its possession. In the continuous struggle between both empires, Mardin, along with other towns of the region, changed hands as frequently as this side or that gained ascendancy. In the 12th century it fell to an Ortokid emir and, with only a minor temporary change or two, has stayed Moslem ever since. Saladin failed to take the city. A Mongol horde also besieged it for eight months without success. A story has it that at a critical time during the siege the defenders made yogurt out of dog's milk and sent some out to the besiegers, a gift that so convinced the Mongol commander the city had ample supplies still, he raised his siege and departed.

Excavations within the inner walls of Diyarbakir have identified what is believed to have been in origin a Mitanni settlement, then a city of the Urartu, then Assyrian. As heirs of Alexander, the Seleucids occupied it, and because it commanded so strategic a crossing of the Upper Tigris, it became an objective of perennial conflict between the Romans and the Persians, then Byzantines against Persians. Under Justinian one siege lasted so long even the supply of rats ran out, and a group of hags took to cannabilism, murdering lonely victims at night, but were brought to justice eventually by the infernal smell of their charnel pots.

Arabs captured the city in 639, and in 660 it became part of the Omayyid Caliphate and, subsequently, in 750, of their Abbasid successors. In 974 the Byzantines under John Tsimiskis succeeded in recapturing Diyabakir, but for only a brief occupation, as the Persians later did for a limited period in the 16th century under Şah İsmail. It became Ottoman in 1515.

The Unveiling

My mother was rebelling against life too—but for a different reason. Her rebellion was, unexpectedly enough, against wearing the veil, for she had noticed that none of the foreign women wore them and that even a few of the more daring Turkish women from good families had ceased the practice also. She used to complain about it to my grandmother, declaring she was sick and tired of keeping her face covered, and I would interrupt, with lordly ten-year oldness, saying I would not have her going about the streets with her face open. I would chastise her too for her many goings-out.

'You are never at home,' I would declare and although usually I was told to mind my own affairs, one day I was very surprised when my grandmother actually agreed with me.

'It is quite true,' she said heatedly. 'You are always out these days. And it is not right for you to complain that you have to wear the veil. Why, many women are still behind the kafes and they never see the colour of the sky, excepting from behind their veils. But at least you cannot complain of that for you tore the kafes from here and it is a wonder to me that you were ever accepted in this street, for you behaved exactly like a fast woman looking for another husband or like a prostitute. Yes, you did!' she assured my mother's astonished face. 'And now you talk of leaving aside your veil. Why, I lived for thirty years with my husband and I never went out without his permission and I had to keep my face covered all the time. If I went out in the carriage with Murat, immediately all the windows were closed and sometimes the blinds were drawn too. I say it is a scandal that women are to-day revealing their faces. God will punish them! Do not let me hear another word from you, my daughter, for surely the sky will open on you for such impiety.'

Never had I heard my grandmother talk at such length or with such obvious passion. My mother replied:

'You are talking a great deal of old-fashioned nonsense, mother! My place is not in the home these days. If I were to sit at home all day, or you either for that matter, who would go to market for us? Do you expect me to stay here all day, reading the Koran and wearing my veil for fear the passers-by should see me from the street? I tell you again, from now on I shall go without my veil!'

And she angrily tore the pretty veil from her face and threw it petulantly on the floor.

My grandmother lifted her hands to heaven.

'I never thought I should live to see this day,' she said.

'Times are changing,' said my mother.

'They will say you are a prostitute!' wailed my grandmother, genuinely distressed, totally incapable of accepting such a fierce gesture as the 'opening' of the face.

'If they do, it will not worry me,' retorted my mother. 'Their words will not bring bread to me. And from now on, you will throw aside your veil too, mother.'

'Oh no, no, no!' said my grandmother in superstitious horror. 'God forbid I should invite punishment upon me!'

But the next morning when my mother went into Beyoglu, with a box of embroidered articles under her arm and her lovely face naked to the world, she was stoned by some children near Bayazit and received a nasty cut on the side of her head. After that she was cautious about going anywhere alone, but was adamant about not re-veiling herself; Mehmet or I would go with her to Beyoglu, my grandmother steadfastly refusing to be seen with her. The reaction to her in the street was mixed. The older ones were stricken with horror, more especially since they had always recognised my mother as a good woman, and now their faith in her was sadly battered. She was still young and attractive—she was twenty-five—and despite the shadows that lingered now and then in her eyes, was so unusually beautiful that people could not help but stare at her, and certain sections of the street wondered if she were trying to catch a husband. They came in their droves, the old men as well, to remonstrate with my grandmother, urging her to put a stop to this terrible thing, and my grandmother, thoroughly enjoying herself, would groan to them that she had no authority left in this wayward family of hers. But the younger women sided with my mother, and some of them even began to follow her example. Their fathers, however, in the absence of dead husbands, took a stick to them muttering piously that no woman in their family would so disgrace themselves. So they put on their veils again in a hurry.

Irfan Orga, Portrait of a Turkish Family

Sights

Gaziantep

In this developing modern city, there is evidence of Seljuk occupation after the 11th century in the **fortress** at the city's centre and in the *medrese* in Karagoz Caddesi. Excavations at an ancient mound on the edge of the city, on the road going east to Nizip, however, uncovered evidence of occupations that go back to the fourth millennium. Among exhibits in the **Archaeological Museum** are a collection of Hittite recoveries.

At 2,000 metres (6,560 feet) on the summit of **Nemrut Dağ**, the great pyramidal-shaped **tomb** is 150 metres (500 feet) wide and 50 metres (164 feet) high. There are reliefs of both Alexander and Darius and of eagles and lions. The entrance is on the north side, with terraces on the other three. Headless Greek and Persian deities sit on a bench as though in heavenly judgement, and on the slope below are their giant heads, looking like characters in a Becket play, buried up to their necks.

On the way up, **Eski Kale**, a castle at Eski Kâhta, has an inscribed relief — dated 50 BC — of Antiochus clasping the hand of Heracles. Here a **Roman bridge** crosses the Cendere River, a tributary of the Euphrates. At Karakuş there are standing columns of the **mausoleum** of Commagene queens.

Carchemish

This was the capital of one of the last of those southern Hittite kingdoms, which fell to the Assyrian Sargon II in 717 BC. From the top of the citadel mound there is a fine view of the Euphrates as it executes a series of loops and throws off several subsidiary streams. On the riverside below the mound are the remains of a **water gate**. The ruins of a **palace** and other buildings of an extensive city lie at the citadel's base; carved supports of black basalt columns stand prominent among the spreadeagled drums. There is a **Sacred Way** within the inner city, as well as two **gates** in the sections of **walls** that still stand. Parts of the site, though, are in a military restricted area. T.E. Lawrence worked under Sir Leonard Woolley on the excavations here, and Gertrude Bell was also a member of an expedition that included D.G. Hogarth of later Egyptian archaeological fame.

Şanlıurfa

Edessa's citadel is still substantially walled and towered, with a deep fosse on two sides. It stands on a high elongated spur in the north of the city; climb by way of a path to a postern **gateway**. Inside the gate a plinth with two standing **Corinthian columns** is known as the **Seat (or Throne) of Nimrud**. In its vicinity are several ruined Byzantine buildings. On the unwalled section of the spur are caves that were the nurseries of suckling gods. These became the shrines of saints, and on the ridge above is a Moslem burial ground with domed tombs of Seljuk and Arab princes.

Below the spur are several connecting pools that may have been created by Justinian's engineers, who rebuilt Edessa's fortifications. The pools are fed from a sacred spring, Calirrhoe, and contain a large shoal of carp that are deemed to be sacred. The citizens feed the carp and do not filch them. Abraham is said to have camped by this spring on his journey from Ur into Canaan. Alongside the longest of the pools is the arched wall of the 17th-century **Abder Rahman Medrese**, in the grounds of which is a small mosque. On the quay at the end of this pool there is a 13th-century **oratory** (a place for prayer), the Malkim el Halil.

In the centre of the old city, near the spur, is the Seljuk **Ulu Cami** of the 11th century, a building influenced by Persian architectural styles. Its minaret is hexagonal, and, for the fact finder, its circumference equals its height. A church opposite this mosque is Nestorian. A Nestorian theological school existed here in early Christian times and continued even after that doctrine had been anathematized. When the Emperor Zeno closed it in 479, the expelled teachers continued as missionaries throughout Persia, Central Asia, India and China — the legendary Prester John is believed by some to have been a Nestorian priest.

The site of **Harran** has revealed Hittite, Assyrian, Persian and Roman occupation, and in Assyrian times there was a **sanctuary** here of the Moon-goddess Sin. There are a number of Byzantine ruins, an Islamic fortress and an eighth-century Omayyid mosque with a tall square minaret.

Mardin

The **citadel** is on a ledge above the town and is Roman in origin but much modified over succeeding centuries. Among the buildings inside the citadel walls are the **castle** and the ruins of two mosques. Off the main square in the town below is the **Sultan İsa Medrese** of 1385, built on two levels, each section having its own portico. The 11th-century **Ulu Cami** has a high-walled court, but the mosque was restored in the 14th century, again in the 15th and more recently in the 19th century. The **Lâtifiye Mosque** dates from 1371, but its minaret is of 19th-century origin. The **Sehidiye Cami** and the restored **Reyhanli Cami** are both 14th-century buildings, and the **Kasim Paşa Medrese** dates from the 15th century.

Mardin had 1,200 Christian families at the turn of this century, though a majority has since then emigrated, mostly to America. It is the seat of a metropolitan Bishop of the Syrian Jacobite Monophysite Church. Like the Nestorian, the monophysite doctrine of Jacob Baradaeus was anathematized by the

early church, though the doctrine is subscribed to still by Syrian Christians. There is a Jacobite monastery in a valley a little to the east of Mardin. The main structure dates from the sixth century, and the monastery is active in that its chapel is used by Mardin's Christians. There is also a boarding school on the premises for orphan boys, and their teacher is appointed from Aleppo. Destitute elderly persons are also given accommodation in the former monastery cells. From the top of one of the craggy peaks that rise above the monastery and its almond groves, the prophet Elijah is said to have ascended to Heaven in the chariot of fire.

East of Mardin is Nusaybin, Assyrian Nisibis in the first millennium BC. As an important junction much fought over by armies from the West and the Middle East, Nusaybin has little to show for its perpetual martyrdom other than a **Roman arch**, an early Christian **church** and a Moslem **tomb**.

Diyarbakir

A full day at least is needed for Diyarbakir. It was Amida for the Romans, who built the walls that enclose an inner city situated on an artificial mound. These walls have three gateways, including one in the main wall, which lead to the outer city. There are four gates in the outer, black basalt walls, which are four metres (13 feet) wide and ten metres (33 feet) high, with a postern and 70 towers.

Of the four gates, the northern one, **Harput Gate**, has semi-circular flanking towers. On the towers are Roman and Arabic carvings in relief; one carving shows a bird with outstretched wings. The columns and arch of the gate are Byzantine, and an inscription refers to an inn or a guest house that had to be demolished to make way for the gate. Another inscription in Greek is a record of the arrival of an emissary sent by Justinian, and a Latin one includes the names of Gratianus, Valens and Valentinian. Arabic inscriptions refer to building operations.

The **Mardin Gate** (Bab el Tell or Hill Gate) is the southern one; the Bab el Rum or **Urfa Gate** and the Bab el Dicle or **Yeni Gate** (or New Gate, Tigris Gate or Water Gate) are on the western and eastern sides respectively. Between the Mardin and Urfa gates, the walls and bastions form a salient known as the Yedi Kardeş (Seven Brothers). A main street, running between the Harput and the Mardin gates, is crossed by another which fades out near the Urfa Gate. Outside the Urfa Gate the **Sari Saduk Türbe's** exterior has attractive tilework.

The finest of the city's buildings is the **Ulu Cami** of 1091, built by the Seljuk Malik Shah, son and successor of Alp Arslan, the victor of Manzikert. Restored in 1155, its superstructure is an Ottoman addition. It has a large rectangular court with two fountains. Reliefs of lions and bulls decorate a main entrance, and on the right as you enter are the columns of a Roman building, their bases almost a column-depth below the present level of the paving. Two-tiered colonnades grace either end of the court. The entrance to the prayer hall is on the left, and the minaret, square in structure and with courses of black tiles, stands apart from the main building. The **Archaeological Museum**, to the west of the Ulu Cami, is in the **Zincirli Medrese**, a late 12th-century Ortokid emirate foundation.

Opposite the Ulu Cami, on the edge of a large square, the 16th-century **Hasan Paşa Han** has a fountain in its courtyard and shops on the ground floor under the colonnade and on the balcony. The entrance to the court has calligraphic decoration. Another 16th-century *han*, the Dellfiller, at the Mardin Gate, stands alongside the **Hüsrev Paşa Cami**, which is Ottoman of 1522–8.

In the market area near the crossroads of the two main roads, the **Behram Paşa Cami** of 1573, with its ribbed minaret, is the largest in the city. The church to the south of this mosque is a monophysite one. Other Ottoman mosques are the **Fatih Paşa** of 1522, the **İskender** of 1551, with its fine porch and pleasant garden, and the **Kasim Padishah** of 1512, situated in an alleyway approaching the Mardin Gate. The **Nebi Cami** (Peygamber or Mosque of the Prophet) dates from 1524 but has undergone frequent restoration.

Although the towers on the inner city walls are Byzantine in origin, most probably of the sixth century, they were reconstructed by an Ortokid emir in the 12th century and again in the 16th century by Süleiman the Magnificent. The mosque within the citadel walls is a 12th-century Ortokid construction, as is the palace. Inside, too, is the Byzantine **Church of St George**.

Black Sea Coast

The forested mountain ranges along the whole length of the Black Sea Coast supply a tranquillizing backdrop to sandy beaches and a sea that frequently is more animated than either the Mediterranean or the Aegean.

Sinop marks the boundary between the western and eastern sections of the Black Sea Coast. Assyrians exploited the mineral resources in the region. As well as gold, Jason's Argonauts may have been in search of minerals: even in our industrial age villagers are said to lay sheepskins in the streams to collect gold dust, thereby transforming the legend of the Golden Fleece into fact.

East of Sinop, the Kızılırmak River finds its way to the sea through Bafra, an important centre of Turkey's tobacco industry. Samsun is Turkey's largest Black Sea port. The Pontic mountains descend abruptly in wooded slopes, and in many villages boat building is a traditional craft. Along the coastal stretch near Ordu, and to the east of it, hazelnuts are under intense cultivation.

Under the Ottomans, Trabzon retained its profitability until overland trading routes were revived, to the port's disadvantage. The coming of the railways in the 19th century also contributed to its diminishing importance. Today, trade and international tourism has, to a great extent, helped to revive Trabzon's prosperity. Turkish Maritime Lines has regular sailings from İstanbul, calling at Amasra and Sinop and other ports on the way to Trabzon; an expanded harbour also caters for larger cruise ships. There is a yacht marina here, and a new five-star hotel has been added.

Getting There

From İstanbul, visits to resorts on the western section of the Black Sea Coast can be made on a daily basis. There is Kilyos on the western side of the Bosphorus, for example, or Şile on the eastern shore. Akçakoca, 140 kilometres (87 miles) east of Şile, is best reached from Adapazari or Duzce on the E5 from İstanbul to Ankara.

From Akçakoca, the coastal road runs to Ereğli (Heracleia Pontica), 32 kilometres (20 miles) northeast, and the large industrial port of Zonguldak, a total of 90 kilometres (56 miles).

Beyond Zonguldak the road turns south, but you can pick up the coastal route again by turning northeast at Çaycuma and then by way of Bartin arrive at Amasra. Amasra (ancient Sesamos) has organized bathing facilities and is picturesquely touched off by a Byzantine fortress that was restored by the Genoese in the 14th century. There are several holiday resorts between Amasra and, 250 kilometres (155 miles) to its east, Sinop.

A coastal journey to the east of Sinop is perhaps better arranged from

242

Ankara, where the 795 road extends the 362 kilometres (226 miles) to Samsun. It passes through Hittite territory, and a visit to Boğazkale, Alaca Hüyük and Yazilikaya can be combined with a journey along the eastern coast. (See pages 215 on the Hittite sites).

After Samsun, on reaching the coast again at Terme, 61 kilometres (38 miles) after a diversion inland, there are a number of small resorts at which a stop can be made, to eat, to swim or to stay the night. Ünye, an attractive port, is 27 kilometres (17 miles) further east. Passing Fatsa, you continue to Ordu, 75 kilometres (47 miles) from Ünye, followed by Giresun, another 51 kilometres (32 miles) along. Tirebolu is 48 kilometres (30 miles) east of Giresun, and beyond Tirebolu it is another 40 kilometres (25 miles) to Trabzon.

Historical Background

Ereğli, or Heraclea Pontica, was named after Heracles (Hercules) who sailed with Jason's Argonauts, at least for part of the journey, tackling one or more of his prodigious labours en route.

Called Sinope by the Milesians of the seventh century BC after they arrived to colonize it, Sinop was the birthplace of Diogenis (Diogenes), the cynic philosopher of the tub. Hercules went down into the Underworld here to fetch up Cerberus. Hittites had settled here. It is Amazon country, too, and it may be that the skirt-like kilt worn by a Hittite warrior became the source of the Amazon legend.

In 88 BC, Mithridates VI, King of Pontus (120–63 BC), raised a coalition of neighbouring states to drive the Romans out of Asia Minor. Several thousand Romans were massacred without achieving this. After three Pontic Wars, in 66 BC the Romans took Sinop and extended Roman rule throughout Anatolia. In the 13th century after the Byzantines had returned to Constantinople, the Genoese, in rivalry with the Venetians, made an agreement with Michael VIII (1261–82), whereby they established trading posts along the Black Sea and elsewhere. Later they negotiated similar agreements with the Seljuks as well as with independent Moslem rulers, who were building castles or modifying existing ones. The Ottoman Mehmet II took Sinop in 1458.

Samsun was ancient Amisus, another Milesian colony. The 12th-century Seljuks preferred Samsun as their major port to Sinop, and of course the Genoese were influential in trade here, even under the later Mongol occupants, who seem to have made more effective use of their opportunities here than elsewhere. After the Mongols, the Emirs of Kastamonu made it part of their independent fief until the Ottomans eventually took it.

Kemal Atatürk landed here on 19 May 1919 and, though carrying the authority of the Sultan, set about organizing resistance to a threatened capitulation to the Western allies and working towards the establishment of a republic.

Terme is on a river that was probably the Thermodon, at whose mouth stood Thesiskyra, a city of the legendary Amazons. Ünye was Oenoe, designated as a place where Xenophon and his Greeks may have arrived at the coast after first glimpsing the sea from the mountains above Trabzon. They trekked and fought their way here from Cunaxa in Persia where they had served as a mercenary contingent in the defeated army of Cyrus the Younger in his revolt against his imperial brother.

Fatsa was the Milesian port of Polemon. Persembe, on the cape to the north of Ordu, was Cotyora, from where Xenophon and the Greek survivors are said by some to have boarded ship for Heracleia. A retreat is never an orderly affair, and it may be that separated contingents of Xenophon's army made use of various means and routes to get themselves home.

Giresun was founded by Milesians from Sinop. Identified as Kerasus, it provided the Greeks with their name for the cherry. Lucullus, the ultimate Roman victor against Mithridates, is said to have taken local cuttings of the cherry back to Italy.

In the territory of the former Byzantine Empire of Trebizond, Trabzon, as Trapezus, was the capital, which survived the fall of Constantinople by eight years. In its origin, Trapezus was colonized by men from Sinope, but later reinforcements came from Arcadia in the Greek Peloponessus. Trapezus gained by staying neutral throughout the Pontic Wars. Some two centuries later Hadrian added a number of buildings, and in the sixth century Justinian reinforced the city's defences. In the seventh and eighth centuries Arab aggression in Anatolia brought a restriction of overland transport, and the port of Trapesus, catering for the consequent increase in sea traffic, flourished. When the Seljuk Keykavus took Sinope, the Comneni Emperor of Trebizond was still able to maintain his independence by signing judicious treaties and entering into alliances with both the Seljuks and the Palaeologi Emperors of Constantinople. The princesses of Trebizond were reputed for their beauty, and this attribute came to be used as a valuable diplomatic pawn, though it was alleged in some quarters that too lavish a use of cosmetics not infrequently mitigated against a princess's natural advantages.

Süleiman the Magnificent was born at Trabzon, and Selim I set out from here to extend the Ottoman power throughout the whole of Anatolia, a process begun by his predecessor, Beyazît II.

Sights

Ereğli has the remains of Byzantine and of Ottoman walls and a castle restored by the Genoese.

An equestrian statue honours Atatürk's stay at **Samsun**, and there is an **Atatürk Museum**, as well as an archaeological one. The site of the city's original foundation is on Karasamsun, to the northwest of the city overlooking the harbour. The **Pazar Cami** is a Mongol mosque of the 14th century.

Ünye's *Belediye* (Town Hall) building is an 18th-century structure of quality. The beach is at Çamlik, and beyond this are the Fok Fok Margaralarya, sea caves that are a breeding haven for seals.

Off the harbour at **Giresun** on an island — Giresun Ada — good bathing can be enjoyed, and there are the ruins of a Byzantine monastery. A **Temple to Ares** on the island is likely to be pre- Milesian. A Byzantine fortress and remnants of city walls stand above the town. In mountain villages above Giresun, 'bird villagers' are said to be able to communicate over long distances by a system of whistling.

More than one castle exists in the bay at **Tirebolu** which was the ancient port of Tripolis, and a Byzantine tower here may have been built as a light house. Further on is **Görele**, with its monastery and a ruined castle.

Trabzon

Houses and buildings of the modern town climb the slopes which rise gently on the west side and rather steeply on the side south of the centre. The ancient **acropolis** is on high ground, a kilometre (.6 mile) or more west of the harbour, with gorges on either side. A connecting bridge stretches over the eastern gorge where sections of old walls and the remains of towers rest.

For the visitor, an essential stop is at **Ayasofya**, the Church of St Sophia, a kilometre (.6 mile) distant on the coastal road to the west. In origin the church was the domed basilica of a 13th-century monastery and was later converted to a mosque. It became desanctified under Atatürk and was declared a museum. In the mid-20th century David Talbot Rice and his team meticulously and patiently uncovered the magnificent wall paintings and decoration from under centuries of plaster and whitewash. As well as the murals, there are sculpted reliefs in the south porch that depict the Temptation.

From the *Belediye* (Town Hall) in Park Square — the Turkish Airlines Terminal is here — go alongside the park and turn left, then right, to reach the **Church of St Ann**, the oldest in the city, which dates from the eighth century but was restored in the ninth. Nearby is the former site of the **Church of St Basil**, of similar date, in use for a long time as a warehouse. Higher up is the Church of St Eugenius, converted to a mosque as the **Yeni Cuma** or New Friday Mosque, with its tall slender minaret, a landmark. Damaged by fire in 1340, the cupola was added later, the nave enlarged and a porch added.

On the other side of the bridge is the Orta Hisar Cami, or the Fatih Mosque, in origin the **Church of the Panaghia Chrysokephalos** (the Golden-headed Virgin), which probably dates from the tenth century but has been considerably modified. It was so named from the gilded copper of the cupola. Going on past the Orta Hisar, out to the edge of what was the old town and over another bridge, you will find the **Hatuniye Cami**, built in 1514 for Gülbahar Hatun, the mother of Selim, and her tomb is alongside.

Back at the terminal, go past the Atatürk memorial and turn left on Maraş Caddesi. Beyond Cumhuriyet Caddesi, on the south side, are the *bedesten* (covered market) and the former tenth- or 11th-century **Church of St Gregory**, in use neither as a church nor a mosque. The **Pazar Kapi Cami** is in this area, as is the **İskender Paşa Cami**, both buildings of the early 16th century. On Böztepe, a hill south of the harbour, is the cave **Church of the Panaghia Theoskepastos**, which had originated as a **Shrine to Apollo**. Nearby is the 13th-century **Church of St Philip**, now a mosque.

Eastern Anatolia

East of Trabzon at the centre of Turkey's tea-growing country is Rize, a town of wooded hills and terraces. Not surprisingly, wood-carving is a local trade. For the walker and mountaineer there is the hinterland with its lovely Georgian valleys and manifold high peaks to scale, and there are trout streams for the angler.

Travelling south of Trabzon, a visit to the Sumela Monastery can be either a part-day excursion from Trabzon or a stop on the intended journey. Until the exchange of populations between Greece and Turkey after the 1920–2 War, the Greek-speaking population of Trabzon was high, and several Orthodox monasteries in the vicinity were then active.

A staging point for coach services from Ankara to Tehran via Tabriz, Erzurum is also a main station on the railway from Ankara to Van and beyond. The train goes on board the ferry at Lake Van; the crossing takes about four hours and is a congenial one at sunset.

As you approach the town of Doğubayazît, Mount Ararat (Ağri Dağı) becomes the focus of attention in a somewhat arid panorama. Renowned as the spot where Noah's Ark came to rest, the mountain is perhaps best viewed from the Iranian border. The striking İşak Paşa Sarayi, built by a Kurdish ruler, stands above a rocky valley outside of Doğubayazît.

Getting There

From Trabzon a traveller may want to continue east 74 kilometres (46 miles) on the coastal road to Rize. Hopa, 118 kilometres (74 miles) east of Rize, is the last Turkish coastal town before the Soviet border.

The Sumela Monastery is situated in the mountains 46 kilometres (29 miles) south of Trabzon. You leave the city on the main road E390 to Maçka, 28 kilometres (18 miles) away. This is the route a majority of travellers are likely to take if they intend to make a journey to Lake Van or to go further east to Iran. From Maçka a road leads off to the monastery — Meryemane — 17 kilometres (11 miles) southeast.

The E390 continues south by way of the grandiose Zigana Pass, 2,010 metres (6,600 feet) high, and at Torul, 88 kilometres (55 miles) from Maçka, turns southeastward in its mountain journey to Gümüshane and Bayburt, then down to the plateau at Askale, 179 kilometres (112 miles) from Torul, to join the E23 leading the 53 kilometres (33 miles) east to Erzurum.

From Erzurum the E23 continues east through Pasinler, Horasan and Eleskurt to Ağri, a total of 177 kilometres (110 miles). The next town is

Doğubayazît, 95 kilometres (59 miles) away, from which it is another 35 kilometres (22 miles) to the Iran border crossing at Gürbulak.

Go back to Ağri, from where road 985 runs southward 81 kilometres (50 miles) to Patnos. Malazgirt, where the historic Battle of Manzikert was fought, is 40 kilometres (25 miles) southwest from here. From Patnos, it is 46 kilometres (29 miles) eastwards on road 280 to Erciş at the northern end of Lake Van. Continue east for 26 kilometres (16 miles) to meet the 975 road going south to Van, a further 63 kilometres (39 miles). The harbour and railway station on the lakeside are two kilometres (1.25 miles) from the centre of town.

The train from Ankara goes on board the ferry at Tatvan on the lake's southwestern end, crossing to Van, a distance of 88 kilometres (55 miles). Like Erzurum, Van has an airport.

From Van the road leads 30 kilometres (19 miles) south to Gevaş, a pleasant market town with a stream tumbling through its central square. A bus destined for Tatvan can take you round the south side of the lake. Six kilometres (four miles) west of Gevaş is a landing stage from where a ferry plies to the island of Akdamar.

Historical Background

Southwest of Ağri, near the town of Malazgirt, the Battle of Manzikert was fought in 1071. Alp Arslan defeated the Emperor Romanus IV and thereby opened up western Anatolia to the Seljuks and to Turkoman tribes harassed by the Mongols from the east.

A kingdom of the Urartu existed at Van, c. 1000–700 BC. Though indigenous to the region, the gods and the language of the Urartu seem to have had some affinity with those of the Hurrians, and through the Hurrians a Hittite association is suggested. Skill at metalworking was among this people's accomplishments.

Queen Semiramis of Assyria, after falling in love with a local prince, built a palace at Van. Following the devastation brought by the Cimmerians and then the Scythians, Armenians settled in the region. By the first century BC, Tigranes had established an Armenian kingdom which spread over what is now the border with Russia. Gregory, the proselytizing Christian, converted Tiridates, who consequently declared his state Christian some 20 years prior to Constantine I's decision concerning Christianity and the Roman Empire. At the conclusion of a period notable for Christian schism and heresies, the Armenian church emerged as Monophysite and hence alienated from both Constantinople and Rome.

Sights

The Sumela Monastery

Founded in the fifth century and dedicated to the Virgin Mary, the monastery is set precipitously at a height of 250 metres (820 feet) above the level of the roadway. The premises were restored under Alexius III of Trebizond (1330–90), who was crowned here. The entrance stairway has 93 steps. Inside, a stairway descends into the main courtyard off which are the principal buildings, including a church constructed under a rock. The frescoes of the church have been restored.

Erzurum

Although the history of Erzurum — Theodosiopolis for the Romans, named after Theodosius II (408–50) — is a long one, evidence of the city's past dates mainly from Seljuk times. The castle, which has endured many changes of ownership and undergone numerous rebuildings, is not open to the public. The most interesting building is the 13th-century Seljuk **Çifte Minare Medrese** with its arched doorway in stalactite design and its fluted 'twin minarets' (for which the *medrese* is named) with their carved bases. The central court has porticos whose arcades are decorated in arabesques and geometrical patterns. The spacious **Ulu Cami** nearby dates from the 12th century, and behind it are a number of **tombs** with the distinctive cone-shaped dome on a circular drum such as the distinguished Mevlana Tekke at Konya.

Mount Ararat

Despite the arid surroundings, the appearance of the mountain can be influenced by weather; its top is frequently shrouded in cloud, with snow invariably decorating its lower peaks. Ararat rises to 5,156 metres (16,922 feet) above the valley of the Aras River. While frequent expeditions search diligently for conclusive proof of Noah's Ark, at least one Turkish pilot has claimed to have seen a ship's timbers up there.

For climbers the best approach to the mountain is from Iğdir, 51 kilometres (32 miles) north of Doğubayazît, or from Aralîk on the Turkish–Soviet border, 15 kilometres (nine miles) northwest of the border crossing.

Doğubayazît, a town of frontier inconsequence, has at least one fantasy to offer. The early 18th-century **İşak Paşa Sarayî**, a palace and mosque, looks out over the valley, six kilometres (four miles) southeast of the town. The walled enclosure, built by a Kurd, is a mixture of architectural styles. There are ruins nearby of a settlement that dates back to the Urartu.

Van and the Lake

On the lakeside, midway between the centre of town and the harbour and railway station, is an 80-metre- (263-foot-) high ridge. It is 2,800 metres (9,200 feet) long and 120 metres (400 feet) wide, surmounted by a **citadel** with towered walls. Cuneiform Urartian texts were found in a funerary chamber here; the town's museum includes a display of Urartian artifacts and inscriptions.

The ancient city itself is below the ridge on the side nearest the lake, and here are the ruins of two Armenian churches and three Seljuk mosques, the **Ulu Cami**, **Kürsünlü Cami** and **Hüsrev Paşa Cami**. Five kilometres (three miles) east of the town, at the site of Toprakkale, is the mound of what is likely to have been the capital of the Urartian kingdom. Recoveries from a **temple** are in the British Museum, along with inscriptions in cuneiform, and items in bronze and ivory. A concealed stairway in the mound leads up to a chamber that could have been part of the **palace**. King Menuas was a canal builder who brought water from the Hosap River to the city. At Hosap (or Gzelsu), 58 kilometres (36 miles) southeast, there is another castle on a spur, with a polygonal keep and a barbican with heraldic lions.

Lying at an altitude of 1,750 metres (5,750 feet), with an area of 3,737 square kilometres (1,442 square miles), Lake Van is Turkey's largest lake, nearly seven times the size of Lake Geneva. Surrounded by mountains, the lake is dominated on its northwestern shore by Mount Süphan, at a height of 4,434 metres (14,552 feet). At the western end of the lake, Nemrut Daği, 3,050 metres (10,010 feet) high, has its own two volcanic lakes, lying 700 metres (2,300 feet) below its wide crater, with hot springs on the west side and ice-cold ones on the east. The wild boar is hunted in season in the woods of Nemrut Daği, and wild geese frequent its lakes.

Lake Van itself is too sodium-slated to encourage fish or wildlife except at the mouths of the rivers emptying into it, nor is swimming here particularly refreshing. Besides gulls and cormorants, the occasional pelican can be seen.

There are several islands in Lake Van, including Kuç, Çarpanak, Adu and, the most interesting, Akdamar, with its tenth-century **Armenian church** and monastery. The external carvings on the church are of pleasing dramatic interest: besides saints and biblical personalities, some of the parables are depicted, including that of Jonah and the Whale. The interior decoration has some colourful frescoes. Of the monastery buildings, little is left now but the grounds, which are maintained by gardeners.

Southeast of Lake Van are the rugged yet inviting Hakkâri Mountains that extend across frontiers into Iran and Iraq, with the Turkish town of Hakkâri lying at 1,748 metres (5,740 feet). In trekking to Hakkâri, an adventurous hiker might well find himself in company with an equally adventurous bear.

Practical Information

Accommodation

Classifications are set by the Turkish Ministry of Culture and Information in Ankara. However, no classification listing has been published since 1987. In the past two or three years there has been an appreciable expansion in tourism development of new hotels, motels and holiday villages — a proliferation of *pansiyons* (pensions) in particular — which have not as yet been classified by the Ministry but have been issued with local operating licenses. In some instances, especially in İstanbul, a hotel that has been remodelled and thereby has bettered its previous star rating may not yet have had its change officially confirmed. By the same token, an unclassified hotel could be in a recent building, and not necessarily of a lower standard than a 1-star rating, but a star rating should ensure at least the minimum comfort of a room with shower and toilet attached.

In a popular holiday centre, current tourism may not yet have reached the level that new development had anticipated; in such a circumstance a visitor is often able to negotiate a room price. The listing below is given as a guide only. Few casual visitors are likely to be looking for a hotel room in the 5-star or 4-star categories. The choice is legion in the lower-rated and non-classified categories, not all of which are listed here. Also, the new phenomenon of the pension can range from hostel- to family-style to one of sophisticated decor with club-like ambience and a fancier price.

The rates quoted apply in the main to İstanbul hotels; prices tend to be on a lower scale elsewhere. Hoteliers in İstanbul estimated a 5–6 percent increase in hotel rates from the beginning of 1990.

Hotels

5-star Luxury Class
Room rate only:
single US$135–84 (£86–118)
double US$184–215 (£118–38)
suites US$468–1,115 (£300–713)

5-star
Room rate only:
single US$110 (£70)
double US$138–50 (£30–96)
suites US$180–275 (£115–75)

Special Class
Rate includes breakfast:
single US$90 (£57)
double US$120 (£76)

NB Special class hotels are those with converted historic buildings of considerable interest.

4-star
Rate includes breakfast:
single US$80 (£52)
double US$100 (£64)
suites US$125 (£80)

3-star
Rate includes breakfast:
single US$40–70 (£25–45)
double US$75–95 (£48–60)

2-star
Rate includes breakfast:
single US$30 (£20)
double US$55 (£35)

1-star
Rate includes breakfast:
single US$20 (£13)
double US$35 (£22)

Unclassified
Room rate only:
single US$8–10 (£5–6.50)
double US$15–20 (£9.50–13)

Pensions: In general, the charge ranges from 8,000–10,000TL (US$3.60–4.50 or £2.30–3.20) per bed and may or may not include breakfast. A single person is likely to be asked to pay for two beds.

İstanbul

Hotels

5-star Luxury Class
Büyük Surmeli Saatçibayiri Sokak 3, Gayrettepe. Tel. 172 05 15/19, 172 11 60; tlx. 26656 SUOT TR. 448 beds, 210 rooms. Airconditioning, indoor parking, restaurant, coffee shop, bar, nightclub, disco, conference rooms, Turkish bath, sauna, swimming pool, hairdresser, casino/slot machines, rent-a-car service.

Büyük Tarabya Kafeliköy Caddesi, Tarabya. Tel. 162 10 00, 162 07 10; tlx. 26203 HTRB TR. 524 beds, 261 rooms, suites. Outdoor parking, central heating, restaurant, bar, nightclub, disco, conference rooms with facilities for simultaneous translation, sauna, beach, room telephone/radio/television/refrigerator, laundry service, barber and hairdresser, casino/slot machines, rent-a-car service. Situated on an attractive bay and flanked by countless seafood restaurants.

Çinar Fener Mevkii, 34800 Yeşilköy. Tel. 573 29 10/09; tlx. 28861 CIN TR. 402 beds, 201 rooms, suites. Airconditioning, outdoor parking, central heating, restaurant, bar, nightclub, disco, conference rooms, sauna, swimming pool, beach, room telephone/radio/television/refrigerator, barber and hairdresser, nursery, casino/slot machines, rent-a-car service. On the seaside outside an attractive suburb of the city, where horse-drawn phaetons compete successfully with taxis. Close to airport.

Etap Marmara Taksim Meydanî, 80090 Taksim. Tel. 151 46 96 (30 lines); tlx.

24137 ETMA TR. 704 beds, 424 rooms, suites. Airconditioning, indoor parking, central heating, restaurant, bar, cocktail lounges, nightclub, disco, conference rooms with translation services, banquet rooms, Turkish bath, sauna, swimming pool, room telephone/radio/television/refrigerator, barber and beauty parlour, reduced rate for children, casino, slot machines, rent-a-car, helicopter service. At the hub of city activity in Beyoğlu, its rooftop restaurant offers panoramic views as well as Turkish and European cuisine. Its shopping arcade includes a baker, patisserie, a watchmaker and, of course, jewellers.

Hilton Cumhuriyet Caddesi, Elmadağ. Tel. 131 46 46; tlx. 22027 ISTH TR. 770 beds, 410 rooms, 13 suites. Airconditioning, outdoor parking, central heating, restaurants, coffee shop, conference rooms, Turkish bath, swimming pool, motor-boat hire, tennis courts, room telephone/radio/television/refrigerator, laundry service, barber and hairdresser, reduced rate for children, casino, rent-a-car, helicopter service. Isolated in its large hillside precinct off the main boulevard. The lounge and the rooms on the Bosphorus side have uninterrupted views of the waterway, as does the rooftop restaurant. The arcade off the entrance lobby is à la mode with its fashion shops and jewellery vendors. In the driveway entrance from Cumhuriyet, there is a THY booking office, bookshop and offices of some travel agencies. The swimming pool and tennis courts are in a large cultivated garden area.

Ramada Ordu Caddesi 226, Lâleli. Tel. 512 81 20, 512 63 90; tlx. 30222 RAHA

TR. 550 beds, 275 rooms, suites. Airconditioning, central heating, restaurant, bar, nightclub, disco, conference rooms, sauna, swimming pool, room telephone/radio/television/ refrigerator, laundry service, reduced rate for children, casino, rent-a-car service.

Sheraton Asker Ocağı Caddesi 1, Taksim. Tel. 131 21 21 (60 lines); tlx. 222729 SHER TR; fax. 131 21 80. 874 beds, 437 rooms, suites. Airconditioning, indoor parking, central heating, restaurant, coffee shop, choice of bars, cocktail lounges, nightclub, conference rooms with translation services, swimming pool and children's pool, tennis, room telephone/radio/television/refrigerator, laundry service, barber and hairdresser, nursery, reduced rate for children, rent-a-car service. Away from the roar of the boulevard, the hotel has a spacious reception area and lounge, high rooms with views and offers Health Club facilities for the wise.

5-star
Divan Cumhuriyet Caddesi 2, Elmadağ. Tel. 131 41 00/11; tlx. 22402 DVAN TR. 191 beds, 96 rooms, suites. Airconditioning, outdoor parking, restaurant, coffee shop, bar, conference rooms with translation services, room telephone/radio/television/refrigerator, laundry service, barber and hairdresser, nursery, rent-a-car service. Breakfast included in room price.

Special Class
Yeşil Ev Kabaskal Caddesi 5, Sultanahmet. Tel. 528 67 64. 20 rooms. Outdoor parking, restaurant, bar, garden.

Ayasofya Pansiyonlari Soğukçeşme Caddesi, Sultanahmet. Tel. 512 57. 120 beds,

58 rooms, suites. Restaurants, Turkish bath.

Hidiv Köskü Çübüklü. Tel. 331 26; tlx. 23346 RING TR. 35 beds, 14 rooms.

Söküllü Paşa Mehmet Paşa Sokak 10, Sultanahmet. Tel. 512 37. 48 beds, 25 rooms.

4-star

Dragos Sahilyolu 12, Cevisli, Kaltepe. Tel. 352 05 03, 352 44 71; tlx. 23214 DRGS TR. Open May–November. 126 beds, 63 rooms. Outdoor parking, central heating, restaurant, bar, nightclub, conference rooms, beach, room telephone/radio/television/refrigerator. Breakfast included in room price.

Dilson Siraselviler Caddesi 49, Taksim. Tel. 152 96 00; tlx. 25689 DIHO TR, fax. 149 70 77. 180 beds, 90 rooms. Airconditioning, outdoor parking, central heating, restaurant, conference facilities, room telephone/radio/television/refrigerator, laundry service, nurse, reduced rate for children, motor-boat hire, sailing. Breakfast included in room price.

Etap İstanbul Meşrutiyet Caddesi, Tepebaşi. Tel. 151 46 46/63; tlx. 24345 BOT TR. 370 beds, 200 rooms, suites. Airconditioning, restaurant, bar, disco, conference rooms, swimming pool, room telephone/radio/television/refrigerator, laundry service, barber and hairdresser, nursery, reduced rate for children, rent-a-car service.

Fuar Namik Kemal Caddesi 26, Aksaray. Tel. 525 97 32/33, 525 98 59/62; tlx. 22220 ZAF TR. 120 beds, 60 rooms, suites. Airconditioning, outdoor parking, central heating, restaurant, bar, con-ference rooms, room telephone/radio/television/refrigerator, laundry service, barber and hairdresser, casino/slot machines.

İstanbul Dedeman Yildiz Posta Caddesi 50, Esentepe. Tel. 172 88 00/19; tlx. 28217 AKO TR. 543 beds, 261 rooms, suites. Airconditioning, outdoor parking, central heating, restaurant, bar, Turkish bath, sauna, swimming pool, room telephone/radio/television/refrigerator, laundry service, barber and hairdresser, reduced rate for children, casino/slot machines, rent-a-car service. Breakfast included in room price.

Maçka Eytam Caddesi 35, Maçka. Tel. 140 10 53, 140 31 03; tlx. 28002 MAKO TR. 361 beds, 184 rooms, suites. Airconditioning, outdoor parking, central heating, restaurant and bar, nightclub, disco, conference room and facilities, sauna, room telephone/radio/television/refrigerator, laundry service, barber and hairdresser, casino/slot machines, rent-a-car service.

Olcay Millet Caddesi 187, Topkapi Gate. Tel. 585 32 20/23; tlx. 23209 OLCA TR. 256 beds, 134 rooms, suites. Outdoor parking, central heating, restaurant and bar, conference facilities, sauna, swimming pool, room telephone/radio/television/refrigerator, laundry service, reduced rate for children, casino/slot machines, rent-a-car service. Breakfast included in room price.

Pera Palas Meşrutiyet Caddesi 98/100, Tepebaşi. Tel. 151 45 60/71; tlx. 24152 PERA TR. 200 beds, 116 rooms, suites. Airconditioning, outdoor parking, restaurant, bar, room telephone/television, laundry service, reduced rate for children.

Breakfast included in room price. The whiff, still, of Edwardian elegance and expansiveness, though fast fading. To be stayed in for at least one night. Many of its rooms overlook the Golden Horn.

3-star

Akgün Ordu Caddesi, Hazneder Sokak 6, Lâleli. Tel. 512 02 62; tlx. 22613 OGUN TR. 153 beds, 87 rooms. Indoor parking, central heating, restaurant, nightclub, room telephone, laundry service, casino/slot machines, helicopter service. Breakfast included in room price.

Bebek Cevdetpaşa Caddesi, 113/115, Bebek. Tel. 163 30 00; tlx. 27201 HOBE TR. 75 beds, 38 rooms. Outdoor parking, central heating, restaurant, beach, water-skiing, motor-boat hire, room telephone/radio, laundry service, nurse.

Büyük Keban Gençtürk Caddesi, 47, Ak-saray. Tel. 512 00 20/23; tlx. 22022 BUKE TR. 232 beds, 132 rooms. Outdoor parking, central heating, restaurant, room telephone/radio, reduction for children.

Büyük Suadiye Plaj Yolu 51, Suadiye. Tel. 358 11 20/27; tlx. 29404 MUSA TR. 209 beds, 109 rooms, suites. Outdoor parking, central heating, restaurant, nightclub, conference facilities, beach, room telephone, laundry service. Breakfast included in room price.

Eresun Topcu Caddesi 34, Taksim. Tel. 150 44 76, 150 33 67; tlx. 24235 NTT TR. 78 beds, 36 rooms, suites. Central heating, room telephone/radio/television/refrigerator, reduced rate for children. Breakfast included in room price.

Gezi Mete Caddesi 42, Taksim. Tel. 151 74 30; tlx. 25751 GEZI TR. 65 beds, 43 rooms. Airconditioning, restaurant, bar, room telephone/radio, laundry service.

Gulsah Piyer Loti Caddesi, Dostluk Yurdu Sokak 6, Cemberlitas. Tel. 512 56 73/74, 512 56 00/01. Outdoor parking, central heating, restaurant, nightclub, Turkish bath, sauna, room telephone/radio/television, laundry service, reduced rate for children. Breakfast included in room price.

Harem Ambar Sokak 1, Selimiye, Üsküdar. Tel. 333 20 25; tlx. 22482 HRM TR. 204 beds, 100 rooms, suites. Outdoor parking, central heating, restaurant, conference facilities, Turkish bath, sauna, swimming pool, room telephone, laundry service.

İstanbul Büyük Spor Caddesi 98, Beşiktaş. Tel. 160 78 60, 158 29 77. Outdoor parking, central heating, restaurant, room telephone/radio/television/refrigerator, laundry service. Breakfast included in room price.

Kaylon Sahil Yolu, Sultanahmet. Tel. 511 44 00/09; tlx. 23364/22999 KLYN TR. 76 beds, 38 rooms, suites. Airconditioning, central heating, restaurant, conference rooms, beach, room telephone/radio/television/refrigerator, laundry service, nurse, reduced rate for children. Breakfast included in room price.

Keban Sîraselviler Caddesi 51, Taksim. Tel. 143 33 10/13. 160 beds, 87 rooms. Outdoor and indoor parking, central heating, restaurant, conference rooms, room telephone/radio/refrigerator, laundry service, barber and hairdresser, reduced rate for children.

Kecik Fethi Bey Caddesi 18, Lâleli. Tel. 511 23 10/13, 538 14 00/02; tlx. 22036 KECP TR. 140 beds, 72 rooms. Outdoor

parking, central heating, restaurant, conference rooms, Turkish bath, sauna, room telephone/radio, laundry service, barber and hairdresser, reduced rate for children, half-pension rate. Breakfast included in room price.

Kennedy Sîraselviler Caddesi 29, Taksim. Tel. 143 40 90, 145 27 90. 143 beds, 79 rooms, suites. Outdoor parking, central heating, restaurant, conference rooms, room telephone/radio/refrigerator, laundry service, nurse, reduced rate for children.

Klas Harikzadeler Sokak 48, 34470 Lâleli. Tel. 511 78 74/77. Central heating, Turkish bath, sauna, room telephone/radio, barber and hairdresser, reduced rate for children. Breakfast included in room price.

Kilim Millet Caddesi 85A, Findikzade. Tel. 586 08 80/82; tlx. 22111 TR. 114 beds, 72 rooms. Airconditioning, outdoor parking, central heating, restaurant, room telephone. Breakfast included in room price.

Konak Cumhuriyet Caddesi, Nispet Sokak 9, Elmadağ. Tel. 148 47 44/45. 39 beds, 21 rooms, suites. Outdoor parking, central heating, restaurant, room telephone/radio/television/refrigerator, half-pension rate. Breakfast included in room price.

Salman Lâleli Caddesi 10, Aksaray. Tel. 511 32 07/08, 527 35 33; tlx. 22440 TR. 90 beds, 46 rooms. Airconditioning, outdoor parking, central heating, restaurant, sauna, room telephone/radio/television/refrigerator, laundry service, half-pension rate.

Sözmen Millet Caddesi 104, Capa. Tel. 523 40 06/09. 125 beds, 74 rooms. Outdoor parking, central heating, restaurant, conference rooms, room telephone/radio, laundry service, barber and hairdresser.

Şehrazat Millet Caddesi 189, Topkapi. Tel. 586 05 25, 585 39 38. 110 beds, 40 rooms. Outdoor parking, central heating, restaurant, room telephone/radio, reduced rate for children. Breakfast included in room price.

Tamsa Namik Kemal Caddesi, Manastirli Rifat Sokak 34, Aksaray. Tel. 523 86 16/19; tlx. 23765 TMOT TR. 240 beds, 120 rooms, suites. Outdoor parking, central heating, restaurant, bar, cocktail lounge, conference rooms, room telephone/radio/television/refrigerator, laundry service, reduced rate for children. Breakfast included in room price.

TMT Büyükdere Caddesi 84, Gayrettepe. Tel. 167 33 34; tlx. 31102 TR. 199 beds, 103 rooms, suites. Central heating, restaurant, disco, conference rooms, sauna, motor-boat hire, sailing facilities, room telephone/radio, laundry service, reduced rate for children.

Topkapi Oğuzhan Caddesi, Finikzade. Tel. 525 42 40/43. 80 beds, 40 rooms, suites. Airconditioning, outdoor parking, central heating, restaurant, conference rooms, room telephone/radio/television/refrigerator, laundry service, nurse, reduced rate for children. Breakfast included in room price.

Yenişehir Palas Asmali Mescit Oteller Sokak 113, Tepebaşi. Tel. 144 13 00, 144 45 47, 148 88 10/12; tlx. 24404 RAHI TR.

Washington Gençtürk Caddesi 12, Lâleli. Tel. 520 59 90/93; tlx. 22094 WAS TR. 104 beds, 56 rooms, suites. Outdoor parking, central heating, restaurant, room telephone/ radio/television, laundry service, barber and hairdresser, reduced rate for children. Breakfast included in room price.

Zurih Vidinli Tevfik Paşa Caddesi, Harikzadeler Sokak 37, Lâleli. Tel. 512 23 50/54; tlx. 30154 ZRH TR. 88 beds, 44 rooms. Airconditioning, outdoor parking, central heating, restaurant, conference rooms, room telephone/radio/television/refrigerator, laundry service, reduced rate for children. Breakfast included in room price.

2-star

Astor Lâleli Caddesi 12, Lâleli. Tel. 522 44 23/25; tlx. 22440 SATT TR. 66 beds, 42 rooms, suites. Airconditioning, central heating, restaurant, sauna, room telephone/radio/television/refrigerator, reduced rate for children. Breakfast included in room price.

Bale Refik Saydam Caddesi, Akarca Sokak 55, Tepebaşi. Tel. 150 49 12/16; tlx. 25515 BALF TR. 112 beds, 63 rooms, suites. Restaurant. Breakfast included in room price.

Bern Murat Paşa Sokak 16, Aksaray. Tel. 523 24 62/63. 104 beds, 46 rooms, suites. Airconditioning, outdoor parking, central heating, room telephone/radio, laundry service, reduced rate for children, slot machines. Breakfast included in room price.

'L'Affaire du Sofa'

T he French Ambassador, the Marquis de Nointel, is summoned to the court of Mehmet IV in 1677. . .

On arriving at the Porte on the appointed day (Sunday, April 22nd), Nointel had to wait three whole hours in the room of the Kehaya—a surly Turk—without conversation or any other entertainment; and when at last he was called in, he found the narrow corridor that led to the Audience Chamber crowded with chaoushes who jostled him most rudely. Truth to tell, this rudeness, at all events, was not premeditated. The poor chaoushes had come in the turbans of ceremony worn on such occasions, but had been ordered by the Vizir to go and exchange them for their ordinary headgear: hence their hurry to get back to their places before the Ambassador made his entry. Nointel, however, whose nerves were already on edge with the long waiting, saw in their behaviour a fresh insult, and he elbowed his way down the passage fiercely flinging the chaoushes to right and left against the walls. In this temper he entered the Audience Chamber, and there he observed something at which his resentment reached the height of exasperation: the stool destined for him was not upon the Soffah, but on the floor below! He ordered his Dragoman to set it where it should be; one of the Vizir's pages brought it down again. Then the Ambassador, in a towering rage, seized the stool with his own hand, carried it to the Soffah, and sat upon it.

When this act was reported to the Vizir, who was in an adjoining apartment, he sent for the Ambassador's Dragoman and commanded him to tell his master that he must move his seat back where he had found it. The trembling Dragoman delivered the message and was bidden by the angry Ambassador to hold his tongue. Next the Vizir sent his own Dragoman, Dr. Mavrocordato, with whom Nointel maintained the closest friendship. In vain did the Greek try to soothe the enraged Frenchman, imploring him to moderate his temper and yield gracefully to the inevitable. Nothing could prevail over M. de Nointel's obstinacy: the pride of the wig was pitted against the pride of the turban, and it must be remembered that both wigs and turbans were then at their zenith. In the end, Mavrocordato, finding argument useless, changed his tone and said, in Italian: 'The Grand Vizir commands the chair to be placed below.' Nointel replied: 'The Grand Vizir can command his chair: he cannot command me.' At that moment the Chaoush-bashi burst into the room, roaring, 'Calder, Calder—Take it away, take it away!'—and before he knew what was happening, Nointel found the stool snatched from under him. In an access of fury, his Excellency dashed out of the room, sword on shoulder, pushed his way through the throng, and, ordering the presents which he had brought to follow him, mounted his horse and departed, exciting, as he boasted by his firmness, 'the astonish-ment of the Turks and the joy of the French'. Kara Mustafa alone remained calm. His comment, when he heard that the Ambassador was gone, was one word: 'Gehennem' (Let him go to Hell).

Such was the beginning of the celebrated 'Affaire du Sofa'—a quarrel which drew the attention of all Europe and nearly led to a rupture between France and Turkey.

G F Abbott, Under the Turk in Constantinople, *1920*

Bristol Meşrutiyet Caddesi 235, Tepebaşî. Tel. 151 38 55/56. 90 beds, 54 rooms. Breakfast included in room price.

Büyük Levent Gençtürk Cadessi 58, Lâleli. Tel. 511 01 06/07. 60 beds, 32 rooms. Airconditioning, room telephonc/radıo/television, laundry service, reduced rate for children. Breakfast included in room price.

Büyük Londra Meşrutiyet Caddesi 117, Galatasaray. Tel. 149 10 25, 145 06 70. 70 beds, 42 rooms, suites. Central heating, room telephone/radio/television/refrigerator, laundry service, reduced rate for children. Breakfast included in room price.

Davos Gençtürk Caddesi, Gümrük Emimi Sokak 21, Laleli. Tel. 527 04 24, 526 54 42, 512 00 96/97. 80 beds, 42 rooms. Breakfast included in room price.

Davos 2 Ordu Caddesi, Yeşil Tülümba Sokak 37, Lâleli. Tel. 522 58 92, 512 29 87. 45 beds, 22 rooms. Breakfast included in room price.

Ebru M. Kemal Paşa Caddesi 29, Aksaray. Tel. 586 75 57/58; tlx. 22123 OKAC TR. 65 beds, 35 rooms. Reduced rate for children. Breakfast included in room price.

Ensar Ordu Caddesi, Yeşil Tülümba Sokak 39, Lâleli. Tel. 520 61 35/36. 43 beds, 23 rooms. Airconditioning, restaurant, reduced rate for children. Breakfast included in room price.

Eris İstasyon Arkaşi Sokak 9, Sirkeci. Tel. 527 89 50/51. Reduced rate for children. Restaurant, breakfast included in room price.

Hamit Gençtürk Caddesi 57, Saraçhane. Tel. 520 92 05, 527 21 56. 62 beds, 31 rooms. Airconditioning, room telephone/radio/television.

Hanzade Selimpaşa Sokak 21–23, Lâleli. Tel. 526 59 17, 527 73 73. 55 beds, 29 rooms. Airconditioning, reduced rate for children. Breakfast included in room price.

Opera Inonu Caddesi 36, Gumuşsuyu, Taksim. Tel. 143 55 28/29; tlx. 25216 HOPE TR. 97 beds, 50 rooms. Airconditioning, restaurant, barber and hairdresser, nurse.

Pizza Kürültay Sokak 113, Lâleli. Tel. 512 59 40, 526 18 78/79. 48 beds, 28 rooms. Airconditioning, reduced rate for children.

Plaza Sîraselviler Caddesi, Arslan Yatağî 19/21. Tel. 145 32 73/74, 145 79 89. 58 beds, 32 rooms. Central heating, reduced rate for children. Breakfast included in room price.

Toro Köska Caddesi 24, Lâleli. Tel. 528 02 73/74. Airconditioning. Breakfast included in room price.

1-star
Ağan Safettin Paşa Sokak 6–8, Sirkeci. Tel. 527 85 50/51.

Bonjour Ihlamur Yolu 7, Nişantaş. Tel. 146 41 20/21.

Cevher Mesih Paşa Caddesi 66, Lâleli. Tel. 520 96 69.

Evren Dullar Cikmaz 3, Topkapî. Tel. 521 66 77.

Gelir Lâleli Caddesi 5, Aksaray. Tel. 520 74 61.

İtalya Şefer Bostan Sokak 2–4, Beyoğlu. Tel. 143 28 58.

Karatay Sait Efendi Sokak 42, Lâleli. Tel. 511 65 55.

Tahran Mehmet Lüfti Sekerci Sokak 21, Aksaray. Tel. 521 46 50.

Ulübat Kalbürcü Mehmet Çeşme Sokak 10, Topkapî. Tel. 585 46 94.

Yasmak Ebussut Caddesi 18–20, Sirkeci. Tel. 526 31 55/57.

Yilmaz Valide Cami Sokak 79, Aksaray. Tel. 586 74 00/01.

On the Black Sea coast near İstanbul:
Gürüp Tel. Kilyos 1-194. 54 beds, 31 rooms.

Kilyos Kale Kale Caddesi 78. Tel. 031-54. 52 beds, 27 rooms.

Asiatic side of the Bosphorus:
Değrmen Plaj Yolu 24, Şile. Tel. 1048-1148. 149 beds, 73 rooms.

Holiday Villages (*Tatil Koyu*)

Miltur Kumbag Tatil Köyü (class A), at Tekirdağ on the E25 road from Ipsala (frontier post with Greece) to İstanbul, 113 kilometres (70 miles), Kumbag. Tel. 2-101. Open 30 May–September. Beach, restaurant, nightclub, sauna, swimming pool, motor-boat hire, sailing facilities, tennis, reduced rate for children, half-pension rate.

NB Other holiday villages are under development.

Motels

4-star
Baler Avcilar Ambarli, Küçükcekmece. Tel. 591 17 56. Open all year. 24 beds, 62 rooms. Restaurant, bar, swimming pool.

Marin Silivriyolu, Kumburgaz. Tel. 102. Open April–November. 300 beds, 150 rooms. Swimming pool, beach, casino/slot machines.

Solu Şemiz Kümlar Mevkii. Silivri. Tel. 03. Open June–October. 52 beds, 29 rooms. Restaurant, beach, sailing facilities.

Yeşilköy Havan Sokak 4, Yeşilköy. Tel. 573 29 95. Open all year. 60 beds, 30 rooms. Restaurant, bar, beach. Breakfast included in room price.

Turban Kilyos Kilyos. Tel. 142 02 88; tlx. 23770 TR. Open May–October. 300 beds, 150 rooms. Restaurant, bars, beach, full board rate.

Ataköy C. Ataköy Şahil Yolu. Tel. 572 08 02/03, 572 49 50. 412 beds, 206 rooms. Swimming pool, restaurant, bars, nightclub.

3-star
Demirköy Ataköy. Tel. 572 49 45. Beach, restaurant, bar, swimming pool.

Unclassified
Yuva Kale Caddesi, Kilyos. Tel. 43. Open 15 April–5 October. Restaurant, bars.

E5 Londra Highway, Florya Kavağî. Tel. 579 20 20. Restaurant, bar, swimming pool.

Asiatic side of the Bosphorus:

4-star
Dr Erdim Ankara Caddesi 232, Kartal. Tel. 353 78 87. Open June–October. Restaurant, bar, beach.

3-star
Motel 212 Eski Bağdat Caddesi, Temenye Köyü, Kaynarca, Pendik. Tel. 354 00 60. Open June–November. 60 beds, 30 rooms. Restaurant, bar, beach, water-skiing, motor-boat hire, sailing facilities, reduced rate for children.

Unclassified
Akkaya Şile. Tel. Sile/Akkaya 10. Open May–September. Beach, restaurant, bar.

Pen Ankara Caddesi 285, Pendik. Tel. 354 50 56. Restaurant, bar, swimming pool.

Sedef Ankara Caddesi, Palmiye Duragi 32, Pendik. Tel. 354 41 60. Beach, swimming pool, restaurant, bar.

Temenye Ankara Caddesi 206, Pendik. Tel. 354 26 26. Beach, restaurant, bar.

Gülay Koyici Meykii, Polonezköy. Tel. 332 25 50/51. Swimming pool, restaurant, bar, nightclub.

Camping

4-star
Ataköy Mocamp Şahil Yolu, Ataköy. Tel. 572 49 61; tlx. 28894 ESAT TR. Open 20 April–29 October. Capacity 1,505 persons. Caravan sites available, water supplied, electricity 220 volts (extra charge for electricity), cooking facilities, electric cooking, laundry facilities, hot water, car washing facilities, store, mechanical repair service, first aid, boat and slipway, beach, restaurant, bar.

Yeşilyurt Kamping Şahil Yolu 2, Yeşilköy. Tel. 573 55 82. Open all year. All facilities as above.

2-star
Kervansaray Kartektepe Mocamp Çobançeşme Mevkii. Tel. 575 19 91. Open April–15 October. Caravan sites, electricity connection, cooking facilities, laundry, hot water, car-washing facilities, mechanical repairs, restaurant.

Youth Hostels

Kadirga Student Hostel Comertler Sokak 6, Kumkapî. IYHF (International Youth Hostels Association) or ISIC (International Student Conference Card) members.

Sultan Yerebatan Caddesi 35, Sultanahmet. Tel. 520 76 76. 14 rooms: 1–4 beds. 10 percent discount to ISIC–FIYTO members. Use of kitchen, bath and showers.

Youth Cerrah Paşa Caddesi, Muezzin Sokak 2, Aksaray. Tel. 521 24 55. July–September. 172 beds (4 beds per room). Restaurant, cooking facilities and television room. 20 percent discount to IYHF (International Youth Hostels Association) members.

Yücel Caferiye Sokak 6, Sultanahmet. Tel. 522 47 90. 60 beds. Cafeteria. IYHF or ISIC members.

Marmara Sea and North Aegean Region

Hereke

4-star Motel
Totaş Tür Tesisleri Tavsancil, Hereke. Tel. 1131. Open all year. 52 beds, 26 rooms. Restaurant, bars, nightclub, sauna, beach, swimming pool, motor-boat hire, sailing facilities, room telephone/radio/ television/refrigerator, barber, hairdresser, reduced rate for children.

Yalova

Hotels

4-star
Turban Yalova Thermal Yalova. Tel. (4905-4908) 23; tlx. 22701 TR. All year. 209 beds, 100 rooms. Thermal baths, Turkish bath, nightclub.

2-star
Ferah Gökeçdere, Yalova. Tel. (4905) 6. All year. 53 beds, 28 rooms.

Gökçedere Gökçedere, Yalova. Tel. 2-84-226. All year. 86 beds, 39 rooms.

İznik

3-star Motel
İznik Gol Kenari 7. Tel. 10 41. All year. 36 beds, 18 rooms.

Bursa

Hotels

5-star
Anatolia Çekirge Meydani, Çekirge. Tel. 36 71 10; tlx. 32055 MARO TR. 186 beds, 93 rooms.

3-star
Akdogan Murat Caddesi 1, Çekirge. Tel. 36 66 10/15; tlx. 3 22229 AKOT TR. 226 beds, 107 rooms.

Büyük Yıldız Uludag Caddesi 6, Çekirge. Tel. 36 66 00/04; tlx. 32060 BUYY TR.

Çelik Palas Çekirge Caddesi 79, Bursa. Tel. 36 19 00; tlx. 32121 CEPA TR. 262 beds, 131 rooms.

Dilmen Murat Caddesi 20, Çekirge. Tel. 36 61 14/17; tlx. 32063 ODIL TR. 176 beds, 88 rooms.

Kirci Çekirge Caddesi 21. Tel. 36 70 00/03. 104 beds, 54 rooms.

2-star
Ada Palas Murat Caddesi 21. Tel. 36 16 00. 79 beds, 31 rooms.

Dikmen Maksem Caddesi 78. Tel. 21 49 95/98. 106 beds, 50 rooms.

Diyar Kültürpark Karşisi. Tel. 36 31 30/32. 80 beds, 45 rooms.

Gönlüferah Murat Caddesi 24. Tel. 36 27 00/04; tlx. 32057 GFTH TR. 119 beds, 62 rooms.

Kent Atatürk Caddesi 119. Tel. 21 87 00/01; tlx. 32062 KENT TR. 94 beds, 54 rooms.

1-star
Artic Fevzi Çakmak Caddesi 123.

Bilgiç Basak Sokak 30. Tel. 20 31 90.

Cağlayan Inebey Caddesi 73. Tel. 21 14 58.

Hünkar Acemler Caddesi 2.

Ipekçi Cancilar Caddesi 38. Tel. 21 19 35.

Ilman Kültürpark Fuar Karşisi 45.

Yat Hamamlar Caddesi 31.

Camping

Kervansaray Künlük Mocamp (class 3) Yalova–Bursa Yolu, six kilometre post. Tel. 11 39 95. Open May–15 October.

Uludag

Hotels

2-star
Turistic Uludağ Gelisim Bolğesi. Tel. 11 88; tlx. 32429 TR. All year. 257 beds, 127 rooms.

1-star
Alkoclar Milli Park. Tel. 11 30. 15 December–April.

Merih Kadiyayla Mevkii. Tel. 181 01. All year.

Balikesir

Hotels

2-star
Konak Arda Yeşilli Caddesi, Ipek Sokak 2. Tel. 17 515. All year. 35 beds, 15 rooms.

1-star
Büyük Cömlek Oto Terminal. Tel. 127 47. All year.

Cömlek Milli Kuvvetler Caddesi 5. Tel. 227 47. All year.

Imanoğlu Orutculer Caddesi. Tel. 113 02. All year.

Kervansaray Istasyon Meydani. Tel. 116 35.

Molam Yeşil Caddesi. Tel. 180 75. All year.

Yilmaz Milli Kuvvetler Caddesi 37. Tel. 174 93. All year.

3-star Motel

Dogan Akçay, Balikesir. Tel. Akçay 34. Open May–November. 74 beds, 37 rooms.

Çanakkale

Hotels

2-star
Anafartalar İskele Meydani. Tel. 44 54. All year. 140 beds, 70 rooms.

Truva Yalibyolu. Tel. 40 88. All year. 132 beds, 66 rooms.

Eden Beach Hotel Ayvacik. Tel. 39 40. All year. 130 beds, 50 rooms.

Motels

4-star
Ida-Tur Küçükküyü. Tel. Küçükküyü 56 102. All year. 142 beds, 62 rooms.

Tusan PO Box 8, Intepe. Tel. 14 61. March–November. 128 beds, 64 rooms.

2-star
Mola Güztlyali Köyü. Tel. 22 79. April–November. 40 beds, 20 rooms.

Camping

Sen Mocamp (class 3), Canakkale–İzmir Yolu, five kilometre post. Tel. Kepezkoyu 1. 1 June–30 October. Swimming pool, sauna, thermal baths.

Akçay

Motels

3-star
Ege Orucreis Caddesi. Tel. Akçay 33.
May–November. 142 beds, 66 rooms.

1-star
Asiyan Tel. Akçay 33. All year. 90 beds,
45 rooms.

Edremit

4-star Motel
Beyazsaray Etiler Caddesi 4, Edremit.
Tel. 22 245. 15 May–15 September. 52
beds, 26 rooms.

Ayvalik

Hotels

3-star
Murat Reis Altinkum Mevkii. Tel. 14
56; tlx. 53939 MURS TR. 1 March–30
October. 376 beds, 175 rooms.

2-star
Ankara Sarimsakli. Tel. 11 95. All year.
117 beds, 57 rooms.

Büyük Berk Sarimsakli. Tel. 23 11; tlx.
52817 BUBE TR. April–September. 193
beds, 97 rooms.

Berk Orta Çamlik 23. Tel. 15 01; tlx.
52817 BUBE TR. 95 beds, 53 rooms.

Ortunç Alibey Ada (an island). Open
May–October. 44 beds, 22 rooms.

Motels

4-star
Bati Motel Tur-Tes Tuzla Mevkii,
Ayvalik. Tel. 2 59. 15 March–1 Decem-
ber. 350 beds, 148 rooms.

3-star
Cam Orta Çamlik, Ayvalik 12. Tel. 15
15. May–November. 37 beds, 19 rooms.

Küçük Başkent Sarimsakli Plaj, Ayvalik.
Tel. 11 16. June–October. 28 beds, 14
rooms.

2-star
Aytaş Sarimsakli. Tel. 12 57. 1 May–1
November. 102 beds, 51 rooms.

Sevo Küçükköy, Sarimsakli. Tel. 11 66. 1
May–30 November. 45 beds, 21 rooms.

Dikili

4-star Motel
Antür Dikili. Tel. 103 269. 15 May–October. 88 beds, 44 rooms.

Bergama

4-star Motel
Tusan Bergama İzmir Yolu. Tel. 11 73.
March–November. 84 beds, 42 rooms.

Central Aegean Coast
İzmir

Hotels

5-star
Büyük Efes Gaziosmanpaşa Bulvari 1.
Tel. (51) 14 43 00/28; tlx. 53341 EFES
TR. 585 beds, 296 rooms.

4-star
Etap İzmir Cumhuriyet Bulvari 138. Tel.
(51) 19 40 90; tlx. 52233 ETIZ TR; fax.
(51) 19 40 89. 231 beds, 128 rooms.

Kismet 1377 Sokak 9. Tel. 21 70 50/52.
114 beds, 64 rooms.

3-star
Anba Cumhuriyet Bulvari, 124. Tel. 14
43 80/83; tlx. 52449 ATAS TR. 296 beds,
148 rooms.

Hisar Fevzipaşa Bulvari. Tel. 14 54
00/04. 140 beds, 70 rooms.

İzmir Palas Vasif Çinar Bulvari 2. Tel. 21
55 83; tlx. 52631 KIZ TR. 296 beds, 148
rooms.

Karaca 1379 Sokak 55. Tel. 14 44 45;
tlx. 53093 KAOT TR. 136 beds, 68
rooms.

Kilim Atatürk Bulvari. Tel. 14 53 40/44;
tlx. 53041 KIZ TR. 164 beds, 88 rooms.

2-star
Katiböğlü Fevzipasa Caddesi 41/2. Tel.
25 41 22. 82 beds, 41 rooms.

Kaya Gaziosmanpaşa Bulvari 45,
Çankaya. Tel. 13 97 71/72. 100 beds, 50
rooms.

1-star
Babadan Gaziosmanpaşa Bulvari 50.

Billur Basmahane Meydani 783.

Holiday Villages

Altin Yünüş Tatil Köyü (class A),
Boyalik Mevkii, Çeşme. Tel. 12 50; tlx.
53868 GOLD TR. All year. 1,030 beds,
515 rooms.

Club Méditerranée Foça Tatil Köyü
(class A), Foça. Tel. 11 47; tlx. 53909
MEDF TR. 24 May–30 September.

4-star Motel
Türban Ilica Dereboyu, Yolu Cat Mevkii, Böyalik. Tel. 21 28. May–15 October.
120 beds, 60 rooms.

Camping

Denizatt Kampi (class 1), Gümüldür.
Tel. 193 66. 1 June–15 September.

Kervansaray Inciralti Mocamp (class
3), Balcova. Tel. 15 47 60. 30 June–15
October.

Y Camp (class 3), Çeşmealti, Urla. Tel.
21. 15 June–30 September.

Şelcuk

Hotels and Pensions

2-star
Ak Kuşadasi Caddesi 14. Tel. 9 (5451)
2161.

Artemis Pazar Yeri Caddesi.

Atlanta Atatürk Mahallesi 1002 Sokak 9.
Tel. 9 (5451) 2883.

Gamza İbrahim Basaran Caddesi.

Güven 1002 Sokak 9. Tel. 9 (5451) 1294.

Victoria Cengiz Töpel Caddesi 4. Tel. 9
(5451) 3203/4.

Motels

4-star
Kale Han Atatürk Caddesi 49, Selçuk
35920. Tel. 11 54. All year. 44 beds, 24
rooms.

Tusan Efes Efes Yolu 38, Selçuk. Tel. 60.
March–November. 24 beds, 12 rooms.

Kuşadasi

Hotels

4-star
İmbat Kadinlar Cenizi. Tel. 20 00/03;
tlx. 58582 IMTA TR. April–September.
278 beds, 140 rooms.

Tursan 31 Mevkii. Tel. 10 94; tel.
52110/10. All year. 126 beds, 63 rooms.

3-star
Club Akdeniz Karaova Mevkii. Tel. 15
21/22; tlx. 58552 TR. March–November.
818 beds, 409 rooms.

Efes Güverçin Ada Caddesi 37. Tel. 36
60/62. All year. 89 beds, 44 rooms.

Özcelikler Atatürk Bulvari, Yat Limani,
Karşisi. Tel. 44 09; tlx. 58569 OZCI TR.
All year. 140 beds, 70 rooms.

2-star
Akman İstiklâl Caddesi 13. April–October.

Aydin Akincilar Caddesi 18. All year.

Marti Kadinlar Denizi. April–October.

Kismet Akyar Mevkii. April–October.

Minik Cephane Sokak 8. All year.

Stella Bezirgan Sokak 44. March–
November.

Holiday Villages

Club Akdeniz (class A), Kuşadasi. Tel.
15 21; tlx. 52838 TR. April–October. 600

beds, 305 rooms.

Club Méditerranée (class A), Kuşadasî.
Tel. 11 35; tlx. 58511 MEDI TR. 17 May–
30 September. 756 beds, 378 rooms.

Küstür Tatil Köyü (class A), 31 Plaj
Mevkii, Kuşadasî. Tel. 41 10; tlx. 52137
KUST TR. June–15 October. 800 beds,
400 rooms.

Club Diana Tatil Köyü (class B), PO
Box 9, Kuşadasî. Tel. 35 50. May–September. 208 beds, 104 rooms.

Omer Tatil Kyü (class B), Kuşsadasî.
Tel. 37 00; tlx. 58519 OMK TR.

Motels

4-star
Ömer Yavansu Mevkii, Kuşadasî. Tel. 37
00; tlx. 52138 OMK TR. 15 May–15 October. 216 beds, 109 rooms.

Unclassified
Turgut Motel Lake Bafa.

Camping

Kervansaray Mocamp (class 3), İzmir–
Kuşadasî Yolu, Ku-20sₛadasî. Tel. 10 87.
May–October.

Inland

Manisa

Hotels

3-star
Alkent İzmir–Ankara road, Taytanköyü,
Salihli. Tel. 55 06. All year. 31 beds, 11
rooms.

2-star
Arma Doğa Caddesi 14. Tel. 19 80. All
year. 68 beds, 42 rooms.

Denizli

Hotels

2-star
Altuntür Kaymakçi Caddesi 1. Tel. 161
76. All year.

Küyümcü Deliklicinar Meydanî 128.
Tel. 137 49. All year.

1-star
Etemağa Istasyon Caddesi 34. Tel. 138
51. All year.

Park Enver Paşa Caddesi 104. Tel. 119
17. All year.

Sarikaya İstasyon Caddesi 72. Tel. 117
60. All year.

Pamukkale

Motels

4-star
Tusan Pamukkale. Tel. 132 06. All year.
94 beds, 47 rooms.

2-star
Esot PO Box 145. All year. 160 beds, 80
rooms. And camping.

Konak Sadi PO Box 102. And camping.

Karahayit Köyü 100 beds, 40 rooms.
And camping.

Mistur 100 beds. And camping.

Pamukkale Turizm 84 beds, 34 rooms.

274

South Aegean Coast
Bodrum
Hotels

3-star
Myndos Caferpaşa Caddesi, Bodrum. All year. 100 beds, 59 rooms.

Sami Gumbet, Bodrum. Tel. 10 48. 230 beds, 100 rooms.

Taraca Gumbet, Bodrum. Tel. 17 21. All year. 110 beds, 48 rooms.

2-star
Baraz Cumhuriyet Caddesi 62. Tel. 17 14. All year. 48 beds, 24 rooms.

Gözen Cumhuriyet Caddesi 18. Tel. 12 27. All year. 48 beds, 20 rooms.

Kalyon Cumhuriyet Caddesi. Tel. 61 41. All year.

Mut Türgütreis. Tel. 11 46. April–November. 90 beds, 36 rooms.

Sinim Akyarlar Mevkii. Tel. 14 20. All year.

1-star
Gala Neyzen Tevlik Caddesi, Yat Limanî. Tel. 19 10. All year.

Mervem Atatürk Caddesi 103. Tel. 26 70. April–November.

Holiday Villages

Torba Tatil Köyü (class A), Torba, Bodrum. Tel. 23 42; tlx. 52585 TR. May–25 October. 900 beds, 350 rooms.

TMT Tatil Köyü (class A), Bodrum. Tel. 14 40; tlx. 52504 TR. 26 April–30 October. 350 beds, 121 rooms.

Club Ekin Pina Tatil Köyü (class B), Güverçinlik, Bodrum. Tel. 27 50 (ext. 1). May–17 October. 200 beds, 95 rooms.

Motels

4-star
Halikarnasus Cumhuriyet Caddesi, Kümbahçe Mah, Bodrum. Tel. 10 73. All year. 55 rooms, 28 beds.

Regal Bitez Yalisi, Bodrum. Tel. Kabakum 58-129. May–October. 32 beds, 16 rooms.

3-star
Kaktus Ortakent, Bodrum. Tel. 10. 36 beds, 16 rooms.

Mütlüm Türgüt Reis, Bodrum. Tel. 11 46; tlx. 6142 TR. 102 beds, 36 rooms.

Bargilya Güverçinlik, Milâs.

Unclassified
Gün Işığı Gölköy, Bodrum. Tel. Gölköoy 86. 15 May–30 September. 40 beds, 10 rooms.

Camping

Ayaz Kamp (class 1), Gumbet, Bodrum. Tel. 11 74. All year.

Aktür Kamping (class 1), Tatilsitesi, Emecik Köyü. Tel. 106. May–15 October.

Mediterranean Coast
Marmaris
Hotels

5-star
Altin Yünüs Içmeler. Tel. 13617.

Münamür Içmeler. Tel. 13606.

4-star
Iber Içmeler. Tel. 14051, 16486.

Marmaris Yüzer 1 June–25 September. 700 beds, 250 rooms.

Turunç Turunç. Tel. 14913.

3-star
Elif Içmeler Mevkii. Tel. 44 91. 1 April–1 November.

Flamingo Siteler Mah, Lidya Oteli Yani. Tel. 40 00/02; tlx. 52286 FLAM TR. 1 April–1 November. 140 beds, 63 rooms.

Hawai Kemeralti Mah, Çildir Mevkii. Tel. 40 03, 05 36. All year. 120 beds, 65 rooms.

Marbaş Içmeler Mevkii. Tel. 29 04. All year. 140 beds, 69 rooms.

Ocaktan Uzonyöl. Tel. 25 60. 18 April–1 December.

Otel 47 Atatürk Caddesi 10. Tel. 17 00. All year. 101 beds, 50 rooms.

Yavuz Atatürk Caddesi 10. Tel. 29 37; tlx. 53832 TR. All year. 108 beds, 51 rooms.

2-star
Atlantik Atatürk Caddesi 34. Tel. 12 36. All year.

Berkit Içmeler Mevkii. Tel. 14 23. 1 April–30 October.

Efendi Içmeler Mevkii. Tel. 44 90. 1 April–30 October.

Karadeniz Atatürk Bulvari. Tel. 28 37. All year.

Kontez Içmeler Mevkii. 1 April–30 October.

Lidya Siteler Mahallesi 130. Tel. 29 40. May–December.

Marbella Uzunyöl. Tel. 10 49. May–December.

Orkide Siteler Mah. Tel. 25 80. May–1 November.

Yunus Uzunyali. Tel. 17 99. 1 May–December.

1-star
Karaaslan Town centre.

Imbat Town centre.

Marmaris Atatürk Caddesi 30. Tel. 11 73. All year.

Murat Han Kenan Evren Bulvari. Tel. 18 50. All year.

Paradise Siteler Mevkii. Tel. 36 37. 1 April–1 November.

Pina Town centre.

Rodos 1 April–1 November.

Holiday Villages

Marti Tatil Köyü (class A), Marmaris. Tel. 49 10. 562 beds, 281 rooms. All year.

Türban Marmaris Tatil Köyü (class A), Marmaris. Tel. 18 43; tlx. 52529 TKOY TR. 510 beds, 246 rooms. 1 May–15 October.

Atlantik Tatil Köyü (class B), Marmaris. Tel. 13 79.

Motels

4-star
Poseidon Kemeralti Mahallesi, Uzunyali 134, Marmaris. Tel. 18 40. 15 May–October. 118 beds, 56 rooms.

Faces of rural Turkey

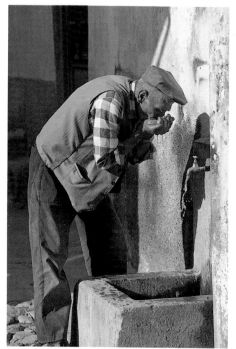

3-star
Club Atlantik Içmeler Mevkii, Marmaris. Tel. 29 07. April–November. 62 beds, 36 rooms.

Halici Cam Sokak, Marmaris 2. Tel. 11 71. May–November. 206 beds, 93 rooms.

Datça

Hotels and Pensions

3-star
Mare PO Box 27, Datça. Tel. 12 11. All year. 109 beds, 50 rooms.

2-star
Fuda Yali Datça. Tel. 10 42. All year.

Holiday Villages

Club Datça Tatil Köyü (class A), Datça. Tel. 11 03. 188 beds, 92 rooms. May–November.

Villa Datça Cokertme Mevki, PO Box 6, Iskele Mahallesi, Datça. Tel (61 45) 15 10; fax. 19 55.

Motels

4-star
Aydi-Tur Resadiye Mahallesi, Karakesit Mevkii, Datca. Tel. 11 02. 1 April–30 November.

Dorya Iskele Mahallesi, Datca. Tel. 10 35. 1 May–31 October. 80 beds, 32 rooms.

Köyceğiz

Hotels

2-star
Ozay Kordon Böyü. Tel. 13 00. All year.

1-star
Büyük Kalinos Cengiz Topel Caddesi 37. Tel. 12 88. All year.

Fethiye

Hotels and Pensions

3-star
Prenses Fethiye. Tel. 13 05. All year. 120 beds, 60 rooms.

2-star
Sema Fethiye. Tel. 10 15. All year.

1-star
Dedeoğlu Iskele Meydani. Tel. 40 10. All year.

Likya Karagözler Mahallesi. Tel. 11 69. April–November.

Motels

4-star
Meri Olüdeniz, Fethiye. Tel. Olüdeniz 1. All year. 150 beds, 75 rooms.

Seketür Çalis Mevkii, Fethiye. Tel 17 05. 1 May–1 November. 70 beds, 30 rooms.

2-star
Ata Hisaronu, Fethiye. Tel. 14 30. 58 beds, 29 rooms.

Motel Mütlü Çalis Mevkii, Fethiye. Tel. 14 30. 74 beds, 37 rooms.

Kaş *1-star* Hotel

Bürak Reis Kalkan, Kaş. Tel. 77.

Kemer

Hotels

3-star
Adonis Oteli Kemer. Tel. 1832, 2482; tlx. 56665 KEM TR. January–December. 70 beds, 30 rooms.

2-star
Dörkuk Iskele 16. Tel. 11 25; tlx. 56625 YDR TR. 15 March–15 November. 66 beds, 36 rooms.

Karahan Inonu Caddesi. Tel. 18 00/3. All year.

Unlisted
Alba Club (class A), Beldibi, Kemer. Tel. 27 66. 1 June–30 November. 900 beds, 450 rooms.

Club Méditerranée Tatil Köyü (class A), Kemer. Tel. 10 09; tlx. 56689 KMR TR. 28 April–30 September. 770 beds, 335 rooms.

Club Salima (class A), Kemer. Tel. 15 24; tlx. 56610 CLSA TR. 5 May–20 August. 600 beds, 252 rooms.

Milta Kemer (class A), Kızıltepe. Tel. 22 33; tlx. 56592 MLTA TR. 30 May–30 October. 900 beds, 402 rooms.

Palmiye (class A), Kemer. Tel. 28 90/96; tlx. 56615 PLYA TR. 1 May–7 November. 1,010 beds, 498 rooms.

Robinson Canyuva (class A), Canyuva, Kemer. Tel. 15 10/18; tlx. 56698 CYA TR. May–November. 721 beds, 332 rooms.

Camping

Türban Kızıltepe Kamping (class 1),

Kemer. Tel. 11 13. 5 May–30 October.

Antalya

5-star
Club Sera Lara, PO Box 444, Antalya. Tel. 311 70/79; tlx. 5670 ALZO TR. All year. 450 beds, 150 rooms.

Talya Fevzi Çakmak Caddesi, Antalya. Tel. 15 600/08. All year. 300 beds, 150 rooms.

Türban Adalya Kaleici, Yat Limanî. Tel. 180 66/67; tlx. 56241 TBA TR. All year. 58 beds, 28 rooms.

4-star
Start Ali Çetinkaya Caddesi, Antalya. Tel. 11 280/26; tlx. 56062 TUAS TR. All year. 120 beds, 60 rooms.

3-star
Antalya Lara Yolu, Nine kilometre post. Tel. 146 09; tlx. 56231 ANMO TR. April–November.

Olimpos Tel. 12 80/82; tlx. 56634 OLIM TR. April–October. 112 beds, 56 rooms.

2-star
Atan Lara Caddesi. Tel. 111 92; tlx. 56014. All year.

Bilgehan Kazim Özalp Caddesi 194. Tel. 151 84. All year.

Lara Lara Yolu, PO Box 404. Tel. 152 99. All year.

1-star
Büyük Cumhuriyet Caddesi 57. Tel. 114 99. All year.

Tatoğlu Kazim Ozalp Caddesi 91. Tel. 121 19. All year.

Yalçin 1253 Sokak 10. PO Box 151. Tel. 141 90. All year.

Yayla Palas Ali Cetinkaya Caddesi 12. Tel. 119 13. All year.

Perge Parkici, Perge Sokak. Tel. 23 60. All year.

Side and Manavgat

Hotels

4-star
Sural Colakli Köyü, Manavgat. Tel. 45 00. All year. 411 beds 201 rooms.

3-star
Defne Side. Tel. 133 13/8. All year. 183 beds, 90 rooms.

2-star
Kara Elmas Side. Tel. 13 50. All year.

Motels

4-star
Cennet Side. Tel. 17 167; tlx. 56199 TR. April–January. 114 beds, 55 rooms.

Türtel Selimiyeköyü, Side. Tel. 22 25. April -November. 92 beds, 46 rooms.

Unclassified
Club Aldiana (class A), Titreyen Göl, Manavgat. Tel. 42 60/62; tlx. 56606 TR. May–October. 650 beds, 300 rooms.

Robinson Pamfilya (class A), Manavgat. Tel. 4702/8; tlx. 56585 ROSI TR. 1 May– 30 October. 824 beds, 284 rooms.

Türtel Turistik Teşişler (class A), Side. Tel. 22 25; tlx. 56683 TTL TR. 11 June– 30 October. 687 beds, 324 rooms.

Sidelya (class B), Colakli Köyü. Tilkiler Mevkii, Side. Tel. 42 85. All year. 250

beds, 100 rooms.

Yakup Ertosan (class B), Side. Tel. 16 30/34. 15 March–30 November. 464 beds, 140 rooms.

Alanya

Hotels

4-star
Alantur Dincayi Mevkii. Tel. 12 24; tlx. 56143 ATUR TR. All year. 198 beds, 99 rooms.

3-star
Aladdin Sarat Mahallesi. Tel. 10 48. All year. 216 beds, 108 rooms.

Blue Sky Bayirli İskele Caddesi 66. Tel. (323) 16487.

Panorama Güllerpinari Mahallesi, Keykubat Caddesi. Tel. 11 81; tlx. 56609 TR. April–November. 472 beds, 240 rooms.

2-star
Alaiye Atatürk Caddesi 82. Tel. 20 48. 1 April–1 November.

Alanya Büyük Gullerpinari Caddesi. Tel. 11 38. 1 April–1 November.

Atilla Güllerpinari Mah. Tel. 22 09. All year.

Aytür Keykubat Caddesi. Tel. 39 55. All year.

Banana Çikçikli Köyü. Tel. 15 48. May– November.

International Güllerpinari Mah. Tel. 11 95. 1 March–1 November.

Kaptan İskele Caddesi 62. Tel. 10 94. All year.

Riviera Güzelyali Caddesi. Tel. 14 22. All year.

1-star
Berrin Yenilmaz Sokak. Tel. 28 30. All year.

Cimen Keykubat Caddesi. Tel. 22 83. All year.

Emel Bostanci Pinar Caddesi. Tel. 25 81. All year.

Günaydin Kültür Caddesi. Tel. 19 43. All year.

Güvenlik Atatürk Caddesi. Tel. 13 14. All year.

Cleopatra Saray Mahallesi. Tel. 39 80/81. All year.

Meşüt Obaköy Göl Mevkii. Tel 13 39. April–October.

Ozen Müftüler Caddesi 38. Tel. 13 39. April–October.

Park Hurriyet Meydani. Tel. 16 75. All year.

Pehlivan Satay Mahallesi. Tel. 27 81. All year.

Wien Güllerpinari Mahallesi. 1 April–1 November.

Holiday Villages

Club Aquarius Alanya Tatil Köyü
Alanya–Konaklikoy, ten kilometre post. Tel. 26 32; tlx. 56589 CAQU TR. 1 April–15 November. 440 beds, 220 rooms.

Motels

4-star
Alantur Camyolu Köyü, Alanya. Tel. 12 24; tlx. 56143 TR. April–December.

Alara Yeşilköy, Alanya. Tel. Avsallar 146. April–November.

Aspendos Avsallar Köyü, Incekum. Tel. 04 91. May–November.

Incekum Avsallar Köyü, Incekum. Tel. 7 120 149. All year.

Selam Keykubat Caddesi. Tel. 12 50. All
year.

Yalihan Avsallar Köyü, Incekum. Tel. 10.
April–November.

3-star
Comertöğlü Avsallar Köyüu, Alanya. Tel.
Avsallar 72.

Merhaba Keykubat Caddesi. Tel. 12 51.
1 April–1 November.

Panorama Keykubat Caddesi. Tel. 11 81.

Yeni International Keykubat Caddesi.
Tel. 11 95. All year.

2-star
Sultan Güzelyali Caddesi. Tel. 13 48.
April–September.

Camping

Alanya Kamp-Motel (class 3),
Okürcalar Köyü, Alanya. Tel. 172. 1
April–1 November.

BP Mocamp (class 3), Okürcalar Köyü. 1
April–1 November.

Anamur

2-star Hotel
Cephe Anamur. Tel. 43. 35 beds, 18
rooms. All year.

3-star Motel
Karan Bözdoğan Köyü, Anamur. Tel. 10
27. All year.

Silifke

2-star Hotel
Olba Taşucu. Tel. 12 22. May–October.
By the sea. 30 beds, 20 rooms.

4-star Motel
Taştür Taşucu. Tel. 45 90 290. March–
November.

Kizkalesi *2-star* Hotel
Yaka Kizkalesi. Tel. 10 41. March–
December. 30 beds, 15 rooms.

Mezitli *3-star* Motel
Marti Erdemli Yolu, Mezitli Mevkii. Tel.
147 41.

Erdemli

Camping

Kervansaray Kizkalesi Mocamp (class
3), PO Box 7, Erdemli. 1 April–15 October.

Mersin

Hotels

4-star
Atlihan İstiklâl Caddesi 168, Mersin. Tel.
24 153/55; tlx. 67374 ATOL TR. All year.
183 beds, 93 rooms.

3-star
Mersin Camii Şerif Mahallesi, 10 Sokak
2. Tel. 216 40/46; tlx. 67180 MERS TR.
All year. 226 beds, 105 rooms.

2-star
Hosta Fatih Kayabali Caddesi 4. Tel. 147
60/24. All year. 118 beds, 52 rooms.

Toros Atatürk Caddesi 23. Tel. 122 01.
All year. 96 beds, 62 rooms.

Turkmen İnönü Mahallesi, Pozcu. Tel.
110 04. All year. 108 beds, 54 rooms.

1-star

Hayat İstiklâl Caddesi 68. Tel. 110 76.
All year.

Hititler Soğüksü Caddesi 40. Tel. 163 27.
All year.

Nobel İstiklâl Caddesi 123. Tel. 112 27.
All year.

Ocak İstiklâl Caddesi 48. Tel. 157 65.

Savran Soğüskü Caddesi 46. Tel. 244 17.
All year.

Adana

Hotels

5-star
Büyük Sürmeli Kürüköprü Ozler Caddesi. Tel. 219 44/48; tlx. 62282 BSOT
TR. All year. 329 beds, 170 rooms.

Sürmeli İnönü Caddesi 112. Tel. 227
01/02; tlx. 62330 SUTU TR. All year.
232 beds, 116 rooms.

2-star
Inci Kurtulus Caddesi. Tel. 226 12. All
year. 67 beds, 36 rooms.

İpek Palas İnönü Caddesi 103. Tel. 187
43/48. All year. 102 beds, 53 rooms.

Koza Ozler Caddesi. Tel. 146 57; tlx.
62802 ADKO TR. All year. 119 beds, 66
rooms.

Set İnönü Caddesi. Tel. 211 30. All year.
87 beds, 42 rooms.

1-star
Anba Abidin Paşa Caddesi 1A. Tel. 106
17. 174 beds, 87 rooms.

Duygu İnönü Caddesi. Tel. 167 41. All
year. 54 beds, 36 rooms.

Erciyes Palas Ozler Caddesi 53. Tel. 188
67. All year. 55 beds, 36 rooms.

4-star Motel
Raşit Ener Türtes Iskenderun Yolu
Uzeri, Gurne Bulvari. Tel. 119 04. All
year.

Camping
Raşit Ener (class 1), as above.

İskenderun

Hotels

3-star
Hatayli Osmangazi Caddesi 2, İskenderun. Tel. 115 51; tlx. 68136 TUNA
TR. All year. 120 beds, 60 rooms.

2-star
Bahadirli 12 Eylül Caddesi, İskenderun.
Tel. 129; tlx. 68019 OBAH TR. All year.
84 beds, 42 rooms.

1-star
Guney Palas Beş Temmuz Caddesi 17,
İskenderun. Tel. 336 97; tlx. 68105 IGPO
TR. All year. 53 beds, 30 rooms.

Hitit Cumhuriyet Meydani 1, İskenderun. Tel. 137 81; tlx. 68168 AKBO
TR. All year. 76 beds, 40 rooms.

Belen *3-star* Hotel
Kamelya Sarimazi evkii, Belen. Tel. 103.
All year. 88 beds, 44 rooms.

Antakya

Hotels

2-star
Divan İstiklâl Caddesi 62, Antakya. Tel.
115 18. All year. 40 beds, 23 rooms.

1-star
Atahan Hurriyet Caddesi 28, Antakya.
Tel. 110 36. All year. 75 beds, 42 rooms.

Harbiye

Hotels

2-star
Hidro Kariyer Mahallesi, Harbiye. Tel. 6.
All year. 32 beds, 16 rooms.

1-star
Cağlayan Urgen Caddesi 6, Harbiye. Tel.
11. All year. 23 beds, 13 rooms.

De Liban Dermasta Mahallesi, Harbiye.
Tel. 54. All year. 65 beds, 29 rooms.

Central Anatolia

Ankara

Hotels

5-star
Büyük Ankara Atatürk Bulvari, 183.
Tel. 125 66 55–75; tlx. 42398 GTEL TR;
fax. 25 50 70. 304 beds, 180 rooms,
suites. Airconditioning, indoor parking,
restaurant, bars, nightclub, conference
facilities, sauna, swimming pool, barber
and hairdresser, casino/slot machines.

Etap Altinel Tandogan Meydani, Gazi
Mustafa Kemal Bulvari 151. Tel. (4) 231
77 60; tlx. 44419 EBOT TR. 360 beds,
175 rooms, suites. Airconditioning, restaurant and bar, conference rooms,
Turkish bath, sauna, barber and
hairdresser, casino/slot machines.

4-star

Ankara Büyük Sürmeli Cinnah Sokak
6, Kizilay. Tel. 230 52 40/54; tlx. 44110
SBO TR. 236 beds, 118 rooms, suites.
Swimming pool, nightclub, barber and
hairdresser.

Ankara Dedeman Büklüm Sokak 1. Tel.
117 62 00/14; tlx. 42408 DEDE TR. 455
beds, 252 rooms, suites. Swimming pool,
nightclub, barber and hairdresser.

Kent Mihtat Paşa Caddesi 4. Tel. 131 21
11/18; tlx. 42424 KENT TR; fax. 34 46
57. 242 beds, 120 rooms, suites.
Nightclub, disco, conference rooms, barber and hairdresser.

Best Atatürk Bulvari 195. Tel. 167 08
80; tlx. 46670 BST TR; fax. 67 08 85.
108 beds, 48 rooms, suites. Conference
rooms, sauna, nightclub.

Stad İstiklâl Caddesi 20, Ulus. Tel. 310
48 48; tlx. 42248 HOS TR; fax. 10 89 69.
397 beds, 217 rooms, suites. Conference
rooms, sauna, barber and hairdresser.

3-star
Altinişik Necatibey Caddesi 46. Tel. 229
11 89; tlx. 42656 LTTE TR. 397 beds,
217 rooms.

Bulvar Palas Atatürk Bulvari 141. Tel.
117 50 20/28; tlx. 42613 BLVD TR. 288
beds, 177 rooms, suites. Conference
rooms.

Elit Olgunlar Sokak 10, Bakanliklar. Tel.
117 50 01; fax. 117 46 97. 80 beds, 40
rooms.

Etap Mola Atatürk Bulvari 80. Tel. (4)
117 85 85; tlx. 42294 MOLA TR. 106
beds, 57 rooms, suites. Conference rooms.

Evkuran Ziya Gök Alp Caddesi. Tel. 133

21 10/13; tlx. 46920 EVHO TR. 120
beds, 60 rooms, suites. Conference rooms.

Eyuboğlu Karanfil Caddesi 73. Tel. 117
81. 106 beds, 53 rooms.

Grand İzmir Caddesi 35. Tel. 117 50.
186 beds, 91 rooms.

Kevkan Fevzi Çakmak Sokak 12. Tel.
230 21. 95 beds, 50 rooms.

Metropol Olgünlar Sokak 5, Bakanlıklar.
Tel. 117 30 60; tlx. 472739 MSOL TR;
fax. 117 69 90. 68 beds, 32 rooms.

Ornek Gülseren Sokak 4, Maltepe. Tel.
230 52. 70 beds, 35 rooms.

Tunali Tunali Hilmi Caddesi 119. Tel.
127 81; tlx. 42142 VEL TR. 96 beds, 54
rooms.

Turist Çankiri Caddesi 37. Tel. 310 39;
tlx. 44103 SER TR. 350 beds, 168 rooms.

Yeni Sanayi Caddesi 5B, Ulus. Tel. 310
47. 130 beds, 65 rooms.

2-star
Akman Tavus Sokak 6. Tel. 324 41 40–
43.

Anit Gazi Mustafa Kemal Paşa Caddesi
111. Tel. 229 23.

Apaydin Bayindar Sokak 8. Tel. 133 31.

Basyazici Çankiri Caddesi 27. Tel. 310
39.

Bayram Cumhuriyet Caddesi 1A. Tel.
111 36.

Ercan Denizciler Caddesi 36. Tel. 312 62.

Ergen Karanfil Sokak 48. Tel. 134 46.

Erşan Meşrutiyet Caddesi 13. Tel. 118 98.

Guleryuz Sanayi Caddesi 37. Tel. 312 41.

Hancioğlu Ulucanlar Caddesi 68. Tel.
320 25.

Hitit Firuzaga Sokak 12. Tel. 310 86.

Melodi Karanfil Sokak 10. Tel. 176 41.

Sultan Bayindar Sokak 35. Tel. 131 59.

3-star Motel
Omur İstanbul Yolu, nine kilometre post.
Tel. 315 39; tlx. 44040 AYAR TR.

Camping

Altinök Süsüköy Mocamp (class 2), İs-
tanbul Yolu, 22 kilometre post. Tel. 243
13 66. 1 May–15 October.

Yayla Mocamp (class 2), İstanbul Yolu,
110 kilometre post. Tel. Kizilcahamam 7.
1 June–30 October.

Yozgat *1-star* Hotel
Yilmaz Ankara Caddesi 14A, Yozgat.
Tel. 1107; tlx. 44852 YOZ TR.

Sungurlu *3-star* Motel

Hitit Ankara–Samsun Yolu, Sungurlu.
Tel. 42-409. All year.

Nevşehir
Hotels
3-star
Göreme Hükümet Caddesi 16, Nevşehir.
Tel. 17 06. 15 March–15 October.

Orsan Kapadokya Kayseri Caddesi,
Nevşehir. Tel. 10 35. 1 March–1 November.

1-star
Lâle Gazhane Sokak, Nevşehir. Tel. 17 97. All year.

Orhan İbrahim Paşa Mahallesi, Nevşehir. Tel. 18 10. All year.

Viva Kayseri Caddesi 45, Nevşehir. Tel. 13 26. All year.

3-star Motel
Paris Asarkaya Mevkii, Nevşehir. Tel. 15-99. All year.

Ürgüp

Hotels

2-star
Büyük Kayseri Caddesi, Ürgüp. Tel. 10 60. All year.

Tepe Teşlimiye Caddesi, Ürgüp. Tel. 111 54. 1 March–1 November.

1-star
Sinasos Mustafa Paşa, Ürgüp. Tel. 14 32. All year.

4-star Motel
Türban Ürgüp Tel. 14 90; tlx. 49613 URMT TR. All year.

Avanos

1-star Hotels
Venessa Orta Mahalle, Avanos. Tel. 201. All year.

Kizilirmak Venessa Bahcelievler Mah, Avanos. Tel. 99. All year.

Niğde

Hotels

4-star
İhlara Sanayi Caddesi 5, Niğde. Tel. 18 42. All year. 122 beds, 64 rooms.

3-star
Vadi Ankara Caddesi 17, Niğde. Tel. 45 26. All year. 144 beds, 55 rooms.

Aksaray

4-star Motel
Orhan Ağaclu Tür Ankara–Adana E5. Nevşehir Kavağı, Aksaray. Tel. 49 10. All year.

Kayseri

Hotels

3-star
Turan Turan Caddesi 8, Kayseri. Tel. 119 68. All year. 135 beds, 70 rooms.

2-star
Hattat İstanbul Caddesi, Kayseri. Tel. 193 31. All year.

1-star
Terminal İstanbul Caddesi 76, Kayseri. Tel. 158 46. All year.

Konya

Hotels

3-star
Sahin Alaeddin Caddesi, Konya. Tel. 12 376. All year.

Selçuk Babalik Sokak, Alaeddin Caddesi, Konya. Tel. 11 12 59/61.

2-star
Ozkaymak Park Otogar Karşisi, Konya. Tel. 337 70. All year.

Yeni Sema Yeni Meram Yolu, Konya. Tel. 13 279. All year.

1-star
Başak Palas Alaeddin Caddesi, Konya. Tel. 113 38. All year.

Dergah Mevlana Caddesi 19, Konya. Tel. 17 661. All year.

Konya Mevlana Alani, Konya. Tel. 166 77. All year.

Otogar Otogar Yani, Konya. Tel. 301 38. All year.

Seljuk Alaeddin Caddesi, Konya. Tel. 112 59.

Sema 2 Yeni Terminal Yani, Konya. Tel. 32 557.

Beyşehir *3-star* Motel

Dilayla Akseki–Antalya Yolu, PO Box 5, Beyşehir. All year.

A Dirty Story

*T*he three of them were sitting on the damp earth, their backs against
the dung-daubed brush-wall and their knees drawn up to their
chests, when another man walked up and crouched beside them.

'Have you heard?' said one of them excitedly. 'Broken-nose
Jabbar's done it again! You know Jabbar, the fellow who brings all
those women from the mountain villages and sells them in the
plain? Well, this time he's come down with a couple of real beauties.
The lads of Misdik have got together and bought one of them on the
spot, and now they're having fun and making her dance and all
that. . . It's unbelievable! Where does the fellow find so many
women? How does he get them to come with him? He's the devil's
own son, he is . . .'

'Well, that's how he makes a living,' commented one of the men.
'Ever since I can remember, this Jabbar's been peddling women for
the villagers of the Chukurova plain. Allah provides for all and
sundry. . .'

'He's still got the other one,' said the newcomer, 'and he's ready to
give her away for a hundred liras.'

'He'll find a customer soon enough,' put in another man whose
head was hunched between his shoulders. 'A good woman's worth
more than a team of oxen, at least, in the Chukurova plain she is.
You can always put her to the plough and, come summer, she'll bind
and carry the sheaves, hoe, do anything. What's a hundred liras?
Why, a woman brings in that much in one single summer. In the
fields, at home, in bed. There's nothing like a woman. What's a
hundred liras?'

Yashar Kemal, Anatolian Tales

Southeastern Anatolia

Gaziantep

Hotels

3-star
Kaleli Hurriyet Caddesi, Guzelce Sokak 50, Gaziantep. Tel. 127 28. All year. 140 beds, 70 rooms.

1-star
Büyük Karagöz Caddesi 26, Gaziantep. Tel. 152 22. All year.

Mimar Hurriyet Caddesi 24, Gaziantep. Tel. 179 92. All year.

Murat İnönü Caddesi 53, Gaziantep. Tel. 122 05. All year.

Türk Hurriyet Caddesi 27, Gaziantep. Tel. 194 80. All year.

Nizip *2-star* Hotel
Belediye Atatürk Bulvari 30, Nizip. Tel. 684. All year.

Şanliurfa

Hotels

3-star
Harran Atatürk Bulvari, Şanliurfa. Tel. 28 60. All year. 120 beds, 54 rooms.

2-star
Türban Urfa Köprübasi, Yüsüfpaşa Mah, Şanliurfa. Tel. 35 20. All year.

Diyarbakir

Hotels

2-star
Demir İzzet Paşa Caddesi 8, Diyarbakir. Tel. 123 15. All year.

1-star
Amid Suakar Sokak 7, Diyarbakir. Tel. 120 59. All year.

Aslan Kibris Caddesi 23, Diyarbakir. Tel. 139 71, 185 74. All year.

Derya Inonu Caddesi 13, Diyarbakir. Tel. 149 66. All year.

Diyarbakir Büyük İnönü Caddesi 4, Diyarbakir. Tel. 158 32. All year.

Saraç İzzet Paşa Caddesi 16, Diyarbakir. Tel. 123 65. All year.

Turistik Ziya Gök Alp Bulvari 7, Diyarbakir. Tel. 126 62. All year.

Nusaybin
4-star Motel
Nezirhan Germeli Köyü Mevkii, Nusaybin. Tel. 84 11; tlx. 72355 VOHO TR. All year.

Black Sea Coast

Sinop

3-star Hotel
Melia Kasim Riza Nuh Caddesi 41, Sinop. Tel. 168. All year. 96 beds, 57 rooms.

3-star Motel
Köskburnu Tür Köskburnu, Gerze, Sinop. Tel. 81-503. All year.

Bafra *3-star* Motel
Bafra Belediye Bafra. Tel. 15 24. May–November.

Samsun

Hotels

4-star
Türban Büyük Samsun Sahil Caddesi, Samsun. Tel. 107 50. All year. 232 beds, 116 rooms.

3-star
Yafeya Cumhuriyet Meydanî, Samsun. Tel. 165 65. All year. 220 beds, 104 rooms.

1-star
Burç Kazimpaşa Caddesi 36, Samsun. Tel. 154 80. All year.

Gökce Ferah Sokak 1, Samsun. Tel. 179 52. All year.

Vidinli Kazimpaşa Caddesi 4, Samsun. Tel. 160 50. All year.

Ünye *2-star* Hotel
Kümsal Gölevi Köyü, Ünye. Tel. 44 90. All year.

Fatsa *3-star* Motel
Dolunay Yaprakli Mevkii, Fatsa. Tel. 15 28.

Ordu *2-star* Hotel
Turist Sahil Caddesi 26, Ordu. Tel. 114 66. All year.

Giresun *1-star* Hotel
Giresun Atatürk Bulvarî 7, Giresun. Tel. 24 69. All year.

Trabzon

Hotels

2-star
Ozgür Atatürk Alani 29, Trabzon. Tel.

113 19. All year.

1-star
Horon Sira Magazlar 125, Trabzon. Tel. 111 99. All year.

Usta İskele Caddesi, Trabzon. Tel. 121 95. All year.

Eastern Anatolia

Erzurum

Hotels

3-star
Oral Terminal Caddesi 3, Erzurum. Tel. 197 40/44; tlx. 74117 HAVA. All year. 161 beds, 90 rooms.

2-star
Büyük Erzurum Ali Ravi Caddesi 5, Erzurum. Tel. 165 28. All year.

Efes Tahtacîlar Caddesi 36, Erzurum. Tel. 170 81. All year.

Kral Erzincan Kapî 18, Erzurum. Tel. 119 30.

Sefer İstasyon Caddesi, Erzurum. Tel. 136 15. All year.

1-star
Akay Kamilağa Sokak 2, Erzurum. Tel 173 30. All year.

Buhara Kâzîm Karabekir Caddesi, Erzurum. Tel. 150 96. All year.

Çinar Ayazpaşa Caddesi 18, Erzurum. Tel. 135 80. All year.

Polat Kâzîm Karabekir Caddesi, Erzurum. Tel. 116 23. All year.

Sivas

Hotels

2-star
Kösh Atatürk Caddesi 11, Sivas. Tel. 111
50. All year.

1-star
Sultan Belediye Sokak, Sivas. Tel. 129
96. All year.

Erzincan
3-star Hotel
Urartu Cumhuriyet Meydani, Erzincan.
Tel. 15 61. All year. 116 beds, 58 rooms.

Doğıbayazit

2-star Hotel
Isfahan Eminiyet Caddesi 26,
Doğıbayazit. Tel. 11 30; tlx. 74238
AROT TR. All year.

4-star Motel
Simer Türtes Iran Yolu, three kilometre
post, PO Box 13, Doğıbayazit. Tel. 22
54; tlx. 74258 KGSM TR. All year.

Van

Hotels

4-star
Büyük Urartu Seriye Caddesi, Van. Tel.
206 60. All year. 150 beds, 75 rooms.

3-star
Akdamar Kâzim Karabekir Caddesi 56,
Van. Tel. 18 100-04-13 036; tlx. 73164
ATOY TR. All year. 138 beds, 69 rooms.

Tekin Küçük Camii Civari, Van. Tel. 13

66. All year. 104 beds, 52 rooms.

2-star
Büyük Asur Turizm Sokak 126/1, Van.
Tel. 18 792. All year.

1-star
Beş Kardes Cumhuriyet Caddesi 34, Van.
Tel. 11 16. All year.

Çaldiran Sihke Caddesi, Van. Tel. 27 18.
All year.

Kent İşbankasi Arkasi, Van. Tel. 24 04.
All year.

Kars

1-star Hotel
Temel Palas Kâzimpaşa Caddesi, Kars.
Tel. 13 76. All year.

Yilmaz Küçük Kazibey Caddesi 114,
Kars. Tel. 10 23. All year.

Restaurants

İstanbul

Beyoğlu

Çiftnal Samanyolu Sakak, Osmanbey. Tel. 140 12 80. Turkish and French cuisine. Open weekdays 12.30 pm–1 am. Medium priced.

The China Restaurant Lamartin Caddesi, Taksim. Tel. 150 84 34, 150 62 63. Medium priced.

Divan Hotel Restaurant Cumhuriyet Caddesi, Elmadağ. Turkish and continental cuisine, plus seafood specialities. Open 12–3 pm, 6 pm–1 am. Medium priced.

Fischer Gümüşsuyu Caddesi, Taksim. German cuisine.

Four Seasons (Dort Mevsim), İstiklâl Caddesi 509, Tünel. Tel. 145 89 41. Mainly French cuisine, with Turkish and international dishes. Open every day 12–3 pm, 6 pm–12 midnight. Medium priced.

Galata Tower at the top of the tower, Küledibi. Tel. 145 11 60. Turkish and French cuisine. Floor show (starting from 8 pm to 1 am). Open every day 12–3 pm, 7.30 pm–1 am. Expensive.

Garden '74 Bestekar Sevki Bey Sokak 74, Balmümcü. Tel. 166 09 77. French cuisine. Reservations recommended. Open every day 8.30 pm–12 midnight. Disco from 12 midnight to 2 am. Very expensive.

Green House at Hilton Hotel Cumhuriyet Caddesi, Elmadağ. Tel. 146 70 50 (ext. 8973). Turkish and international. Terrace overlooking the Bosphorus. Open every day 6.30 pm–12 midnight.

Günay Cumhuriyet Caddesi 349/1, Harbiye. Tel. 140 83 95. International cuisine with some house specialities. Boulevardier atmosphere after midnight. Open every day 8 pm–4 am. Expensive.

Haci Baba İstiklâl Caddesi 49. Tel. 145 43 77. Turkish cuisine. Terrace overlooking courtyard of the Greek Orthodox Cathedral. Open 12 noon–12 midnight. Moderately priced.

Haci Salih 3 İstiklâl Caddesi, Anadolu Han 201/1. Tel. 143 45 28. Traditional Turkish cuisine. No alcohol. Small restaurant. Open daily, except Sunday, 12 noon–12.30 am. Moderate in price.

Hasir Kalyonçüküllügü Caddesi 94/1, Tarlabaşi. Tel. 150 05 57, also known as the Greek Taverna. Turkish cuisine with specialities. Open every day 11.30 am–12 midnight. Moderate in price.

Japanese Restaurant Cumhuriyet Caddesi, Taksim.

Kulis Corc (George) İstiklâl Caddesi 209A, Beyoğlu. Tel. 143 20 46. International cuisine with specialities. Open 12 noon–12 midnight. Medium cost.

Liman Rihtim Caddesi, on the third floor of Karaköy Boat Terminal. Tel. 144 10 33. Turkish and International cuisine of the highest standard. Open for lunch trade on weekdays only, 12–4 pm. Terrace overlooking Bosphorus and Marmara. Medium cost.

Mazgal Nispetiye Caddesi 12, Etiler. Tel. 163 35 50. French/Turkish cuisine. Piano music in the evening. Open daily 4–11 pm. Disco (upstairs) 11 pm–4 am.

Otag 85 Steak House, Yeni Tarlabaşi Caddesi 7, Taksim, and 3 Taksim Square. Tel. 145 42 51. Wine bar and restaurant. Open 12–3 pm, 8 pm–1 am. Medium range.

Orient Express at the Etap Marmara Hotel Taksim Square. French cuisine, and rated by some the best of its kind in town. Open daily 12–3 pm, 7–10.30 pm. Reservations recommended. Very expensive.

Pera Palas at the hotel, Meşrutiyet Caddeşi, Tepebasi. Classic Edwardian setting with Turkish and French cuisine. Piano in the evening. Open 11–1 am. Medium cost.

Pronto Valikonağı Caddesi, Süleiman Nazif Sokak 3/A, Nişantaş. Tel. 148 77 26. Italian cuisine. Open daily 12 noon–12 midnight. Moderate in price.

Rejans Olivo Çikmazi 15, Galatasaray. Tel. 144 16 10. Russian/International cuisine. Reservations recommended. Open daily 12–3 pm, 6–11 pm.

Ristorante Italiano Cumhuriyet Caddesi 6B, Elmadağ. Tel. 147 86 40. Italian cuisine. Open daily 12–3 pm, 7–11 pm. Reservations. Moderate cost.

Swiss Cumhuriyet Caddesi 14/1, Elmadağ. Tel. 140 46 18. Swiss/French cuisine and Turkish dishes. Open daily 12 noon–12 midnight. Expensive.

On the Bosphorus

Abdullah Emirgan Körü Caddesi 11. Tel. 163 63 06. Turkish/French. Good but expensive.

Ali Baba Kireçburnu Caddesi 20, Sarîyer. Tel. 162 08 89. Fish restaurant. Simple style, moderate in price.

Balîkçi Karatütük Caddesi 172, Yenimahalle, Sarîyer. Tel. 142 37 77. Fish restaurant on sea front. Moderate in price.

Bosfor Çayirbasi Caddesi 312, Büyükdere. Tel. 142 03 64. Fish restaurant. Recommended. Medium price range.

China Palace (Huang Kung), Kireçhurnu Caddesi 19, Tarabya. Tel. 162 26 57.

Chinese cuisine. Overlooking water. Expensive.

Erol Kilyos Yolu, Nalbantçeşme, Sarîyer. Tel. 142 15 26. Turkish cuisine, interesting specialities. On a hill. Medium cost.

Filiz Kefeliköy Caddesi 168, Tarabya. Tel. 162 01 52. Fish restaurant. Superior dishes, moderate prices.

Han Yahya Kemal Caddesi 4, Rumeli Hisar. Tel. 165 28 68. Fish restaurant. Good food, moderate prices.

Hüzür 1 Caddesi 23, Arnavütköy. Tel. 163 42 19. Fish restaurant. Medium prices.

Kiyi Kefeliköy Caddesi 126, Tarabya. Tel. 162 00 02. Fish restaurant. Medium prices.

Kösem Kefeliköy Caddesi 90/92, Tarabya. Tel. 162 01 58. Fish restaurant. Consistent quality and service. Moderate pricing.

Marti Karakütük Caddesi 2, Yenimahalle. Tel. 142 06 64. Fish restaurant. Consistent and unpretentious. Moderate prices.

Nese Büyükayazma 29, Arnavütköy. Tel. 165 10 93. Turkish cuisine. In the hills (downhill from Etiler). Very moderate.

Telli Baba Rumelikavağî Yolu, Telli Baba Mevkii. Tel. 142 03 00. Fish and meat restaurant. Picturesque setting. No frills, good and moderate in price.

Yeni Bebek Cevdet Paşa Caddesi 122, Bebek. Tel. 163 34 47. Turkish and French fish dishes. High standard of food and service. Medium price range.

Old City

Borsa Yali Köskü Caddesi, Yali Köskü Hani 60/62, Sirkeci. Tel. 522 41 73. Turkish cuisine. Food rather than decor. Midday only. Moderately priced.

Cemal Balîk Capariz Sokak 27, Kumkapî. Tel. 527 22 88. One of the better of the several fish restaurants in this fisherman's wharf area. Moderate in costs. Noon to midnight.

Çinaralti Capariz Sokak 12, Kumkapî. Where fishermen eat fish and drink. Open 11 am–12 midnight. Moderate cost.

Büyükcekmece and Küçükcekmece, by a lake out of town to the west via the E25, are places where citizens of İstanbul go to eat meat. Set among fine bridges built by Sinan, several restaurants are in the area.

Kapri İstanbul Caddesi 44, Yeniköy. Tel. 573 44 84. Turkish and international cuisine. Expensive.

Marmit İstanbul Caddesi 64, Yeşilköy. Tel. 573 85 81. French/Turkish cuisine. Game dishes. Three-course set menu with wine. Evenings 6 pm-12 midnight. Reservations. Expensive.

Olimpiyat 2 Canli Balîk. This is one of eight fish restaurants situated under Galata Bridge. Some meat dishes, too. All moderately priced. A tradition that might end when the bridge is replaced by the new one, now under construction.

Pandeli Mîsir Çarşîsî 1, Eminönü. In the Egyptian or Spice Bazaar, on an upper floor. Tel. 522 55 34, 527 39 09. An İstanbul institution that should be attended at least once. Book in advance. Midday only. Medium cost.

Bursa

Anatolia Çekirge Meydanî. Tel. 36 71 10/18.

Öz Kent Kültür Parkiçi. Tel. 36 76 66.

Selçuk Kültür Parkiçi. Tel. 36 76 58.

Şerman Atatürk Caddesi, Oba Ishan, first floor. Tel. 21 61 93.

İzmir

Bakus Etap İzmir Hotel, Cumhuriyet Bulvarî, Alsancak. Tel. 14 42 90/99.

China Town 1379 Sokak, Efes Is Hani 57A, Alsancak. Tel. 25 73 57/58.

Efes Büyük Efes Hotel, Cumhuriyet Meydanî, Alsancak. Tel. 14 43 00 (ext. 849).

Golden Atatürk Caddesi 314/A, Alsancak. Tel. 22 03 41.

İkizlar Fevzi Çakmak Caddesi, 163 Sokak 1, Bornova. Tel. 18 30 85.

Palet Yali Caddesi 294/1, Karsiyaka. Tel. 11 84 36.

Park Kültür Park. Tel. 13 96 20.

Yengeç Cumhuriyet Bulvarî 236, Alsancak. Tel. 21 73 68.

Ankara

China Town Köröğlü Sokak 19, Gaziosmanpaşa. Tel. 127 70.

Hulya Hösdere Caddesi 199/A, Çankaya. Tel. 138 29 61.

Karadeniz Karanfil Sokak 11, Kîzîlay.

Kazan Ahmet Agaoğlu Caddesi 26, Cankaya.

Liman İzmir Caddesi 11/15, Yenişehir.

RV Tahran Caddesi 13, Kavaklidere. Tel. 127 03 76.

Yahha Hemseri Sokak 28, Gaziosmanpaşa. Tel. 137 83 48.

Yakamoz Köröğlü Caddesi 38, Gaziosmanpaşa. Tel. 134 37 46.

Washington Bayindir Sokak 28A, Kîzîlay. Tel. 131 22 18.

Recommended Reading

Arrian. *Anabasis of Alexander* (in translation) (New York: Loeb, 1929).

Barber, Noel. *Lords of the Golden Horn* (London: Pan Books, 1973).

Baynes, Norman H. and Moss, H. St L.B. *Byzantium* (Oxford: OUP, 1948).

Bean, George E. *Aegean Turkey* (London: Benn, 1979).

Bean, George E. *Lycian Turkey* (London: Benn, 1978).

Bean, George E. *Turkey Beyond the Maeander* (London: Benn, 1980).

Bury, J.B. *The Eastern Roman Empire* Everyman edition (London: J. and M. Dent).

Cook, J.M. *The Greeks in Ionia and the East* (London: Thameir Hudson, 1962).

Cuddon, J.A. *The Owl's Watchsong* (London: Barrie and Rockliffe, 1960).

Czalpluka, M.A. *The Turks of Central Asia* (London: Curzon Press, 1973).

Fox, Robin Lane. *Alexander the Great* (London: Allen Lane, 1973).

Gibbon, H.A. *The Foundations of the Ottoman Empire* (London: Frank Cass, 1965).

Gurney, O.R. *The Hittites* (London: Pelican, 1952).

Herodotus. *Histories* (in translation) (London: Penguin, 1954).

Kincaid, C.A. *The Successors of Alexander* (Chicago: Argonaut Inc, 1969).

Kinross, Lord. *Within the Taurus* (London: John Murray, 1954).

Kinross, Lord. *Ataturk, The Rebirth of a Nation* (London: Weidenfeld and Nicholson, 1964).

Liddell, Robert. *Byzantium and Istanbul* (London: Longman, 1956).

Luke, Sir Harry. *The Old Turkey and the New* (London: Godfrey Bles, 1953).

Macaulay, Rose. *The Towers of Trebizond* (London: Collins, 1956).

Maclagan, M. *The City of Constantinople* (London: Thames and Hudson, 1968).

Menzies, Sutherland. *Turkey Old and New* (London: W.H.Allen, 1880).

Moorehead, Alan. *Gallipoli* (London: Hamish Hamilton, 1957).

Nichol, Donald. *The Last Centuries of Byzantium* (London: Rupert Hart-Davis, 1972).

Ostragorsky, G. *The History of the Byzantine State* (Oxford: Blackwell, 1956).

Penzer, N.M. *The Harem* (London: Spring Books, 1966).

Rice, David Talbot. *Byzantine Art* (London: Pelican, 1954).

Rice, David Talbot. *Constantinople: Byzantium - Istanbul* (London: Pelican, 1965).

Rostovtzeff. *The Social and Economic History of the Roman Empire* (Oxford: OUP, 1926).

Runciman, Stephen. *The History of the Crusades* (Cambridge: CUP, 1954).

Sherrard, Philip. *Constantinople Iconography of a Sacred City* (Oxford: Oxford University Press, 1961).

Stark, Freya. *Alexander's Path* (London: John Murray, 1958).

Vasiliev, A.A. *History of the Byzantine Empire* (Madison: University of Wisconsin, 1952).

Index